PRAISE FOR *MAD CITY*

"Thrilling . . . Ranks among the most important books to rise from the dust of the true-crime explosion."

—M. William Phelps, host of *Dark Minds* and *New York Times* bestselling true crime author

"Written by the internationally renowned criminologist and criminal humanist Michael Arntfield, this book is remarkable in several ways—it provides deep, penetrating insight into the nature of the criminal mind via an eclectic approach, and it sheds light on the kinds of internal pathologies that guide the behavior of many criminals. This is required reading for experts and the general public alike. A truly great read."

—Marcel Danesi, PhD, Director of the Program in Semiotics and Communication Theory and Professor of Linguistic Anthropology at the University of Toronto

MAD CITY

MAD CITY

The True Story of the Campus Murders That America Forgot

Michael Arntfield

Published by Little A, New York
www.apub.com

ISBN-13: 9781503942653 (hardcover)
ISBN-10: 1503942651 (hardcover)
ISBN-13: 9781503942646 (paperback)
ISBN-10: 1503942643 (paperback)

Cover design by Rex Bonomelli

Printed in the United States of America

First edition

For the victims and their families, and for Linda Schulko (née Tomaszewski) and retired Detective Sergeant Pat Postiglione. The latter for reaffirming my faith in police work; the former, my faith in humanity.

CONTENTS

MAD CITY

PROLOGUE

Flagstaff

There is no heaven but revenge.

—Thomas Nashe, *The Unfortunate Traveller*

March 28, 1979

The dash clock read 10:56 a.m. The meter read $8.75. She flipped the driver a ten spot and told him to keep the change. The ingrate drove off muttering a backhanded "Thanks, lady." Typical fare.

She looked up to see a sign bearing due east: **Cable TV. Air Conditioning. Hourly Rates.** Across the street, two more signs, opposite lots. To the north: **Repent**. To the south: **All Day Breakfast**. She pulled a battered take-out menu from her back pocket to double-check that this was the place. The menu was a relic of her last overnight stop, a sad travelogue of the last six weeks on the road from Michigan to Arizona—an impromptu scratch pad. The face of the pamphlet read, **Great Wall Chinese Diner, Ypsilanti, MI**. That was then. Beneath the delivery number was an address scribbled in blue ballpoint—*this* address. She'd had to hole up in some seedy joints before, while throwing good years after bad, but this one took the cake and then some. This was now.

In the other pocket, a Flagstaff Chamber of Commerce brochure—glossy to the max—with page 8 dog-eared, the panoramic city vista on page 1 not looking like much of anything she'd seen since breaching the city limits. It was, after all, where the road led, where he—the monster—had fled. He was circuitously retracing the same route he took from '65 to '68 before dropping anchor in the Mad City. Before *it* happened. Back on an I-40 off-ramp, her Chevy Malibu Classic—bronze on midnight black—half off the road, half on. Two Michelins straddled the fog line, the hood propped, the rad blown. She'd hit the Chamber just before closing time after thumbing a ride downtown from near the interchange the day prior. She'd glommed the complimentary mag from a spinning four-sider at the counter on her way out, studying it at an all-night diner within walking distance until first light. Page 1 was a typical bait-and-switch tourist trap skyline scam. But page 8 was pure pay dirt—Northern Arizona U. He'd go there. He'd have to. His compulsion would lead him back there to hunt. Old hat. Hardwired.

Holding her breath the whole time, she checked into room 214, a one-star "junior suite" bookended by the stairwell on one side and an ice machine on the other. A sign read, **Out of Order**. A scan of the room revealed a thirteen-inch DuMont with rabbit ears riveted to a lazy Susan—*American Bandstand* on mute, left on since who knows when by who knows whom. On the bedside table, an old, wet wipe—desiccated—lay crumpled in an amber ashtray. Beside it, a General Electric clock radio flashed 12:00 a.m. in 3/4 time. Attached to the room door was a fire-escape route map occluded by an unidentifiable stain. Two night chains, three dead bolts. The room balcony was no-man's-land—a sliding door seized shut since time immemorial. Through the cheesecloth curtain veiling the mildewed security glass, a translucent vista. It was a bird's-eye view of a pawnbroker kitty-corner to the east, a small bar-windowed storefront. It was local neighborhood color. Its current circumstances also made it something more, an eerie flashback of tragedies past—the

Mad City in the spring of '68. Two Flagstaff PD prowl cars and a morgue wagon sport-parked across the sidewalk attended to a local matter. The street-side cabaret spelled robbery-homicide. She'd seen it before. Beside the prowlers, an unmarked Impala—olive green on parchment brown. A sign on the dash read, **Official Police Vehicle**. A print man in plain clothes carrying an attaché case slouched in the middle of a uniform confab. The coroner stood to the side and chained cigarettes. A pair of sawhorses kept back looky-loos. Yellow crime-scene tape galore.

Fast-forward—same day, high noon plus fifteen minutes. Daytime surveillance outside *his* west-end bungalow—the monster's lair. His latest abode scored with fake creds, eerily close to the university campus as usual. A dump of Social Security numbers on the sly by a friend on the inside had kicked loose a known alias on the lease for the place, the details leaked to her while still back in Michigan. By 1:00 p.m., she'd closed to within fifty feet with a fake "lost dog" cover story to avoid suspicion, the whole time eyeballing and then daring to open the mailbox—stuffed to the max. Publishers Clearinghouse and Franklin Mint mailers, a "final notice" from the electric company, a dozen more items with mechanically typed labels. Nothing personal. On the lawn, a pair of *Daily Sun* daily editions chucked there by a keener paperboy. The monster was AWOL again, gone at least two days. She'd need to follow her intuition and hit the NAU campus library—give or take a twenty-minute walk. Unless he'd blown town for another spot on the map, there's nowhere else he could be. He'd be there watching, waiting, stalking. She'd stop him this time. She'd have to. It was, after all, her purpose in life, a world shaped by torment and obsession. It was an all-consuming calling—alpha to omega.

On the way now, walking along the most direct route. Out of nowhere, a speed trap came into view. She scoped a motor cop in aviators doing point-and-pulls on the north side of West Franklin. As she passed by on foot, the city band on the cop's Kawasaki KZP kicked in. The disembodied voice of a shrill dispatcher spewing ten-code and other alphanumeric gobbledygook suddenly reverted to plain English. An "all units" alert went live: "Nuclear emergency in the State of Pennsylvania." Her ears perked up—anything nuke related in '79 was a Cold War wire in the blood. On cue, the cop stowed the radar gun, punched the Harley into gear, and sped off hell-bent.

Linda half walked half ran to the next block—where West Franklin became East Franklin—to find a student stereo shop having a spring sidewalk sale. A marked-down Hitachi hi-fi facing the street shot out more details on a local lefty AM station: "Partial meltdown . . . Three Mile Island evacuated . . . Governor Thornburgh urging calm." Turned out not to be a duck-and-cover drill or doomsday scenario, just some half-wit asleep at the switch back near Philly, a reactor or two overloaded. Nonetheless, it was national news, a national scare. People didn't understand nuke radiation other than that it was terrifying. Even as far away as Arizona—almost 2,200 miles away—the Three Mile Island catastrophe in the making had people on edge, boxing up preserves and incanting the anthem, reciting Our Fathers.

By 1:40 p.m., Linda touched down on the university campus, the lawns teeming with freaked-out new-wave types variously talking about the meltdown, radiation poisoning, cover-ups, and red scares. It was like UW transplanted from a decade prior except that the men and women were harder to tell apart, the causes to be angry about slightly revised, the clothes a tad baggier. It was the same hot mess of aimless student activism, same prefab rhetoric and defiant verve. Different haircuts. Through a clearing of coeds sprawled out on a contiguous set of tattered afghans—an improvised reefer picnic—she eyeballed a manicured moraine in the distance. Brushing past a girl in a cropped "Blue Oyster Cult '78" tour shirt, her gangly boyfriend in a denim vest replete with pins—Black Flag, the MC5, the Ramones—Linda made her way to the clearing.

There, over the crest of the hill, she found a walking path crossroad and a sign that read, **LIBRARY**. The signs on this campus, Linda thought to herself, were in better shape than the ones back at UW. The way the patina of age wrought by a Midwestern winter worked the edges of the letters on signs there and inscribed them with a certain character was notably absent in a campus located smack-dab in a desert oasis, something of a varsity timeshare holiday. Sure enough, like any timeshare, the place had that never-lived-in look, like a model home staged to approximate the nonexistent lives of nonexistent people. It was catalogue perfect—like Christine was before UW. Before *he* found her. Before *it* happened.

Now, at the library entrance, double hinged and palatial. On the door on the right, a sign read, **Use Other Door.** *Inside*—the library proper—a montage of every library: stacks upon stacks, Dewey decimals, card drawers, old tables, errant paper airplanes, the white noise of aimless muttering, extraneous coughs, and dragging chairs. A sign at the circulation desk read, **Quiet Please** and was predictably disavowed wholesale. All the while, Linda made her way toward more interesting fare—the library smoke pit.

In spite of their obvious differences, Linda realized that Flagstaff in '79 was a transplanted Mad City from '68, at least in one key respect. You could light up, smoke, and flick ashes just about anywhere—hospitals, day cares, grocery stores, lecture halls, and courthouses—but *not* in libraries. It was the one and only place on the UW campus where an enforceable sign reading, **No Smoking** was ever treated with any semblance of seriousness. It was that same sign that the monster in a roundabout way had used to make his first move on Christine in the spring of '68. Smokers as captive audiences for other smokers are inevitably forced to listen, forced to acquiesce to a time-honored social code. The corollary of asking for a light is to ask more questions; the corollary of providing that light is to offer up more answers. The paradoxical subculture of smoking is one that defies, but at the same time strangely upholds, tradition—one that flips off yet simultaneously embraces conformity. Often misleading, contradictory, yet time-honored, answered questions from smokers only beget more questions from other smokers—and even more responses. And so it went. And so it goes.

But in the spring of '79, like the fall of '68 when she first starting piecing it all together, no one saw the hunter for what he was—no one, it seems, but Linda. No one but she chased him. No one but she listened. No one but she ever tried—ever. Two dozen one-star detectives were back in Madison, all purportedly "hot on the trail" of the Capital City Killer while Linda—and Linda alone—was the only one after the *real* killer. He was a serial killer before it became a household term, a media darling, a cottage industry. No one paid any attention. Not then. Not now.

Back inside the library, a dejected Linda—the smoke pit empty. Grasping at straws and days wasted, she beelined for the open space beyond the stacks. If it was like UW, she thought, he also might be trolling near where the librarians kept the daily newspapers, where those same broadsheets hung precariously on dowels away from the more academic fodder. While the stacks drew the bookish types, the dailies were where the dreamers hung out. It was where dreamers like Christine—picturing herself as an enterprising reporter, a cosmopolitan career girl—could find her muse. At all libraries, public and campus alike, the dowels were the breakaway space with comfy chairs where regular folk could drop in to read, see, and be seen. That's where, after all, Christine was seen—where *he* saw her. It was where, for being in the wrong place at the wrong time, the final countdown on her life started. If he was still in Flagstaff, he would be there. Old habits die hard. Compulsions live forever. Christine, his own brother, the family he cut to pieces—they were just the beginning. Ten years later he was now honing his craft—more dangerous than ever. There would be more victims until he was stopped, until he was permanently put out of business one way or another. As the clock back at the circulation desk chimed 2:00 p.m. MT, she thought to herself: like an angel getting its wings, a cop back in Wisconsin just got another electroplated "meritorious service" trophy. They might just make hay out of the Capital City Killer theory forever. In the meantime, she and she alone would chase him.

But while Linda relentlessly gave chase and threaded her way across Middle America and back, little did she know that it was all beginning again, back where it all started—back in the Mad City. The very day she arrived in Flagstaff chasing one killer, sixteen hundred miles away, a young Madisonian was being taken by another—again. Another Madisonian vanishing; another girl on or near the university campus gone into thin air; another missing person presumed dead; another case cold before it started. It was a familiar refrain. History, it seems, was starting over, turning the soil, wreaking havoc. History was sadistic. It was opportunistic. Time melts away but it also refreezes. It liberates some while trapping others beneath the ice—forever. While he was here in Flagstaff, his methods were still back there, on rerun back in the Mad City. It was happening all over again. Eleven years later and the song remained the same.

Before long, a police interagency press conference would be held in Madison to address the latest whodunit—Julie Speerschneider vanishing. It was the latest example of Midwestern witchery that would trigger a flashback to that once fateful spring of '68. Mental images took form and revealed the sights and sounds of what Linda saw back in May of that year—the sights and sounds of every police conference in Madison that ever was and would be again: off-the-rack jackets and ties, lieutenant's bars, shorn heads, double-talk, and double-dealing. Faces and names listed brought back caustic memories with a vengeance, disturbing premonitions about what would happen next. "University Avenue," "unknown male companion," "hitchhiked," "out of character." The details deemed fit to publicly disclose would spell *Christine redux* but Linda's sniff test told her *copycat*—just one of many to come to the Mad City in the monster's wake. Blood begets blood. Time melts away nothing.

But now, out of time and looking to make her way out of the library—back to the road for the next town on the map as she chased ghosts and stale-dated clues all alone—Linda made a U-turn. She cut left down a dog-legged corridor where a window was throwing in Arizona afternoon sunlight. Once there, it was revealed to be a dead end. It was apropos. It was a revelation that summarized her life's last ten years. Looking up to her right, a sign on the wall foretold the next ten: **No Exit**.

Chapter 1

Midwestern Gothic

The evil that men do lives after them.

—William Shakespeare, *Julius Caesar*

Picnic Point

Every city, from two-bit hick town to cosmopolitan metropolis, has what might be called a main drag. Or, perhaps, *the* main drag. Every October 31—that time of year when the Celts once thought that the barrier between the living and the afterlife was at its thinnest, the protective membrane keeping us safe from the spirit world compromised to the point at which some ghouls were able to cross back over—the main boulevard in Madison, Wisconsin, transforms itself into a macabre pedestrian piazza where costumed drunks get their scare on. Of course, what never dawned on the Celts as the creators of All Hallows' Eve and, by extension, the Madisonians at "Freakfest" on State Street every year is that it's not the dead who should frighten us: we should be more afraid of the living.

True to form, the annual Freakfest is just one of countless Madison originals that has earned the city its reputation as a quintessentially "mad" place, a locale where eccentricity and idiosyncrasy prevail as being among the city's marquee qualities. Monikers such as *Mad City* and *Madtown* aren't just catchy abbreviations and truncations of the city's official name, one coined in honor of founding father and third American president James Madison. Rather, they're well-earned pseudonyms that appropriately capture—and celebrate—the city's uniquely unhinged character. These pseudonyms—not unlike Denver as the "Mile High City" or Birmingham as the "Tragic City"—appropriately underscore Madison's distinct and precarious position in the American landscape and national conscience at once. It's not only a place seated along a picturesque isthmus and circumscribed by four lakes when viewed on a map from above, but also a place shunted squarely in the mouth of madness once you're actually on the ground. As time and space battle it out, Madison is a city surrounded by reality on all sides yet still defined by a certain surrealism. It is, in fact, less a physical place as much as an idea or metaphysical construct of that same place. It's an abstraction of America and the requisite American Dream while at the same time, curiously enough, serving as the state capital. Bureaucracy, fantasy, and a conceptual anarchy all occupy the same real estate that was an unlikely urban center to begin with—nineteenth-century swampland in both the literal and figurative sense bought for a song by a federal judge in 1829. The capital city was thus in some sense always destined to be the Mad City, and then some.

Today, however, Madison has a number of well-earned bragging rights that might surprise some people. The Mad City actually rivals comparatively better-known locales such as San Francisco, New York, Austin, and Nashville as a center of creative, intellectual, and political action—officially eclipsing cities in terms of intellect and livability that have celebrated histories in the American imagination and tend to be seen as destinations in and of themselves. Wisconsin, however, doesn't usually make people's bucket lists—not the *short* list anyway. Ditto with Madison as its capital. It's not the type of place people stereotypically earmark to go and "find" themselves, whatever that means. But for many years it was, in fact, just such a place. In many respects, it still is. With currently just over half a million people in its metro area, and having been variously and previously saluted as the best metro area to live in America, the most educated city in America, and the healthiest city in America, it might be said that Madison is a book of well-kept secrets. Of course it's always the best-kept secrets that also conceal the most unsettling truths.

Beyond Madison as its capital, the State of Wisconsin has a lesser-known but inarguably sordid criminal past, one many have tried to forget. Peter Kürten, the first serial killer for whom the term "serial killer" was actually coined and also known as the "Vampire of Düsseldorf," actually has a strange Wisconsin connection—in spite of being German born and committing his murders in that country's Rhine Province. His aberrant acts of sexual violence claimed at least nine confirmed victims and as many as thirty suspected victims in the late 1920s; they were described by the police at the time as heinous acts of *serienmörder* (serial murder). Kürten was eventually caught and guillotined in the city of Cologne on July 2, 1931. His severed head was later preserved and his brain studied by scientists in an attempt to better understand what made Kürten tick; they sought to identify and document any physiological abnormalities that might explain his years of horrific offenses culminating in the murders of several schoolchildren in 1929. As luck would have it, that same specimen was later stolen by a unit of American GIs invading Germany in the final days of World War II and made its way back to the United States as a morbid spoil of war. Today, Kürten's mummified head remains a roadside attraction at a museum in the small theme-park city of Wisconsin Dells—the first documented serial killer in the world now calling the Dairy State "home." Or, at the very least, his *new* home. Like other serial killers to follow in his footsteps, the Dairy State is where, for one way or another, he would eventually end up.

Two hundred miles north of Wisconsin Dells where the Vampire's gruesome decapitated head remains on display under glass, in the similarly unheard-of Vilas County, the area's iconic Little Bohemia Lodge once served as a clandestine hideout for the infamous Dillinger Gang during America's bloody "Public Enemy" era. In April of '34, the place looked like the Alamo when the then Bureau of Investigation surprised Dillinger, Baby Face Nelson, and other Chicago gangsters and, in a frenzied firefight, revealed to the world for the first time how the seemingly benign Wisconsin hinterland had actually become the criminal underworld's preferred spot to sojourn. Later, the state became home to "Plainfield Ghoul" Ed Gein, a serial killer and body snatcher whose crimes inspired the Robert Bloch novel and subsequent Alfred Hitchcock film *Psycho*, as well as the comparatively down-market *Texas Chainsaw Massacre* franchise that followed. Gein, who died in Madison in 1984, endures as of one of the state's more noteworthy former residents, as he fashioned sex dolls and even living room furniture out of the bodies of his victims.

Thirty years later, "Milwaukee Cannibal" Jeffrey Dahmer horrified the world with his own similarly ghoulish crimes that involved serial murder, cannibalism, necrophilia, and—in retreading Gein's fetishes—the use of body parts as decorative items and novelties in his squalid lodgings. Contemporaneous with Dahmer, "North Side Strangler" Walter Ellis also stalked the streets of the same Wisconsin city, Milwaukee, claiming the lives of at least seven prostitutes between 1986 and 2007. In the meantime, not one but *three* other innocent men were charged with the Strangler's murders and two of them were wrongfully convicted at trial, serving between six and twelve years in prison while Ellis continued to kill with impunity. These same local patsies were later cleared on DNA evidence once Ellis was finally arrested. As the city cut checks for a few million dollars in hush money and scrambled to settle lawsuits and sweep up the mess, Ellis died in a Sioux Falls hospital after serving only two years for the string of sex slayings. More recently, the 2005 murder and mutilation of Teresa Halbach, the crime at the center of the controversial yet epochal 2015 Netflix docuseries *Making a Murderer*, brought renewed attention to what really goes on in a state many would consider to be the epitome of sedate. It is, after all, the same state where, in the township of Waukesha in the spring of 2014, two twelve-year-old girls lured their friend into the woods to sacrifice her to the Internet meme known as "Slender Man." So infatuated were the two demented grade-schoolers by the faceless online concoction—the Internet's first boogeyman—that they genuinely believed that they could summon him forth from cyberspace by murdering their classmate to win his affection and murderous approval. While the victim managed to narrowly escape being the first human sacrifice to a purely digital entity, the incident would punctuate what had been a protracted dark age in Wisconsin—one that few are willing to talk about. It's a history that today reminds us that the state's pastoral and peaceful veneer hides a sinister and largely forgotten history. But that's only the beginning.

One of countless online and typically anonymous renderings of the macabre Internet meme known only as Slender Man. In May 2014, two Wisconsin schoolgirls obsessed with the faceless ghoul tried to sacrifice their classmate and friend to him in the woods outside Milwaukee in order to conjure a real-world, off-line version of the creature.

From the scenic shores of Madison's postcard-worthy Picnic Point, an iconic mile-long peninsula along the south shore of Lake Mendota—one of the four lakes circumscribing the city's signature isthmus—one might be inclined to forget that same forgotten and irreparably blighted history. Within that same vista, the Mad City cleans up especially nice, as most cities do, from an untroubled distance. It's a distance from which the skeletons long since buried are no longer visible through the kaleidoscope of the naked and optimistic eye, none of the pain and trauma wrought upon the city visible from the proverbial nosebleeds of Madison's outer limits. Like every postcard snapshot ever bought and sold, it's a panorama that serves as a window into what was and what could be—what residents and visitors alike think it is now or otherwise hope it might be again. It is, if nothing else, a compelling and emotive sight that's drawn countless locals and tourists alike, all of whom flock there in the summer months to glom on to one of the best views in all of the flyover states.

A view of Madison's iconically serene Picnic Point on Lake Mendota in the early morning twilight, a halcyon reminder of the city's perceptively peaceful past. Courtesy: Wisconsin Historical Society.

The truth is, that same view—a snow-globe menagerie depicting life in the state capital, known almost as much as the Mad City as the Capital City—is also part of a much bigger story. *This* is that story. It is perhaps the greatest story never told in American history, at least the history of American crime. Moreover, even bigger than the Mad City itself, it's a story that begins and ends with two girls, each from seemingly faraway worlds, but whose lives collided right there in Madison as perhaps the unlikeliest of places. Two girls whose lives became soldered together in a chance meeting on an otherwise unremarkable afternoon in the dying days of the legendary summer of '67. It's also the story of what happened next—the travelogue of a thousand dominos toppling with tragic consequence. It's the story of sliding doors set in motion as the lives of dozens of others were to soon become mired in the same tragedy without end. It's the story of ineffective leaders who betrayed the people and the public trust alike. It's the allegory of ineffectual cops everywhere—well-intentioned in some cases, but ineffectual nonetheless—chasing a serial killer who never existed while ignoring the real killers in their midst. At the same time, it's a tale of bravery incarnate, a tale about how one city changed the course of events for so many and—ultimately—the definition of American justice.

The story begins and ends in the same place, the campus of the University of Wisconsin (UW) at Madison. Simply put, every state university system is "at" somewhere—it has to be. Whenever a state establishes a network of public universities, the city is a suffix that brands that campus as its own animal. Eventually, the U-and-whatever state abbreviation gets dropped and only the city remains, as though the campus were a stand-alone entity. Once upon a time, UC Davis simply became Davis. Ditto for UC Berkeley, UNC–Chapel Hill, and UVA Charlottesville—truncated to become Berkeley, Chapel Hill, and Charlottesville respectively. UW–Madison is the inverse, another proverbially quirky Mad City outlier. As the flagship campus of the UW system, consistently lauded as one of the top public research universities in America and what's known as a "Public Ivy," it was and remains simply known as UW. Any reference to UW is to refer to UW–Madison by default. The city where the campus is situated therefore only ever needs to be mentioned in cases when it's *not* Madison. But in this case, it is. It first began back in the summer of '67 when everything started coming up Madison.

Young Americans

One can, not surprisingly, see the prized UW campus from Picnic Point, the university campus, like in many cities, having been gobbled up as the most prime and picturesque real estate during Madison's earliest days. On a spring evening sometime around the equinox of '65, one sixteen-year-old Linda Tomaszewski—third generation American, descended from Polish immigrants, tough as nails—took in that view and smelled the air and, before long, carved out a plan. It was just over sixty miles door-to-door—about seventy-four minutes in daytime traffic—from Linda's two-story prewar home on South 39th Street in Milwaukee to the gates of UW. By the standards of blue-collar, God-fearing Catholic Southside Milwaukee, it was also worlds away—two destinations poles apart. In the spring of '65, Linda was only a sophomore at nearby St. Mary's Academy, an all-girls Catholic school split eighty-twenty between Poles and Italians, run by some of the most notoriously ascetic nuns in all the Midwest. But it was there and then that it first dawned on the feisty redhead that UW was, like the moon landing already in the works, out of this world yet still within grasp. It was just far enough to get away and cut the cord to her old neighborhood but not *too* far to draw the ire of her Old World parents or the stringent St. Mary's nuns. As the first of her family set to go to college, the UW campus would still be within range of her fireman father's protective reach—a proverbial force field that extended to Madison but no farther—and also close enough to abate the worry of her doting grandparents who rented out the second-story granny suite of the family home. But it was also distant enough to allow young Linda, at long last, to come up for air. In time, however, in her search for freedom, she'd get more than she bargained for.

Unlike most other St. Mary's girls, Linda knew by her senior year that she needed to parlay her gold-plated GPA into a one-way ticket out of working-class tedium in Southside Milwaukee. It was an escape hatch from either one of the two lives to which most of her classmates had resigned themselves to inheriting: life as a homemaker like their mothers and mothers' mothers or, like their neighbors with a color Zenith and maybe a second car, life in the typing pool at the Allen-Bradley Company headquarters. It was a local calling that, like a coal mine in a northern town, or the docks in a coastal community, was often seen as the only option for young Milwaukee women at the time. If one were to get *really* lucky, a Southside career woman of that era might even land a gig as a "senior" secretary and get a reserved parking space—a brass nameplate on the desk to boot. But young Linda always made her own luck. By August of '67 that meant hitting the road to UW and never looking back. By then, she had, of course, absolutely no idea what forces had already been set in motion—what fate had in store for her. By the next time she made it to Picnic Point to take in that same panorama that had once inspired her to pull up roots from Southside Milwaukee, she'd end up longing for the simple life as an Allen-Bradley typist—for a life doing anything other than what the universe had thrown at her. But a little over halfway through her freshman year, someone burned down Linda's world. In so doing, they awoke a sleeping giant.

Fast-forward to a decade later and across America, the summer of '77 would become infamously known as the Summer of Sam. Amid a suffocating heat wave, a psychotic creep named David Berkowitz toting a .44 caliber revolver kept New York City, and by extension much of the country, under siege. Citizens locked themselves in behind latched doors and tightly fastened windows, without air conditioning, in most cases. All the while the killer reveled in the mass panic, ginning up further fear by sending taunting communiqués to the local police and newspapers. He called himself the Son of Sam, claiming to be controlled during his murderous deeds by a demonic force channeled through, of all things, his neighbor's dog. What a difference a decade makes. Precisely ten years earlier was the endless summer of '67—what became known as the Summer of Love. With San Francisco's Haight-Ashbury district as its epicenter, the Summer of Love was also a distinctly national phenomenon that transcended the celebrated Bay Area, sending out a seismic wave of psychedelic drug use, sexual experimentation, and self-righteous dissolution that made its way east across America, swallowing up unsuspecting cities like Madison in an unwashed wave of hippie zealotry. It was the Pandora's box that kicked off a larger cultural paradigm that—presto change-o—soon became known as the Age of Aquarius.

The Summer of Love never made it to Linda Tomaszewski's neighborhood in Southside Milwaukee. By the fall of '67, however, the Age of Aquarius would run roughshod over the Mad City—the new place she called home. At UW, Linda arrived as a bright-eyed if not overwhelmed freshman to find a counterculture agitator's delight. The pep rallies and Sadie Hawkins dances she'd expected, and which the UW recruiters visiting St. Mary's had extolled to her guidance counselors and senior administrators, had by then been summarily cannibalized by student protests and rowdy sit-ins. The time-honored homecoming parade came to feature draft card burnings as a requisite sideshow, one that diverted attention from the hundred-year mainstay of ticker-tape beauty queens marching in soldier formation down State Street. Fraternities and sororities saw their rush-week pledges rivaled by fringe activist groups such as the Students for a Democratic Society, otherwise abbreviated as SDS, while the more violent Weather Underground recruited some pledges of their own. One of the infamous Chicago Seven—a faction of malcontents charged with inciting a riot at the Democratic convention in Chicago the following year—had matriculated at UW and was already stirring the pot in Madison that same autumn. Students in bell-bottoms and profs in houndstooth jackets talked about Grace Slick as the new Plato and actually meant it. A pedantic English TA recited Chaucer by day and pushed H by night. Any sloganeering down-and-outer with a six-string or tambourine was the proverbial big man on campus. Anything 'Nam was fair game for attack—a good reason to get stoned and chew the rag. By September of '67, someone had turned on the faucet. *Free love* was little more than a euphemism for *powder keg*—and the wick was lit.

Just shy of its 120th anniversary, the UW campus had, to some extent, also become a microcosm of Madison proper—or at least what people thought it was. It was hoped that the crowning intellectual achievement of a state whose motto ("Forward") might appropriately capture Wisconsin's thirst for progress, innovation, and expansion, UW was a tolerant, creative, and most importantly a *decent* place in the late '60s. That's why, after all, aside from the short drive, Linda's parents let her abscond from church life and daily chores to study there. The truth is that the campus, though fitting all of these descriptions and embodying all of these features, actually couldn't have been more of a blank slate—a place untested once in the throes of social upheaval and thus primed for a new radicalism once the Age of Aquarius dawned. For a city like Madison—the capital of America's dairy land and a quintessentially Midwestern locale—it was the equivalent of throwing kerosene on a smoldering fire clamoring for oxygen. The city or, more accurately perhaps, the new generation at UW, was a kinetic force desperate to grow and expand. And it did.

When Linda first set foot in the Mad City as a UW freshman, the campus had become an event horizon for a counterculture she never really knew. But amid the incipient mayhem, a buttoned-down Polish Catholic girl with one-inch spectacles from Southside Milwaukee, completely out of her element and subsumed by almost everything the sisters at St. Mary's had warned her about, found the most unlikely of allies. The girl she met turned out to be her new best friend, in fact. Her new crony and confidante was studious, just like Linda was. She was also modest and personified kindness when she didn't have to. She was dedicated to family, friends, and faith—without exception. She loved origami, art, and poetry. She loved the outdoors, animals, and, most of all, her Motown records. Her name was Christine Rothschild. In time, Linda would learn to call her Chris. In time, the Mad City newspapermen called her something else—the first victim.

Soft Target

Christine's background in the Edgewater section of Chicago was the antithesis of Linda's upbringing in Milwaukee. Maybe that's why they gelled. Linda's working-class origins were at once a badge she'd wear close to her heart and also a blight she'd keep concealed from the blue-blooded and boringly repetitive New Englanders with whom she shared lecture halls and dorm bathrooms at UW in the fall of '67. Many were predictably messed-up trust-fund punks from NYC and metro Boston who couldn't cut the Ivy League and whose folks had sent them to UW to play grown-up for a few years, flunk out, and then come home humbled and supplicating—with hat in hand. But Christine was different; from day one Linda knew that she was a notable exception. She was a genuine outlier whom Linda read like an open book: old money, cerebral, yet humble—even vulnerable. Hailing from a five-star family in a manicured north-end neighborhood in lakefront Chicago, Christine's father was a wealthy industrialist who, among other things, reportedly held the first patent on what would later become the automated parking garage boom gate. Christine grew up in a three-story, quintessentially Federal-style home on Kenmore Street, just minutes from Wrigley Field, and was an honors graduate of the tony Senn Secondary on nearby Glenwood Avenue. There she had managed to graduate fourth in her class of five hundred while also serving as all-school class president, a member of the French club, and both writer and editor for the school newspaper. But despite her privileged upbringing and modeling gigs—a regular for *Teen Fashion News Sheet* and other look books for Magnificent Mile clothiers—Christine epitomized modesty. Not only modesty, in fact, but thoughtfulness. She wore no jewelry, only donned flat shoes, and sported little if any makeup. Unlike her friends back home in the Windy City, Christine cared more about the UNICEF initiatives in Africa than who wore what at the Academy Awards. Then there was her mother.

A well-heeled woman and well-intentioned dilettante, Christine's mother, Patria, had by the summer of '67 when Christine matriculated at UW, already buried two sons, dead in separate tragedies. By that same fall, she had also taken to toiling in hobbies in which women like her always seemed to excel—buying and collecting things that weren't for sale. She could be found setting out doilies one day and hanging a Picasso—a *real* Picasso—on the dining room wall the next. She was an immaculate hostess and an inveterate aesthete, a big-city socialite if there ever was one. But ahead of Christine's departure for UW that same August, her mother bought her something that actually *was* for sale—an opal ring purchased on first sight from a glass case at Bloomingdale's on the city's famed Magnificent Mile. It was one of the few pieces of jewelry that Christine ever wore outside of a Chicago-area catalogue—the only one she wore to UW. Christine's mother would later go to her grave believing unequivocally that that same ring, like the Hope Diamond before it, was hexed. That it was an augury of evil—a harbinger of pain.

By the time Christine arrived at UW, she, like Linda, was keenly aware that—despite her parents' best intentions—she was in the wrong place at the wrong time. She'd always wanted to attend an East Coast college, maybe the same Ivy League campuses that the moneyed detritus of UW, now her peers and classmates, never got into. Maybe a university in Canada or Scandinavia. Her parents had flat-out forbidden it. Maybe Columbia and then go on to become a journalist for a major NYC daily, she once thought; maybe Princeton and, from there, a political columnist—a witty pundit and satirist. Maybe Smith in Northampton, maybe Vassar in Poughkeepsie. Although Christine loved to read and to write—and loved to travel even more—the schools that really jazzed her and opened up the world for her were summarily deemed off-limits by her Christian Scientist family. New England, and especially New York, were out of bounds—full stop. Christine needed to be closer to home, her parents asserted, forever within reach—always on a short leash. Of those colleges within the perimeter of that leash, her parents thought the safest campus for their little girl was UW. Her parents thought wrong.

Left: A key turning point in the history of the Mad City. As a crowd of gawkers looks on, the very public 1954 Russ family murder-suicide marked a rude awakening for many about the violent underbelly of Madison that would reach critical mass just over a decade later. Right: By the late 1960s, arrests along Main Street and near the UW campus, the perceived sanctuary of the city, were increasingly common. In this case, a Madison police officer pursues a cavalier suspect who saunters away from the scene of a theft. Courtesy: Wisconsin Historical Society.

In reality, the protective cocoon her parents were weaving for Christine was a mechanism that kept her from escaping as much as it was one that prevented danger from getting in—a double dead bolt on the only exit in a burning building. By the time she first arrived at UW, Christine was also severely bulimic, depressed, and had left her Mag

Mile high-end Chicago threads back home. She had by that fall taken to wearing garments—mostly shifts—sewn by her sister, Roxanne, which were typically a couple of sizes too large. The clothes also managed to serve the secondary purpose of masking just how ravaged her body had become by the fall of '67; the Christian Scientists had told her that disorders of the body and the mind alike were mere illusions and forbade her from seeking medical attention or intervention—period. In reality, life behind closed doors on uptown Kenmore Street wasn't as perfect as it seemed, or as it ever appears to be anywhere. Subsisting on Folgers and garden salad—the consistently banal binge that prefaced each and every purge—years of catalogue modeling in Chicago for stores such as Marshall Field's, Saks, and the litany of high-end boutiques and clothiers along the downtown "Loop" had sanded down Christine's identity as much as it had her bodily frame. It had whittled her down to being little more—in her mind at least—than a sentient shop-window mannequin first, Christine Rothschild as a person second. But when Christine and Linda first met by happenstance, sharing a laugh when some generic UW stoner of the day tripped over a brochure rack and fell ass over teakettle onto the floor of Dean Ruedisili's waiting room in South Hall in late August '67, the ice was summarily broken. It was there and then—the only two students in the waiting room that day—that Linda saw the *real* Christine for who she was and in the flesh. Christine saw Linda back. She saw herself back—her reflection smiling for the first time in years in Linda's eyes. Soon, they were kindred spirits. It was a chance meeting that would change their lives. It was a chance meeting that would change a city and state's criminal history at once. It's a history that, until now, it seems few have ever known about.

During that late summer and into the balmy autumn of '67, following their separate arrivals at UW, Linda and Christine weren't the only strangers in a strange land. By September of that year, Madison was a place that, in good faith it seems, lowered the drawbridge and invited in trouble. It had unwittingly become a veritable helipad for psychopaths landing there from all over the Midwest and beyond. If conventional criminology prior to the 1960s taught us anything useful, it's that amid this same type of cultural upheaval and social disorganization, much like the metaphysical curtain that the Celts thought was pulled back every Halloween night, such pickings are prime targets for predators looking to walk into—and destroy—the lives of innocents when they aren't looking. Cities such as Madison and places such as UW were to become the proverbial soft targets that many larger and even stereotypically more "dangerous cities" could never offer up so easily. Before the clinical and forensic literature on psychopaths, which was to later come and ultimately verify what the annals of crime had already shown, a more anecdotal history confirmed that perceptively safe cities caught up in great migrations and celebrations tend to simultaneously invite in and ignore homicidal threats at a rate rarely seen in more perceptively perilous locales. Consider, by way of comparison, the World's Fair of 1893 in Christine Rothschild's hometown of Chicago. It was, ostensibly, a celebration of the four hundredth anniversary of Columbus discovering America. It also ended up being what likely remains the single greatest protracted bloodbath on American soil at the hands of an American citizen.

Known at the time as the Columbian National Exposition, the 1893 iteration of the now iconic World's Fair was hosted in Chicago between May and October of that year, seeing millions of international tourists descend on the city without much of a plan—much less a care. Their objectives were little more than to take in some sights, soak up the town, and find a place to bed down for a few weeks. Many of the exhibitors, promoters, and performers would, of course, be staying for several months—for the entirety of the event—as would the service-class workers who sought out Chicago as something of an Industrial Era oasis with tourists inevitably paying and tipping in cash. Beyond that, no one knew where their friends, coworkers, or loved ones would be at any given time or would be staying for any prolonged period, much less when they arrived in Chicago or when they planned to leave. It was a psychopath's delight and, all the while, one man lay in wait—Herman Mudgett, aka H. H. Holmes.

At the corner of 63rd and South Wallace in South Chicago, Holmes by 1893 had built an ostentatious structure the locals ominously coined "the Castle." Well ahead of the World's Fair but predicting the opportunities it would provide in terms of a stocked pond of easy victims—soft targets—Holmes began bankrolling construction of the fortified building with blood money. His first step was to murder his employer at the pharmacy across the street from the building site and then to remortgage the store's assets to first get shovels in the ground. The Castle that was later built, and on initial appearance, was deemed to be a stately hotel catering to visitors to the Windy City and, more specifically, the upcoming World's Fair. In reality, it was a built-to-suit deathtrap designed so that guests would check in and never check out—literally. There were suite doors with no interior handles and lace curtains drawn across false, bricked-up windows—all to prevent escape following check-in. Some rooms were disguised gas chambers and others torture chambers. The basement boiler room was a proverbial hell on Earth where the victims—guests, visitors, employees, deliverymen—were stripped of flesh and their bones reassembled for sale to medical schools as articulated skeletons for study by students unaware of the ghastly origins of the specimens used by their professors. By the time of his arrest by Pinkerton agents in November of 1894 after fleeing north to Canada and hiding out—and killing—in the city of Toronto, Holmes's imposing edifice back in Chicago had become the awe of Southside schoolchildren. They assigned it a new name that the press would ensure to make headlines worldwide—the "Murder Castle." The new moniker was beyond well deserved. Holmes is thought to have lured up to two hundred people to their deaths and subsequent acid baths over the course of the World's Fair, including migrant service staff who were hired off the books in many cases and never seen or heard from again. Yet, despite the magnitude of his crimes, Holmes remains simultaneously the least understood and most understudied serial killer in American history, in large part due to the vintage of his crimes and the deplorable state of police record keeping at the time. What we do know, however, as author Erik Larson theorizes in the book *The Devil in the White City*, is that Holmes was America's first verifiable serial killer by modern definition, and, potentially, to this day its worst. More importantly, he was the first known serial or mass murderer to settle in a city and premeditate his crimes based on the specific social ecology of that same city. In some sense, Holmes *profiled* Chicago as his hunting ground based on its dynamism and disorganization—the fact that people would arrive there while swept up in something bigger than they were and inevitably let their guard down. With the Chicago fair of 1893, the malevolent psychopath was born and, with it, the great American city became a dangerous place. A hunting ground writ large.

True to form, H. H. Holmes was a criminal psychopath—that fraction of the roughly 1 percent of the population who are existing psychopaths—those with the power to change history, destroy lives on a grand scale, and change the social complexion of entire cities forever. Although only a small number of that same 1 percent of psychopaths actually amount to violent sexual predators in the vein of H. H. Holmes, sadly, they're also what might be called the "vocal minority," the most motivated and prominent of psychopaths. Cities such as Madison in '67 amid the Age of Aquarius would have been, as was *fin de siècle* Chicago for H. H. Holmes, noteworthy places for earmarking by men of a similar mindset—destinations on their radar from the get-go. The Mad City was by the Summer of Love a proverbial chessboard where there were pawns to be summarily scarified and more coveted prizes to be had. In search of such spoils, men such as Holmes would be drawn there. In Madison, some of these same types of men would also be drawn there; some would stay, and at least one would come and later go. After he did so, Linda would follow him from the city and stay on his tail—forever shadowing him to make sure he never struck again. She would ensure that he never settled in another soft target city to pick up where he left off, as he did in Madison. She would ensure *it* never happened again.

Penny Dreadful

The fact that no one can estimate with any certainty just how many victims were lured to their death in the Chicago hotel of horrors constructed by Holmes reflects the stark reality that a great deal of murder investigation was—and still is—pure guesswork. In fact, today there are no fewer than twenty of the largest American cities where, if you're murdered right now while reading this book, the chances of your killer being apprehended are no better than 15 percent. The odds are even worse if you're killed at random, which in some cities accounts for over 90 percent of unsolved homicides. The numeracy is both unassailable and inscrutable—not to mention terrifying. It also reflects the fact that denial for many otherwise intelligent people is a necessary survival skill. It confirms that we all prefer stories, whether fact or fiction, that have a discernible villain, as evidenced by Holmes's tell-all for the Hearst newspaper empire printed immediately prior to his execution—he thus became the first of countless cases of serial killers to be anointed as a celebrity by the commercial media of their day. In the end, it's easier to process the idea of a single criminal psychopath being the sole cause of so much mayhem rather than to spread responsibility among many—to acquiesce to the stark reality that a greater number of murders than previously thought might actually be separate, random events.

The uncomfortable alternative would be to believe that, as far back as 1893, Holmes may have killed as few as two hundred people while another eighteen hundred or so of the suspected two thousand murders that occurred in Chicago and the surrounding area during this period might have been the product of multiple offenders, each with varying methods and motives. The idea that Holmes single-handedly killed all of them is, not surprisingly, more palatable than the thought that these tourists and wage laborers might have been dispatched in an assortment of random incidents by an equally random assortment of discrete offenders. Psychologically, humans as a species need answers—a face, a name, a reason. We don't want to believe, even in a city like Chicago that's been racked by violence since its founding, that a monster like Holmes could exist alongside other killers—murderers who were themselves never caught. We need to make Holmes the beginning—and end—of it all. But it's when there is no face and no name to assign blame to—no villain to simultaneously titillate and terrify—that things really unravel and history gets it wrong. Of course, five years before H. H. Holmes began murdering in earnest, Jack the Ripper had become a household name not only in London, England, but also across Europe and the Americas. And while there is no question that women in the East London slum of Whitechapel were being slaughtered during this same period, the explanation for these deaths would go on to become pure fiction.

A September 1888 headline in the British "penny dreadful" Illustrated Police News *marked the beginning of the mass hysteria that came to define the Whitechapel murders still credited to the mysterious Jack the Ripper. In reality, the total of eleven murders committed in East London between 1888 and 1891 are the work of multiple killers, the Ripper having become the criminological equivalent of Bigfoot and other modern-day legends and hoaxes.*

The truth is that fiction disguised as history and legitimized by people who ought to know better is still fiction. The multimillion-dollar murderabilia and dark tourism industry spawned by those same Whitechapel murders initially began with the penny papers of the era, or "penny dreadfuls" as they were known—cheap, lurid, and exploitative, somewhere between comic book and tabloid—and went from bad to worse from there, setting the stage for twentieth-century disinformation tactics by the media to increase circulation. The fact is that the Ripper legend is little more than just that—legend. His existence in nineteenth-century London marked the predictable creation of a character to whom the police and the public alike could attribute blame and work into a believable narrative, the Ripper simply being alchemized into existence through a complicated yet cumulative threefold phenomenon. This included: firstly, overzealous reportage by an often unscrupulous news media; secondly, a public with a penchant for legend and superstition at the expense of fact; and, lastly, the ease with which what are known as *false linkages* can be made, especially when police are in over their heads—not to mention desperate for a patsy. If this sounds familiar it's because it would happen again. And again.

Before long, the Ripper becomes the Strangler in Boston in 1963, once again through false linkages and media meddling. He later transmutes into the Freeway Killer in 1970s California, which was three separate serial killers, all later caught, their discrete victims' deaths for years having been wrongly connected to a single sex slayer. Later, he's the North Side Strangler, already mentioned, in Milwaukee where three men get erroneously linked to and blamed for one's man's reign in murder. Between erroneously inflating and deflating the number of suspects for whom the police should be looking, the annals of history are sadly chalk full of such errors of homicidal arithmetic. In the meantime, in the Mad City—1968 through 1984—the Ripper reemerges, this time as the so-called Capital City Killer. Same myth, different city. Different moniker, same incompetence.

The truth is that there wasn't a single Jack the Ripper—there were several. He didn't write letters to the newspapers. Two of the three key documents were confirmed as forgeries created by an unscrupulous newsman named Thomas Bulling. Nor did he conform to the profile cooked up by Dr. Thomas Bond—the forensic pathologist overseeing some of the autopsies, and who later threw himself out a window—who suggested the killer was a society man wandering through the London fog in a black cape and top hat. The killers didn't include Lewis Carroll or Sir Arthur Conan Doyle or the physician to the British royal family as some have ridiculously speculated. The purported Whitechapel Ripper certainly wasn't some globe-trotting maniac who moved from America where he had reportedly been the Servant Girl Annihilator of Austin, Texas—only to later decide to move *to* America to become the Axeman of New Orleans as many self-avowed "Ripperologists" have often argued. In fact, given the criminal ecology of London's Whitechapel district at the time, the murders are just as likely to be message killings between the rival gangs who ran prostitution rings and street-level opium dealing in East London as much as they are the work of one or even two or more serial killers. In truth, the Ripper theory is just as likely a nineteenth-century version of the *femicide* later seen in Juárez, Mexico, where hundreds of young women, working mostly in the maquiladoras and other sweatshops, have been murdered over the last two decades. With varying motives and MOs, about a third of the tragic Juárez slayings involve sexual assault, and others robbery or extortion. Some are dispatched quickly while others are mutilated in the same fashion as the Whitechapel victims. The circumstances and victim profiles are actually quite similar with one difference—no one is claiming there is a single Juárez Ripper or offering spooky walking tours of the murder scenes. There is no money to be made off of the Mexican femicide, no kitsch industry of novelty mugs, ten-cent tours, or T-shirts. From Whitechapel to Juárez, Madison—it turns out—is the proverbial Rosetta stone. The Mad City is the missing link in explaining how and why cities make murderers.

Room 119

The Mad City was, for a time, a Whitechapel in silk stockings. While the houses were nicer and the air cleaner—no London fog, no slanty shanties—the antecedents were in place to recreate the same conditions that allowed the Ripper myth to be borne out of the violence that once deluged East London. In the end, however, Madison didn't have a "canonical" five victims as the traditional Ripper legend holds. It had a canonical seven. All told, seven victims would be slain at the hands of an equally fictional Capital City Killer—a mythical Wisconsin Ripper. Like Whitechapel before it, some of these city murders were connected to each other and a common offender, and some weren't. Like the Boston Strangler, the Freeway Killer, and other more recent American serial killer cases mired in false linkages, Madison would soon have its own Ripper myth courtesy of snap judgments and overblown egos. In time, they'd call him the Capital City Killer—a Midwestern Ripper. A man for all seasons.

As with the equally fictive Ripper before him, the crimes attributed to the Capital City Killer actually happened—there is no arguing that. There is also no arguing that they were nothing short of horrific. The trouble is that, just like the Whitechapel murders, nearly a century before the slayings started in Madison, the myth quickly took over and subsumed any remnant of objectivity. Reality was soon something of an obscure and less interesting footnote to the main story—the preferred folktale—that few ever bothered to fact-check. Like the Age of Aquarius before it, the lore of the Capital City Killer at once swallowed the Mad City and its rag-tag assemblage of police departments. These included the city cops—the Madison PD—as well as the Wisconsin State Police, the Dane County Sheriff's Department, and—last but certainly the worst hit—the UW campus police. Before long, hack reporters fanned flames while campus scuttlebutt trumped official press releases from the authorities. Eventually the press releases stopped and only urban legend prevailed—the same legends that clouded the facts and enabled false linkages in a series of killings that would cast a twenty-year shadow over UW, Madison, and even the entire Midwest. From Jack the Ripper to the Capital City Killer, it seems that history and myth can make strange bedfellows. Sometimes, it might even suit the interests of those in charge.

Initially a theory rejected wholesale by police, the legend of a single serial killer stalking the campus and area surrounding UW ultimately evolved into a war of attrition and took on a life of its own. Before long, it was Capital City Killer *here*, Capital City Killer *there*. He was everywhere, wanted and on the lam for every crime—ever. If the dates might have realistically lined up, local cops, politicos, and the opportunists newly freed from the Wisconsin woodwork would have put him on the grassy knoll for the JFK snuff in '63, on a ladder outside the Lindbergh home in '32, and at Calvary for the crucifixion.

But Linda Tomaszewski knew better. She knew by the summer of '68 that whoever killed her new best friend, Christine, didn't stay in the Mad City. He wouldn't. He couldn't. He would keep moving as he had before—as he always would. He would be forever walking into the lives of vulnerable young women when he knew they weren't looking. He had an eye for them, for young girls like Christine—trusting, naïve, pure.

Sometimes, he'd strike closer to home—against those who trusted him most. But while the cops chased mirages for years on end and the Capital City Killer became the proverbial boogeyman of Madison—especially in the hallowed halls of UW—Linda was chasing a real serial killer.

A tale of two dorms. Left: Two female UW students are squired by a young man to the front doors of the monolithic Witte Hall, built in the Brutalist style and designed to maximize occupancy. Right: The more traditional and quiet—and isolated—Ann Emery Hall, where Christine Rothschild lived in room 119 for the final months of her life while attending UW. Courtesy: UW–Madison Archives Collection & Wisconsin Historical Society.

Linda's freshman year at UW was spent living, as many young women at UW did, within the confines of the dormitory known as Witte Hall. In the fall of '67, the building looked more like the YWCA than it did a traditional dorm. It still does. Ten stories spread across two towers—a concreted-poured exterior, punch-hole windows—bisected by a central common, the place is a perfectly uninspired cube of conformity. Once upon a time, it also packed in thousands of students at two to a room, all females. Against a more traditional collegiate Gothic backdrop, the monolith of Witte Hall was quite clearly the unwanted stepchild of campus buildings, one built in the raw, fortress-like Brutalism that defined much of the new construction of the 1950s and '60s. But, with history at UW soon set to change, it was also a place that offered safety in numbers.

Christine, on the other hand, lived at the much more private and reclusive Ann Emery Hall during her freshman year, less a dormitory itself as much as it was a traditional boarding house. It was intended by her father to serve as a not-so-secret prelude to the type of exclusive living Christine's life might allow if she didn't stray too far from the nest—if she exorcised what she had to at UW and came home as expected.

Between Linda and Christine, the dichotomy of Witte Hall and Ann Emery came to underscore their odd-couple pasts as much as it did their present circumstances—and their tragic shared future. An old and stately looking Tudor Revival–style structure, Ann Emery Hall had an assortment of aged housemistresses who kept eyes on the first-year girls who lived there. They were girls who came and went through a dated yet opulently furnished front parlor—luxurious English country pieces, richly polished Comtoise clocks—all of which could easily be mistaken for the velvet-pillowed lobby ornaments of the old-money Ridgemoor Club back in Christine's native Chicago. It was also a space unspoiled by modern conveniences and security mechanisms. There was no controlled entry, no intercom, no cameras or convex mirrors, and no sign-in book. For a motivated predator, Ann Emery Hall would prove to be the perfect soft target.

On a typical day after class, Christine would head back to room 119 at Ann Emery Hall—single bed, single occupancy, no visitors—without a care in the world, and throw an Aretha Franklin album on her turntable before flipping open something by Yeats or Keats. Sometimes she would take pen to paper and write her own prose and poetry, much of it dark and solemn. One such poem, written in free verse, she titled "You're a Sad Campus, Wisconsin," digging into what she saw as the counterculture facades that many students and faculty, otherwise scared half to death of the real world, adopted as a pretense in and out of the classroom.

By spring thaw, it had been a long and sad winter for Christine while living at Ann Emery Hall and at UW generally. The shorter days also meant longer nights—endless nights it seemed for "Chris," as Linda called her, who, by the spring of '68, also knew that she had an unwanted nightly caller outside her ground-floor window. There was someone, some invisible but sentient force, lurking in the seemingly interminable darkness of an endless Wisconsin winter behind the threadbare curtains of her dorm room. Someone was stalking her—a peeper, prowler, some kind of twisted sleepwatcher, she wasn't sure. By the time April came around, he had also started calling her room. It began with the typical heavy breathing and guttural groaning, or what psychology textbooks call *telephone scatologia*—someone who obtains sexual arousal and power from the fear elicited through making, typically repeated, anonymous and menacing calls. In time, he began to do more than just breathe and make bizarre noises. In time, he came to speak. With an intentionally demonic sounding and dramatized tenor, the caller would tell Christine what she was wearing, what time she got home, what time she turned out the lights—even how her body looked when she was asleep. He could see her through the translucent curtains. He could see *everything*. Well before the clinical and forensic literature had assigned the name *somnophilia* to describe this bizarre and dangerous fixation on sleeping and helpless people—typically women—a particular brand of peeping linked with all sorts of other disorders, including necrophilia, the caller made it clear that he wasn't going away anytime soon. On the contrary, he was escalating—and quickly.

Unfortunately, at age eighteen and feeling invincible as any eighteen-year-old does, Christine still had no idea by late April of '68 just how much danger she was actually in. She had no concept of the events that had already been set in motion—the laws of inertia at work behind the curtain, both literally and figuratively, and the finality that had already been wrought. She would bring up the unsettling calls in passing to Linda when they'd meet for their daily coffee outside Bascom Hall, a bench situated in the shadow of President Lincoln's statue at their usual meeting spot. Other times, it might be at Rennebohm's, the most popular milkshake and short-order joint among students at UW. As she explained to Linda, Christine wasn't sure if the figure she could discern through the cheesecloth curtains of room 119 was real or illusory—if the calls were real or part of the spate of nightmares she'd been having about someone following her. She was too afraid to pull back the curtain to make sure—too paralyzed by fear to call the phone company to check, much less call the police. She thought, and perhaps even hoped, that her mind might have been playing tricks on her, her starvation diet and a bout of Wisconsin cabin fever having ravaged her cognition to the point of imagining it all.

One thing for certain was that, if the calls were real, they were getting more frequent, more intense, more foreboding. Linda implored Christine to report the nighttime calls to the cops of jurisdiction, the UW Five-O, just to be sure. Linda also asked her to think about who might be behind the calls, who exactly the self-admitted sleepwatcher and night stalker could be. Perhaps it was someone from class or perhaps an overzealous member of the First Church of Christ, Scientist she attended while in Madison at the insistence of her loving but inevitably domineering parents. As Linda already knew from Christine's other weekly tales, there was no shortage of courtiers and creeps at both locales to populate a list of likely suspects. The truth was, however, that, by the time she let Linda in on the dark secret of the man haunting her room at Ann Emery through the curtains and by telephone, Christine had already figured out exactly who it was. She also knew—tragically—that there was no stopping him.

Chapter 2

The Sleepwatcher

It was written I should be loyal to the nightmare of my choice.

—Joseph Conrad, *Heart of Darkness*

April Fool

In March of '68, roughly a month before the night stalking, sleepwatching, and twisted phone calls started in earnest, Christine had taken to sequestering herself in UW's Memorial Library reading room between classes and even on weekends. It was perhaps the last vestige of solitude amid the social turbulence of a rowdy campus where she could find some alone time and marshal her thoughts. The place was something of a cozy hideaway within the hub of the library proper, drawing in that special type of bookworm seeking a respite from the vexing rowdiness that pervaded the rest of the building. It was quieter, less crowded, and more intimate. The downside was that the room was also a veritable fishbowl where everyone inside was backlit and on display—cluelessly voyeurized—within a self-contained glass terrarium. It was the perfect place to sit and watch, to sit and wait. It was the perfect locale to beset a coveted prize from a distance. It was the perfect spot to spring a trap.

Enter Niels Bjorn Jorgensen, MD. Forty-two years old, a lecherous, unrelenting narcissist, and a pathological liar to beat the band. Standing a lanky six feet on the dot, thinning blond hair with steely blue eyes that looked reptilian black in the right light. He was nothing if not an unsettling presence when he officially arrived on campus on April Fools' Day '68—a natural-born bedlamite. As a self-proclaimed veteran of the Battle of the Bulge, he said he was a field medic sergeant assigned to the 117th—said he took shrapnel in the leg while crossing the Ardennes on Christmas Eve '44. Now, out of thin air, it seemed, he'd materialized in Madison. He arrived in the Mad City, he said, to button up his medical residency, drawn there from Michigan via California, from as far away as South Africa before that. He hailed from nowhere in particular and yet everywhere, it seemed—a veritable nomad—and had come to UW to begin his third year med school residency in general surgery. Apparently he was completing his residency on some sort of odd piecemeal installment plan at universities that would take him here and there. In the spring of '68 the "here" was, for reasons that no one ever really knew, the city of Madison—the UW campus hospital, a teaching hospital, as his home base. It didn't take long before Jorgensen started giving coworkers there—doctors, nurses, even the orderlies—the heebie-jeebies. Cold and arrogant with a shallow affect, he would soon also prove to be a convincing social chameleon when it suited him. A textbook psychopath, Jorgensen appeared in town like an apparition, touting faraway credentials and reveling in what he called the "opportunities" a place like the Mad City offered him. No one was ever really sure what that meant, what he was really about, or where he came from. He simply showed up one day and that was that.

Niels Jorgensen arrived at UW to begin his latest medical school residency in general surgery at the campus hospital in April of 1968. At age forty-five, Jorgensen was roughly twenty years older than his peers and had a strangely suspicious résumé that seemed to go unverified. Soon enough, his true colors would come to the fore.

Jorgensen's backstory before getting into medicine as a midlife career was a mystery long before anyone started to look into it. It was an ever-changing series of yarns, all of which were really never anything less than arcane. What was clear was that his spare time, as best anyone could tell, was spent aimlessly prowling the campus or sitting for hours on end in the Memorial reading room—usually when Christine was there. Later, it was *only* when Christine was there. The problem was that he never checked out any books. Nor was he known to ever talk about books, save one—something called *The Love Pirate* that would soon be published. Had anyone gone looking, they'd have known the pages of that manuscript were a codex of Jorgensen's real past deeds—the book provided the elusive answers to who and *what* Jorgensen really was by the time he arrived in Madison; the book was the dark backstory of where he was and what he had done before he mysteriously matriculated at UW. It was also a window into an even darker future.

But by the end of that same April, Christine knew exactly who Jorgensen was—what he really was about. After targeting her for most of that month, shadowing her in the library and peering at her from between the shelves, prowling around outside her bedroom window at Ann Emery and calling her room, he escalated to the point of following her out to the library smoke pit as she indulged in her hourly compulsion. It was there that he made his first real approach. But Christine instantly made the connection. True to form, she was weirded out and summarily rebuffed him, crushing out a newly lit cigarette and heading back inside. She had immediately recognized his game, and her instincts spelled "trouble" in living Technicolor. Humans, Christine knew, were the only species on the planet to have socialized themselves out of the evolutionary survival instincts. She knew that girls would get in cars, talk to strange men, or even reveal their names and addresses when asked, afraid of looking rude or ungracious even when their primordial gut instincts told them it was dangerous—even when their gut instincts told them that there was really nothing random about random chance encounters. Women, she knew, had in some sense come to place outward appearances and ladylike decorum ahead of listening to those same instincts. Predators knew it. That's how, after all, girls got talked into cars, why they never ran for help when they thought they were being followed. But Christine trusted her gut instinct, a female intuition refined over tens of thousands of years of evolution and shaped by her life back east in the big city. So when the good doctor feigned being in need of a light for a battered old cigarette,

Christine recognized it as a textbook prop and called him out on it—told him to take a hike and made her way back into the library on the double to find safety in numbers. But it was all of little help in preventing the inevitable. At that time and place, for reasons beyond Christine's control, the die was cast. The plaster had set.

By then, Jorgensen had been to the reading room enough to know when Christine came and when she left—and most importantly where she went after she left. Christine had led him right back to Ann Emery—right to her ground-floor room. He soon began watching her there from a distance, a sinister foot surveillance conducted by hiding in plain sight amid the daily cabaret that was the disjointed herd of eclectic characters roaming the campus. It was the perfect place to blend in, to watch from afar, and to get Christine's routine down pat. Somehow he obtained her first name and then later her last name, perhaps from the Ann Emery lobby directory, perhaps by just asking around. We will likely never know. He then might have even obtained more personal particulars from her medical records, to which he would have had access at the UW campus hospital where Christine twice the previous fall had received treatment for her bulimia. It was the same MO that had worked so well before—he'd been there and done that. However he went about it, in a matter of days, Christine moved from being Jorgensen's pet project to a point of fixation, what we classify today as *stranger-sexual predator* stalking. Unlike other forms of stalking behavior, such as *stranger-obsessional* or *domestic-anger* stalking, which are associated with either some type of personality disorder or severe mental illness, the stranger-sexual predator knows precisely what he is doing and how it will end. It is also, not unsurprisingly, the stalker typology most commonly correlated with serial rape and serial murder.

Through the looking glass: This shows one of the countless windows, some facing outdoors and some facing into the library proper, that encircled the Memorial reading room. Students seeking solace there soon found themselves continuously on display. It was here that Jorgensen first set eyes on Christine and set his sinister plan into action. Courtesy: UW–Madison Archives Collection.

Night Swim

On the morning of May 24, 1968—a Friday—Linda made her usual trek from Witte Hall to Ann Emery to call on Christine. In fact, not so much to call on her but to let her know that their usual Saturday night routine of watching the swim team meet at the campus natatorium—the UW "Nat" on Observatory Drive—had to be kiboshed at the last minute. Thrown under the bus simultaneously by her English lit, geology, and philosophy profs, and drowning in term-paper assignments, Linda would have to abandon the campus for the weekend to pull consecutive all-nighters back home in Milwaukee. Trying to pull all-nighters at UW, especially at Witte Hall where everyone had spring fever—and on a weekend no less—was little more than a recipe for aggravation and wasted time. Linda knew it to be true, even with the advertised but unenforced "quiet hours" and a nightly curfew imposed to buoy good study habits before term finals. So she booked herself a one-way ticket on the Badger Bus to get back to her folks' place in Milwaukee. Her father would be working at the firehouse and her mother, a freelance waitress and catering maven, would be, no doubt, serving highballs at a swanky downtown hotel—like the Astor, the Pfister, or the Knickerbocker—at yet another banquet or wedding. Their mutual absences would therefore leave Linda with the main floor of the home to herself for the better part of two days and nights. Silence and solitude were great gifts for the studious and cerebral Linda after a year living in a dormitory at UW, always well worth the road trip back to the old neighborhood.

The Badger Bus, a campus "shuttle" in the form of a chartered chrome-yellow school bus ferrying students from campus to outlying cities on weekends for a mere buck or two, would get her home, with stops, in just under two hours. Before boarding, Linda made what would be the final trek to Ann Emery to see Christine and relay a message. But Christine wasn't there. She was back at the Memorial reading room—the fishbowl—where Jorgensen was putting his final plan in motion. Although Linda didn't know it then, the last time she would ever see Christine alive had already come and gone. It was two days earlier almost to the hour—Wednesday, May 22.

On that morning, just after 11:00 a.m., Linda, while waiting at the crosswalk outside South Hall, saw Christine hiking up Bascom Hill on campus. Linda recognized her new pair of black thigh-high boots, or Jane Fonda boots as they were known by the spring of '68 following their prominence in the campy sci-fi film *Barbarella*. She also recognized the art attaché that Christine was toting and was never seen without. At the time, Christine was making a beeline with that same signature art case straight toward two campus cops on foot patrol. Linda squinted to make out their faces, ones she'd later never forget. On the right was Officer Roger Golemb, green and straight out of the academy—apparently declared "police essential" and sent to cop school instead of being drafted to Vietnam. On the left was Reinhold "Tiny" Frey—called "tiny" because, of course, he wasn't. Christine caught a glimpse of Linda and waved while yelling, "See you for the swim meet Saturday night." Linda nodded and gave a flick of her right-hand fingers as if to convey, *that's right.*

Linda had just remembered that gesture, the subtle *see you then* pantomime, as she knocked on Christine's door at Ann Emery Hall after rushing there on Friday to let her know that she couldn't meet up with her after all. But with no answer at room 119 and the Badger Bus warming up and the seats quickly filling—first come first served—Linda pulled a scrap of lecture-hall paper from her tote bag and scratched a quick letter to be wedged in the doorjamb:

> *Chris,*
> *Headed home for weekend . . . getting papers done. Sorry I have to miss the swim tomorrow night. Call me at my parents' number if you like. Probably staying until Monday. Will come by again Tuesday if I don't hear from you.*
> *Linda*

Without much of a second thought, Linda folded the note lengthwise and shimmed it in the door frame before heading back to the bus and splitting for three days—a seventy-two-hour pass from UW, from Witte Hall, from the unforeseen things yet to come. What Linda didn't know when she'd passed Christine was that she had been talking to campus cops about Jorgensen. Christine had put two and two together and figured out that he, the older creepy medical resident who introduced himself in the smoke pit, was in all likelihood her nocturnal stalker, the Peeping Tom, and the sleepwatcher whom she knew paid a visit to her window and lurked in the bushes outside night after night. Ever since she had blown him off in the Memorial Library smoke pit, his presence in the reading room had remained constant and unflinching. A presence, however, that had also become more intense—more ominous by the day. By May 22, she was also certain that he was following her every move since she regularly caught glimpses of him between classes in the corridors, his face mostly concealed by a newspaper or an umbrella at Rennebohm's and most of her other usual hangouts. Once armed with this same information on Bascom Hill, the sage advice offered by Officers Frey and Golemb amounted to precious nothing. They assured her that it was likely all in her mind. If not, she should do what many girls did for peace of mind and to guard against trouble should it ever happen—buy a rape whistle. It wasn't until after it was all over—said and done, dead and buried—that Linda discovered all of this. But it wasn't gleaned from any official reports, because there were none, but instead from Golemb himself—one of countless interviews Linda later took on all alone. It turned out that this was neither the first nor the last time in life, and later in death, that Christine would be failed by those she was taught to trust.

Back in Milwaukee, in the wee hours of what was by now Monday morning, the twenty-seventh—Linda, still up and writing a biographical essay on Lord Byron for her English lit class—the rotary dial phone on the kitchen wall rang. She snagged it off the receiver by the end of the first ring for fear it would wake her grandparents two floors up or her mother on her lone night off. A gruff voice on the other end quickly kicked in. Identifying himself only as "Officer Hendrickson, UW Campus PD," the caller asked Linda to confirm her name. She did—hesitantly. "What's this about, officer?" she offered as a rejoinder, hardly believing that a campus cop would be so cavalier as to call her at her parents' home at such an hour—the clock stove reading 2:17 a.m.—much less that he had any important reason to do so.

"Do you know Christine Rothschild?" he added, doing so with a wary tone. Given the hour and her time-honored sense of teenaged invincibility, Linda failed to recognize the call for what it was at the time—a real cop, and a very real problem. The cop then did what cops do and followed up with an immediate second question: "When's the last time you saw her?" Linda, doing what perceptively invincible young people do when they're caught off guard and fail to see the truth of what's unfolding in front of them, then flippantly answered that question with a tongue-in-cheek question of her own. "What, did someone spike her fruit punch at the First Church?"

Click. The line then went dead—the man calling himself Officer Hendrickson had hung up, apparently receiving all the information he needed. But Linda still resigned herself to the belief that it must have been a crank call. If not, then at most it had to be a young campus patrolman—someone crushing on Christine and overstepping his authority to play good cop a little too earnestly—calling some known associates at an inappropriate hour as part of some half-assed courtship scheme. What Linda didn't know is that she wasn't a known associate. Christine Rothschild didn't have "known associates," not at UW—not anywhere. The police had obtained Linda's name from the note left back at room 119 at Ann Emery Hall. The cops had been to the room. They had been *in* the room.

Later that same morning following her tortuous all-nighter, Linda, somewhere between half awake, half asleep, and a state of caffeine intoxication—shakes and nausea galore—sat down with the local yellow pages to call and confirm the time the next Badger Bus left for campus. At the same time, her father, just home himself from the firehouse and comparatively well rested after a quiet night, flipped on the Zenith stereophonic console tuner to catch the late-morning news flash on local MTMJ, 620 AM. To Linda, who by that time had been at UW for nine months and had seen the latest array of newfangled gadgets the moneyed New Englanders had—the nine-track cassette, the Lear Jet Stereo 8—her parents' hulking mahogany-encased hi-fi looked more like the type of sarcophagus Howard Carter might have dragged out of King Tut's tomb back in November of '22 than what most people of the day would call a radio. But from the depths of that dark wooden chest bought on layaway two decades prior, the disembodied voice of a Midwestern newsman strung together a series of words he called the local top story: "Eighteen-year-old coed found murdered yesterday has now been identified as Christine Rothschild, a native of Chicago." It was an announcement that would alter Linda's life course—a story that would change the criminal complexion of the Mad City forever.

Dew Point

A day earlier, just after noon on the twenty-sixth, three days before the end of term and the campus eerily quiet, a family from the nearby town of Waukesha—later made infamous in the Slender Man stabbing case of 2014—pulled its station wagon onto the private, winding roads of the

UW property as part of a usual Sunday drive. In the late 1960s, it was apparently something of a Wisconsin state pastime to load the family into the car on rainy spring Sundays to tour the local UW campuses—La Crosse, Whitewater, and of course Madison—in order to take in the architecture and landscaping. It was a weekly sightseeing indulgence, an opportunity to unapologetically people watch.

Overnight on May 25 and into the following morning, the local temperature had dropped to the dew point in the Mad City. The moisture that had been held in the air for nearly a week was unleashed shortly after 8:00 a.m., leaving those locals who found themselves rained out of Little League games and spring picnics to take to the campuses and go driving—to aimlessly burn leaded fuel. As this particular Waukesha family's car, having traveled from over an hour away, pulled onto UW's flagship campus in the Mad City and then drifted past the gargantuan physics building known as Sterling Hall, the small boy in the backseat made a passing comment about a mannequin discarded in the grass near a hedgerow. Through the fogged-up rear window, as raindrops beaded down and broke up the clouded film that covered the glass, the small boy managed to catch a fleeting glimpse of what two earlier security perimeter patrols had apparently managed to miss. The boy's parents didn't make much of the utterance, dismissing it as either their child's imagination or some remnant of the generally unremarkable year-end high jinks of UW physics students. Had they stopped to look closer, they might have altered the course of events to come. But they didn't.

Four hours or so later, that same family was back home in Waukesha when Phil Van Valkenberg, senior science student and part-time lab assistant at Sterling Hall, popped in behind a hedgerow off the building's main front staircase. It was a location that one wouldn't know without either visiting or scoping out the building regularly. Indeed, Phil knew from experience it was a shortcut to a lower block of basement windows. It led to the lower lab rooms where he'd been working along with a weekend peer group, including a buddy of his who'd pulled the weekend detail cleaning and organizing the place. Phil, deciding to call on his friend just before 4:00 p.m. that afternoon, would normally have made his way through the main doors and then navigated the labyrinthine building down to the basement. On this occasion, he instead chose to turn right at the first landing on the steps where the hedgerow met the railing. He then jumped down behind the foliage and staircase landing to rap on the first visible window he found. It was the usual routine to get his friend's attention to come out for a smoke or a quick bite—a sort of impromptu dinner-bell system. But when Phil vaulted down onto the wet grass this time, he lost his footing, the still-spitting rain having soaked the earth following a day's worth of showers. After slipping forward slightly and landing in a frontward crouch, he laid eyes on, just inches from his face, what the family of four had dismissed as a mannequin just a few hours earlier. Said mannequin was actually Christine Rothschild—or what remained of her.

Left: The main staircase to Sterling Hall, including the half wall that Phil Van Valkenberg jumped from to discover the partially concealed body of Christine Rothschild on the fateful afternoon of May 26, 1968. Right: Christine Rothschild as she appeared immediately before her death and as she is still remembered today. Courtesy: UW Madison Archives Collection & Linda Schulko.

Phil Van Valkenberg had unknowingly fallen forward into a grotesque tableau that had been carefully arranged to provide a very specific message once found. Christine, her body left there since the early morning and exposed to a day of rain, had been intricately posed on her back with her head resting on the cement ledge of the foundation window on which Phil had been intending to knock. Beneath her bloodied head was a calling card, a man's cotton handkerchief—big-city expensive, something sold nowhere in Madison. Its purpose there was puzzling, one part taunting clue and one part the killer's twisted fantasy as he engineered a very specific image for both himself and for whoever found his victim. Christine's head with the hanky underneath had been turned to the side and ravaged, both sides of her jaw shattered and her face pulverized. The first blow from whatever blunt object was used on her would have incapacitated her and knocked her out cold; she probably didn't feel anything that came after. Gruesome as it was, what particularly caught Phil's attention made him freeze with horror. Christine's blue shift dress was matted with red crimson and gore; it was later confirmed that her torso had been stabbed a total of fourteen times with some comparatively obscure type of finely sharpened weapon the cops would later describe as "some type of medical utensil." Translation: a surgical scalpel.

Pulling it together and with a massive dump of adrenaline, Phil retraced his route around the hedges that had kept the body hidden all day and made his way back to the front steps. He sprinted through the front doors of the hall, nearly putting his arm through the glass after pushing when he should have been pulling. He ran to the first open office he could find on the main floor and called the police—all lines on campus ringing directly into the campus PD headquarters rather than the Madison city switchboard. As luck would have it, there were two campus cops right around the corner—ETA less than a minute. Those two cops—Roger Golemb and Tiny Frey—were the same ones Christine had sought out for help just four days earlier. They arrived to find, and later reap, what their earlier indifference had sown. But as it turned out, they still weren't finished doing wrong by Christine.

Trampling the scene and destroying evidence, no doubt unwittingly due to a lack of training in major crime-scene management, the first officers on scene also did precious little to contain what was by then a gaggle of gathering students ranging from concerned coeds to morbid curiosity seekers. When the ambulance arrived about a minute later, just three minutes after Phil Van Valkenberg's call to police, the medics realized that rigor mortis still hadn't set in. In spite of the gore and obvious signs of biological death, the medics ensured one final indignity to the girl who was once the go-to talent and cover girl for Chicago's *Teen Fashion News Sheet*. The UW cops, again with zero semblance of training in crime-scene control, gave the medics free rein. Grabbing Christine's mutilated body by the hands and feet and using a quick-rigged hammock carry, they rushed her down the slippery embankment to the road before flinging her—no gurney, no blanket, no nothing—into the back of the ambulance where she landed in a heap. Any lasting evidence on the body was at that very moment severely cross-contaminated with the vehicle interior and summarily destroyed. The medics then transported her the roughly 150 feet across the street to the UW campus hospital where death was immediately pronounced after missed evidentiary opportunities due to crime-scene blunders—blunders that were by that time still carrying on unabated back at Sterling Hall.

Before Christine's body was moved a second time, this time to the morgue wagon in order to be ferried over to nearby St. Mary's Hospital for a full autopsy, campus police sergeant Trimmer—on a short list of able and conscientious investigators at UW—arrived to snap exposures of the young girl's body as it lay lifeless on a metal table in a private room at the campus hospital ER. If the evidence at the scene noted by the first responders—the posing on the windowsill and the man's handkerchief—wasn't odd enough, then the evidence gleaned at the hospital spelled overkill with a sadistic twist. While Christine had been severely beaten and stabbed fourteen times with a surgical scalpel—the ferocity of the stabs so frenetic, so teeming with both rage and excitement that four ribs were shattered in the process—the killer also went to some extra and unusual steps to ensure death. They were steps that prolonged the killer's time spent at the scene and should have been interpreted for what they were at the time—sexually motivated peri-mortem and post-mortem activities that were not *instrumental* to the crime, or part of the killer's MO, as much as they were *expressive* acts of violence helping to verify the presence of a criminal *signature*. While MOs come and go and can prove highly variable from crime to crime, a signature on the other hand is difficult to fake and largely impossible for sexually motivated killers to refrain from acting out. Because it is in fact why they kill in the first place, it should be taken as among the best indicators that the murderer places great erotic value on destructive and sadistic behaviors. In other words, such a murderer would do it again—he would be compelled to.

This was all missed when an inventory of Christine's possessions was completed and her body was given the once-over and photographed ahead of the official autopsy in the days to come. Although Christine's murder predated the extensive body of knowledge that exists today concerning sexually motivated killers and their criminal signatures, other plain-as-day clues should have led to some obvious deductions. For instance, Christine's prized Jane Fonda boots, devoid of mud or grass in spite of the soaked ground conditions, could only mean that she hadn't been, as was the early working theory, dragged to where she was found; rather, she couldn't have traveled any significant distance in the wet grass and certainly never kicked or dug in her heels as she would have if she thrashed and fought with her attacker. But that inference was never drawn. The logical yet elusive conclusion to be made was that Christine had taken a route similar to that of Phil Van Valkenberg, voluntarily going—most likely lured—to the concealed site by the window and behind the hedgerow before being attacked and killed there.

Also, no one at the scene or afterward managed to pick up on what are today recognized as telltale indicators—and signatures—of sexually motivated murderers. Christine's boots had been removed by the killer and then placed back on the body after her textured panty hose were removed and taken as a souvenir. Beyond this, there had been no obvious touching below the waist and there was an absence of evidence of sexual penetration. Christine's beige, quilted trench coat was still on her body with the interior lining torn out, to be used as a garrote after she was apparently already dead. In fastening the garrote around her throat and slowly tightening it to close off and eventually crush her windpipe, the killer, current training would tell us, was an obvious control freak and paraphiliac boasting numerous twisted fetishes. One of those paraphilias would seem to be necrophilia, which involves sexually motivated interference, posing, and ravaging of the body *after* death. One of the related "preparatory" paraphilias closely linked with necrophilia—a type of precursor or warm-up routine—is what's known as somnophilia. In other words, sleepwatching.

The improvised garrote—a tourniquet with an elaborate knot made with cooled nerves and fine motor precision in the throes of a horrific murder—reflected not only a seasoned psychopath and killer, but also someone adept at fastening restraints and likely accustomed to working with his hands. The ligature was applied as part of a twisted choke job fantasy to act out on a defenseless but still-warm body, one half of an even more specific and paraphilic signature—one that cops of the day had no idea how to interpret. As Sergeant Trimmer methodically and meticulously photographed each step of his removal of the garrote, it became too much for one of the two uniforms serving as scribes and taking notes at his side. Suddenly reaching for a metal wastebasket stowed beneath a nearby desk, the officer watching the examination found himself projectile vomiting in, on, and over the opening at the top of the can. His reaction was visceral, instinctive. He had just seen, as had others in the room along with Trimmer as he continued photographing, exactly what the killer had done before he crushed the girl's throat. In fact, the garrote might have been less about simulating strangulation—to keep air from getting in—than it was an attempt to ensure that something left for the authorities to find never got out.

Recovered from deep within Christine's throat were her tan sheepskin Kerrybrooke dress gloves—both of them inserted postmortem. Rather than the killer making sure she was dead with the use of the improvised ligature, he was instead taking his time to create a very specific visual—something not only paraphilic but iconographic. He carefully carried out a process he'd been mentally rehearsing for weeks or months, the sadistic memory of which would fuel new delinquent fantasies for years to come. To help make sure of it, he took reminders—items that would allow him to rewind and replay the whole scene as a type of brain movie in the future, to relive the scene whenever he held or gazed upon the souvenirs of his work. That's why he took her pantyhose. That's why—as was later confirmed—he also took the blue Sunday ribbon from her hair and the brass lighter from the right pocket of her trench coat but left behind her money and the jewelry on her fingers—including the fateful opal ring her mother had gifted to her.

Souvenirs—unlike "trophies" taken by killers, which are typically living tissue such as locks of hair or actual body parts—have long shelf lives, and can be secreted in a variety of places or even carried out in the open without arousing suspicion. Although the bow and pantyhose would have been part of his private collection, the lighter could be hidden in plain sight, used in day-to-day functioning. Only he would know its sinister origins while reliving the excitement of the crime every time he pulled the lighter to use or show it. He might even go out of his way to use it—to have others use it—expressly for this purpose. All the while it would hold the added symbolic value of a memory about how he had first acquired his target, how he had begun to stalk his prey. After all, the whole thing started when he had asked her for a light. The Memorial Library reading room. The smoke pit. April of '68.

Black Umbrella

With the preliminary processing of Christine's ravaged corpse at the UW hospital taunting Sgt. Trimmer and the other officers present for the rest of their days, back at the crime scene one final and puzzling item was found left on display by the Sterling Hall window well where Christine's body had been carefully posed by her killer. It was a calling card, either part of the larger necrophilic signature or a separate one altogether, part of a discrete deviant fantasy fueling her murderer and designed to upset investigators and the entire campus alike. It still does today. It's a signature that has reappeared in at least one other murder in America—a campus murder no less.

Inserted into the grass immediately in front of Christine's feet was her designer black umbrella, in itself innocuous given the rainy weather that day. Rather than taking the umbrella as a twisted keepsake as he did with the other items, or rather than merely discarding it, the killer took the time to elaborately set up something of a macabre diorama. It was one intended, it seems, to accompany the posing of the body—a paratext that told an expanded story, one that opened up a widened view into the killer's mind. It's also one that dramatically extended his time spent at the scene. Murdering and later posing a victim outdoors in broad daylight, at great risk of being seen immediately beside the body, makes an extraordinarily detailed statement about the mindset and paraphilic drives of any murderer. In this case, however, the time spent setting up an umbrella is essentially as individuating as DNA evidence—a one-in-a-million outlier in terms of crime scene behavior.

A detail first eyeballed by the student who had stumbled across the murder scene, one missed by many of the first cops to arrive, was that Christine's umbrella hadn't just been speared tip-first into the rain-soaked ground like some type of javelin. It had also been inserted with precision at a ninety-degree angle with the handle pointed to the sky, the umbrella opened, and each of the metal stays, or stretchers as they're sometimes called, either manually snapped or cut one at a time around the entire circumference of the canopy.

The umbrella itself was mutilated, just like Christine's body, to suit a certain aesthetic scheme. The question was—and remains—what exactly that scheme was. Bearing in mind how little police agencies, much less campus law enforcement agencies, knew at the time about paraphilias, signatures, psychopathy, and serial indicators, it's easy of course, using existing standards, to armchair quarterback about what was missed during those critical first few hours of the investigation. The fact is that the body of knowledge on these subjects was then limited and nowhere close to being as evolved as it is today. That said, there were still numerous glaring indicators that whoever killed Christine—someone with extraordinary visual fixation and focus on sadistic process and paraphilic specificity—would kill again or had done it before. Maybe both. These were indicators that, putting aside present knowledge and training, especially in the days immediately following the murder, should have immediately cast a net around one or two people. These included Niels Jorgensen if witnesses had been forthcoming about what they knew. Today, this same heuristic process is called *suspectology*, a term that applies to stalled investigations, particularly when investigators start scrutinizing the post-offense behavior of any and all people of interest with a view to creating a viable short list of suspects.

Suspectology, as known today, was initially depicted in a roundabout way in Charles Dickens's Gothic novel *Bleak House*, first published in 1853. The book's protagonist, Inspector Bucket of Scotland Yard, is generally accepted as the first fictional literary treatment of a police detective in a murder mystery written in English. Thus, while the term suspectology is on the newer side, the method is not. It certainly existed in 1968 and had for some time—over a century in both theory and in practice.

Suspectology is, in essence, both the art and the science of recognizing a suspect's "tell." It operates on the assumption that, just as when playing cards for cash or other stakes, the ability to convincingly bluff will only last for so long before natural instincts and autonomic responses begin to give a person away—begin to erode a carefully rehearsed façade. In some cases, this might mean changing one's routine, quitting one's job, spending or hoarding money—any number of actions that, depending on the subject's relationship to the victim, can prove incredibly illuminating. One of the cornerstones of suspectology, actually first posited by Dickens, is for police to attend the victim's funeral, wake, or memorial—not only to pay their respects but also to scope the crowd for giveaways. The thought is, an idea first conceived in fiction but later adopted by most large urban police forces by the mid-twentieth century, that discreet surveillance at these events can sometimes ultimately reveal leads that more conventional methods such as interviewing, interrogation, and even search warrants and wiretap affidavits cannot. In order, however, for suspectology to work in short-listing viable suspects, someone actually needs to be watching their movements. To this end, there is no evidence that anyone was watching Jorgensen, certainly not during the critical "first forty-eight" of the investigation anyway.

By the time the critical first two days of the investigation had wound down—the probability of any case being solved diminishing exponentially every day from that point forward—campus detective Charlie Lulling, the early lead investigator in Christine's murder, publicly announced that the case was already "at a standstill." This wasn't rhetoric or part of some cloak-and-dagger investigative strategy the campus cops had cooked up. Rather, the UWPD actually had no clue where to begin—it was a Midwestern whodunit writ large. What the cops did manage to accomplish, however, was the inverse of suspectology—what's known as *victimology*. Such an investigative analysis, an entire subfield of study and expertise within criminology, is focused on how and why a victim and his or her attacker came into contact. It also seeks to address how and why a particular victim was selected and what his or her relationship was, if any, to the attacker. A canvass run of the campus, including the occupants of Ann Emery Hall, regulars at the Memorial Library, and, of course, the overdue conversation with Linda, all kicked loose some key details that slowly got the victimology ball rolling—albeit too late.

The Final Forty-Eight

Since the first forty-eight hours of a murder investigation are key in terms of maintaining momentum with boots-on-the-ground collection of evidence, corralling of witnesses, short-listing and interviewing of suspects, and leveraging departmental resources to the hilt, cases that stay open beyond that period frequently have bleak futures in terms of solvability. There is, however, another component to an investigation, this one moving backward in time. Although victimology describes digging into how and why a victim and a killer came to meet, which sliding doors were set in motion and by what forces, there is also a process now known as a *psychological autopsy*, which often accompanies the physical autopsy carried out by a medical examiner or forensic pathologist. A psychological autopsy is often just as disturbing—sometimes more. While much of a murder investigation takes place in real time during the critical first forty-eight hours, the psychological autopsy instead looks at the *final* forty-eight—the last two days of the victim's life and what that person did, who they met, where they went and, perhaps most importantly, what their frame of mind happened to be. It's a retroactively assembled chronology, whether through witnesses or supposition, of every decision made right up to the time of death, including how the victim reacted to a particular attacker. In Christine's case, the final forty-eight turned up a biography of what should have been the lowest-risk victim in the Mad City save one fact—she had met the sleepwatcher.

Christine had told Linda about her stalker, including her theory it was Jorgensen, the unmistakable forty-something medical resident whom she'd noticed tailing her since their smoking encounter at the Memorial Library. Christine had also confided in the campus police but had received an implicit "we've got better things to do" brush-off. Christine had additionally shared with Linda the precautions she had taken to make sure she wasn't in compromising situations or didn't find herself in circumstances that were "dangerous" in the conventional sense. These precautions are what are known as *avoidant behavior strategies* taken by people who often feel powerless to prevent imminent victimization. She avoided going out at night, at least alone; she kept her doors and windows at Ann Emery locked; she had even started looking into getting her name removed from the directory in the lobby. But Jorgensen had already killed before—at least twice. In so doing, he had learned to wait out his victims and to strike when the situation was *not* perceptively dangerous. He waited until his targets would be doing something they did all the time—when their guard would be down, the structure of the routine dulling their instincts, their radars down.

Niels Jorgensen, a high-functioning psychopath, sexual sadist, and sleepwatcher, also fit yet another category. A decade after Jorgensen dropped anchor at UW, a pair of innovative criminologists named Marcus Cohen and Lawrence Felson would go on to develop what they called *routine activities theory*. Jorgensen, as it turns out, was the unofficial poster boy when it came to an offender fitting this theory about how predators find their targets, even before it was developed. The theory is premised on the notion that, when a motivated offender and a suitable victim converge in a space and time, a crime will inevitably occur in the absence of an obvious deterrent, or what Cohen and Felson called a "suitable guardian." Sometimes these crimes are opportunistic and reflect locations where attackers know people's routines will bring them, and where an offender will then simply lie in wait. Examples would be a park path known to be frequented on summer evenings by young women jogging or an underground parking garage known to be used by office workers commuting in expensive cars at the start or end of a scheduled workday. Other times these crimes are contoured to the specific routines of individual victims known as *targeted strangers*—a type of victim within the parlance of both criminology and victimology. These are people who don't know their attackers, but who, in many cases, have been specifically selected for attack; they have been obsessively stalked and their routines tracked—their usual hangouts and routes were eyeballed during reconnaissance missions for the purposes of identifying an ideal time and place to strike.

Jorgensen, as a sleepwatching somnophiliac and inveterate peeper, was inherently voyeuristic, his penchant for twisted surveillance activities forming part of a larger set of psychosexual dysfunction known as a *courtship disorder*. The average, psychologically well-adjusted male who has identified someone to whom he is attracted, and who may be a suitable intimate partner, will proceed through a series of socially acceptable steps of courtship to meet them, gain their attention, and increasingly progress toward dating or sexual activity. The courtship-disordered male such as Jorgensen, however, will instead use a supposedly random meeting of the type he had with Christine in the Memorial Library to fuel incipient or escalating sexual deviations. In some instances, the stranger is also stalked and, once the initial fantasy is played out, that person becomes the target of more specific and violent paraphilic acts. As a courtship-disordered necrophile, Jorgensen was a virtual smorgasbord of violent sexual depravity and had at least two successful kills—murders he'd managed to skate on—already under his belt when he landed at UW in April of '68. Forecasting routines and tracking his prey was the secret of that success. By the next month, he had Christine's Sunday ritual down pat.

It was also the predictability of that Sunday morning routine that explained why the psychological autopsy of Christine's final forty-eight didn't turn up anything immediately unusual. It seemed to be the same as every other weekend she'd spent since matriculating at UW and moving from Chicago to Madison. It was precisely because of this normality that investigators should have seen the murder for what it was. But no one got a clue until it was too late. What the cops *did* know, however, is that Christine had received the note wedged in her ground-floor dormitory door on the afternoon of Friday, May 24. The note, later found on her dressing table, was where UW officer Hendrickson first obtained Linda's first name; he then later searched registration records to obtain complete particulars, including her home telephone number in Milwaukee. Beyond that, Christine's Saturday night, including whether she perhaps attended the swim meet alone, has never been accounted for. Nearly a full twenty-four hours of her last forty-eight hours alive were left in the dark, and that should have been all the more reason to move as quickly as possible on any leads, including Jorgensen's name being given to detectives by Linda though a series of frantic phone messages left impaled and piling up on a memo spike in the UWPD squad room. Christine's Sunday—her final few hours alive—were, despite the gaps with Saturday, a bit clearer, some events easier to nail down.

On that morning, the twenty-sixth, investigators confirmed that Christine was awake by 5:00 a.m. when she was seen walking into a bathroom at Ann Emery by the assigned housemother, a doting old woman named Gertrude Armstrong—a widowed and senior campus mentor of a bygone era. Christine's murder marked Gertrude's last day at Ann Emery as well as the final weekend for many of the Hall's young girls. Once the news of the murder broke, one of Christine's fellow Ann Emery residents dropped out and never reenrolled—anywhere. Another was sent a can of Mace via Western Union from her parents back home in Lexington. She transferred to the University of Missouri the next year and spent the rest of her days afraid of the dark. She still is. Another girl's parents did one better and couriered her a can of antiquated army-issue CS gas, fallen off the back of a truck—as they say—somewhere back at Fort Dix. The girl had no clue what to do with it; she didn't need to. The mass exodus from the campus had already begun.

When Christine left Ann Emery just before 6:00 a.m., she had unwittingly already predetermined the course of things to come. In her mind, she was headed to the same place she went every Sunday—a routine that anyone who knew or even knew of Christine would also know. Every Sunday at 10:00 a.m., Christine would be at the sermon and Sunday-school lecture at the First Church of Christ, Scientist, at 315 Wisconsin Avenue, just a few blocks from campus. Built in the same neoclassical style as many of the Mad City's more formidable and official structures, it was where Christine went each and every Sunday to carry on the family tradition of Christian Science, her father having renounced Judaism within days of his own bar mitzvah as he headed down a new road.

Christine never made it to the First Church on Wisconsin that morning. Between 6:00 a.m. and 9:45 a.m., the hour she would normally be due to arrive at the church, her precise movements are unaccounted for. Speculative theories remain just that: speculative. What is known for certain is that both she and Jorgensen were out early that day. What's also known is that Christine's routine before church would have taken her directly past the steps of Sterling Hall across from Jorgensen's workplace—the hospital where that same Sunday he was due to work the day shift. But when and why Christine ended up in the somewhat secluded Sterling Hall location where she was later found remain the enduring questions—the still unsolved mystery. One way or another, this was the day Jorgensen had chosen to kill her. He knew her routine. He knew she would be passing Sterling Hall. That Jorgensen killed Christine is a given; the specifics of the murder are clear. The specifics of the time leading up to the murder are not.

Sterling Hall would have been deserted on that fateful Sunday morning, the hedgerow beside the main staircase devoid of prying eyes. But there was also one additional benefit to Jorgensen's plan. Not only was Sterling Hall within easy reach of UW hospital, it also housed the US Army Mathematics Research Center. On top of providing an ideal scenario for a supposedly coincidental meeting, it had to be the mother lode of locations for a necrophile toting a purloined scalpel and a phony military uniform. As fated, Sterling Hall was where it would all come together for Jorgensen—charlatan doctor, fraud GI medic, army imposter. A serial killer hiding in plain sight.

Sentinel

Within a week of Christine's murder, the spring term—and school year—at UW was over. People left the campus, many for good, and went back to their lives in homes scattered across the nation. After the murder hit the national newswire, UW could no longer duck and cover. The genie was out of the bottle and couldn't be put back in. Most exams were canceled and final grades estimated. Those few people who still lingered in what had by then become a ghost town of a campus turned the murder scene at Sterling Hall into something of a makeshift memorial, or at least they tried. Any flowers, candles, and other goods that were left were collected and summarily turfed by campus administrators. So instead, the eerily vacant scene devolved into a macabre curiosity and attraction. People from all over Dane County—from all over the state of Wisconsin—had already made a point of driving to UW on the weekend to sightsee. But now the destination provided something of a morbid attraction to visit in its own right—the place where it all went wrong and the Mad City got its wake-up call. Only it didn't. Christine's parents had sent her to the Mad City because they thought it was a decent place, a safe campus. The truth is that she was simply in the wrong place at the wrong time—as were over ten thousand other girls, any one of whom could just as easily have been Jorgensen's victim that spring. Sadly, some of them would in fact later be victims themselves at the hands of other killers who sought to emulate him—once the copycats moved in.

By the summer of '68—already the most socially and politically volatile year in American history since the Civil War—Linda had resigned herself to the inevitability that, as long as Jorgensen was on campus amid the upheaval and avoiding police radar, he would soon be looking for his next kill. The same pattern, she knew, would carry on in perpetuity for years upon years, from campus to campus, city to city. It was with this uncanny prescience by late June of that year that Linda pivoted in a new direction. Christine had been forced to check out early—a victim of what the Mad City's social upheaval and endless distraction had managed to invite in. It was then that Linda realized that, at least for the foreseeable future, she could never leave UW—at least not as long as Jorgensen was still there or able to return. An honors degree in lieu of a bachelor's, she thought to herself, just to stay that extra year. Then, maybe a master's, maybe a doctorate, maybe a postdoc—professional student par excellence. Maybe she'd end up on the faculty one day, maybe on staff—maybe even on the campus PD. In the meantime, using Madison as her base, she'd follow him when she could—track and stalk Jorgensen just as he had stalked Christine. Although the shoe was now on the other foot, she'd first have to cut her teeth as a skip tracer and amateur detective. Next stop would be a Milwaukee newsroom. It was the truth foundry where she'd simultaneously unearth the past and mold the future, plan the route—what would turn out to be the next forty years of her life. The road would end only once one of them, either she or Jorgensen, was dead. Maybe both.

Beginning as a summer intern at the Milwaukee *Sentinel* back home that same June, Linda collected a meager paycheck every second Thursday as she toiled amid secondhand smoke in the newspaper's art department, tasked with fetching black-and-white stock images as well as clipping and cropping ad nauseam. Her boss was a salt-of-the-earth man and old-school editor named Bill Share, a working-class Brew City local like her and a living embodiment and doppelganger of television's famed fictional newsman Lou Grant. In time, Share would eventually rise to become the newspaper's president, perhaps its most respected ever. His hours on-site that summer of '68 were spent mostly fact-checking stories on the one hand and chasing down the whereabouts of his own reporters—some with bottles in their desks, others MIA by noon daily—on the other. His recurring distractions left Linda plenty of wiggle room to get her own system down pat. Finishing her own work by lunch, she'd then make herself busy by researching Christine's murder on the sly, sometimes on the clock, sometimes after hours. For her, time was immaterial; it stopped just before 10:00 a.m. on May 26 without ever starting again. In an age when people measure their self-esteem by digital "likes," being helicopter parented and mollycoddled into social and intellectual paralysis by the time of their freshman years, Linda provides a stark contrast that stands the test of time. Though her world had just been turned upside down, her best friend murdered, and her sense of good irreparably shattered, the resolve, tenacity, and foresight that she possessed as a nineteen-year-old was and remains in a class all its own. Unbeknownst to her, it was also about to get a lot more dangerous.

Any number of proverbs, motivational sound bites, and recycled memes talk about finding light in darkness, using a low as a springboard, and finding an open window in a locked room. They rank among the countless hollow platitudes that extol the virtue of finding oneself at a low point. But long before writers were paid to put these taglines on Hallmark cards and motivational office posters, Linda lived those same parables. She not only found light in the darkness but also *became* darkness when needed. In short order, she would use Jorgensen's own tactics against him—she would become him in order to catch him. She would bird-dog him for as long as it took. In due course, it would have to be her, and her alone, when no one else seemed to be looking—when no one else seemed to care. No one knew which way was up, least of all, with some exceptions, the campus police who, well in over their heads, somehow managed to maintain carriage of Christine's case long after the first forty-eight had come and gone—long after the case went cold.

While everyone else in Milwaukee was taking in the first-ever lakefront Summerfest—the Brew City's emulation of Oktoberfest and today a venerable yearly city institution—Linda was playing the long game, battening down the hatches. Whether under a desk lamp at the *Sentinel* or under the lamp in the kitchen in her parents' home, she persevered. After discreetly purloining—and later dutifully returning—art department negatives of the Sterling Hall murder scene, early drafts of the headline stories, and the names and numbers of potential witnesses, she carved a path forward with her own investigation into not just Christine's murder, but a trail of mayhem left by Jorgensen across Middle America.

As the summer of '68 was winding down and people began tiptoeing their way back to UW, hoping the coast was clear, Linda was still back in Milwaukee thumbing through images and scouring them for possibly missed clues when something new caught her eye. About a month after Christine's murder, a stringer with the Associated Press had reported that Madison city cops had located a blood-soaked set of dungarees in a dumpster behind a commercial plaza located just a short drive from the campus square. Linda knew that the campus square was a Seussian Whoville where the UW students did everything, seldom venturing out too far from there. Even fewer owned cars to travel the short distance to the plaza; fewer still would probably know that the plaza existed in the first place. If the denim overalls, owner unknown, were in fact connected to the campus murder, few undergraduate students would be inclined or have the means to travel that far to dispose of the evidence. A short time later, Linda found the follow-up piece—buried in the newspaper's police blotter, no byline—confirming that police had already ruled out the dumpster find as evidence in Christine's murder.

Linda's mind then went down a different path. What choices were available if the killer did need to dispose of his clothing on the quick? The murder scene suggested that the killer, possibly covered in Christine's blood, would have few places to do so other than the campus hospital—right across the street no less. It occurred to her that the killer could even have been inside the hospital at the time Christine was being pronounced dead and the photos of her mutilated body were being snapped. With cops crawling all over the corridors, the killer, she speculated, could have walked among them, hiding once again in plain sight. The bloodied clothing, the murder weapon, all of it might still be *at* the hospital. She wasn't ruling out anything.

As Linda clocked out on her last day at the *Sentinel* and made her way home to pack for year two at UW—returning as a sophomore to the campus where her friend had died—she was on a short list of people who would need to keep the momentum of Christine's investigation going, her memory alive. She had already come this far working in a newspaper art department and piecing together her own leads. From that day forward, Linda would make sure she had her own all-points want on Jorgensen. From the UW campus and later from the road, she vowed to herself that she would keep tabs on him, sweat him wherever he decided to hole up next, and the time after that—and the time after that. If he knew he was being watched, she reasoned, he might not hurt anyone else. In reality, Linda had no idea whom she was dealing with or what she was getting into, what else Jorgensen had already done and what he was prepared to do again. She also had no idea that Christine's murder had been the tipping point—a foray into a new era for the city of Madison and its beloved UW campus. With Christine's murder, someone had pulled his or her finger out of the proverbial dike, and soon a slow leak became a deluge that would ultimately consume the city. As file number 68-78994—what the local cops called the "Rothschild job"—went from cold to colder, new women were already in danger. It was now the fall of '68, and the other shoe had just dropped.

Chapter 3

Sterling Hall

It is the bungled crime that brings remorse.

—P. G. Wodehouse, *Love Among the Chickens*

Swing Shift

After 1968, summers were no longer endless. As August became September that year, before the official onslaught of her fall school assignments, Linda already had some other significant homework nagging her. Jorgensen, even at an eclectic campus such as UW, had been the proverbial fish out of water. The one thing Linda believed she knew about Jorgensen was that he trolled campus smoke pits, using various sinister pretexts to identify the habits of unsuspecting young women, parlaying their naïveté into dark and destructive necrophilic fantasies. The end result was that she worked what would be the first of countless undercover details—all self-assigned and self-taught—over the coming years and decades. The *Sentinel* had simply been spring training.

By that fall term and beyond, Linda, immersed in something of a pennant race with mile-high stakes, would be forced out of her comfort zone. She'd pose as a smoker, a lost freshman, a loner oblivious of her surroundings—a quintessential soft target like her surrogate sister Christine before her—anything that might allow her to ingratiate herself in any environment, to break the ice and elicit a statement from a reluctant witness, even to serve as a decoy for another Jorgensen. She knew that with the real Jorgensen now in the wind, there would soon be others to follow his work. It was a case of doing almost anything that might enable her to get the scoop on a new angle, or, by sticking out her own neck, to expose those like Jorgensen who might also still be in hiding at UW.

It was in that same fall of '68 when Linda caught her first break doing as Christine had once done. Linda soon learned that "smoke breaks" were not only taken at the Memorial Library smoke pit but also at the campus hospital in a common area, itself a smoke pit by default, near the rear employee entrance. Making her way there for the first time that September, Linda found no shortage of hospital staff and med students willing to talk about Jorgensen almost before she could even finish getting out all three syllables of his surname. Not surprisingly to Linda, most of them had never been ID'd or interviewed as potential witnesses by police, their wards and floors never canvassed. Just as Christine had told Linda shortly before her death, the predominant descriptors related to the unsettling *je ne sais quoi* about his odd demeanor.

Although somewhat elusive in terms of its specific delinquency, that demeanor was sufficiently menacing—unquestionably unsettling—enough to raise the antennae of most of the female employees on the wards where Dr. Jorgensen had made his rounds. Other adjectives got thrown around too, some profane and others more akin to what Linda would expect from bookish people like herself working at the campus hospital. They called him prurient, maladjusted, and malevolent. Others labeled him as disaffected and disordered, even sociopathic: the now largely outmoded term still in vogue at the time—one used, with a certain scientific affect, to describe any dislikable person. None actually proffered the more accurate "psychopath" designation, that term still barely a decade old since being popularized by pioneering American psychologist Hervey Cleckley, and still poorly understood and inconsistently applied at the time. All the while, Linda made extensive notes. It was good for a first canvass run, her premiere assignment completed that fall. Three days later she was back at the hospital again, a new rotation of staff—doctors, nurses, residents, interns, clerks—on the day shift. Two days later, the night shift. And so it went for her first week back at UW. In time, Linda came to know the rotations of the various units—who was on shift and who was off shift, who was on call and who was on overtime—until she had spoken to nearly everyone who might have simply met Jorgensen in passing or have been exposed to his chilling presence during those fateful two months he'd spent at UW.

The first few times Linda made her way to the smoke pit and feigned being one of them, she tried her best to pretend inhaling so she didn't appear to be a complete imposter. She'd picked up a few tricks from watching Christine, who, she figured, not only smoked herself thin but also needed to keep her hands busy without actually drawing smoke down all the way. She later learned this was easier if she did as Christine did—rolled her own and cut the tobacco with shredded lettuce. It was a trick she'd never seen before or since, one Christine apparently picked up from some other teen models back on the Chicago Loop. Her next best option was to buy a pack of Virginia Slims. New to market by the fall of '68, a whole pack could be picked up, in some cases, for less than the cost of the lettuce and raw tobacco. By sometime in October, however, she'd abandoned the ruse altogether. The people at the hospital by that time knew who she was and what she was about. Linda in turn knew she'd likely have limited time before word of her freelance note-taking investigation got to the higher-ups and eventually over to UWPD. While at the *Sentinel*, she'd learned that two lead investigators, detectives Josephson and Lulling—the latter notorious for never taking notes—were now officially running with Christine's case. She fully expected to be sandbagged by them or to be put on official notice by Dean Ruedisili—who was notorious for *always* taking notes. In the meantime, Linda just had one more group of employees she'd not yet hit—the weekend swing shift.

Not every hospital has a swing shift; there were few then and certainly even fewer today. Often referred to as the "third watch" by those police departments still using a fixed eight-hour shift plan—an NBC crime melodrama of the same name set in New York City ran from 1999–2005 about it—the term describes that precarious time slot, between the early afternoon and the late evening shifts, that bridges the day and night shifts, often to cover lunch breaks or unexpected days off. From her time at the newspaper and from her father's job at the firehouse, Linda soon figured out that weekends at the hospital would often be staffed by junior people, many of them not yet full-time, covering areas such as housekeeping, maintenance, and even the morgue. It's frequently these same people who also see and hear everything, what late French philosopher Michel Foucault once referred to as the capillary level of power held by fundamental frontline workers as the eyes and ears of everything. Unlike higher-ups, holding symbolic power but often lacking awareness and intuition, the frontline workers possess an intimate knowledge of the bigger picture. In other words, sometimes you're better off knowing a garbage man than the mayor. In fact, you're always better off. It was on an otherwise unremarkable Sunday evening in mid-October when Linda met a man wielding that same type of capillary power—untapped knowledge which, for Linda at least, would blow the case—the so-called "Rothschild job"—wide open.

Happening upon a mild-mannered hospital custodian on his dinner smoke break, the worker had no sooner flicked open his Zippo lighter when Linda engaged him in small talk as an inroad to her real reason for talking to him—a trick she'd picked up back at the *Sentinel*. Sure enough, he soon cut to the chase as though he'd been waiting for the chance—chomping at the bit to spill the beans. The janitor spoke of Jorgensen taking an unusual interest in his access to the bowels of the building—the morgue in particular. Their initially idle chatter, which began as passing exchanges in the corridors, later progressed outside where Jorgensen, a nonsmoker, apparently spent his spare time in the hospital common smoking area, a favorite trolling spot of his. His spare time when off shift was of course devoted to the Memorial Library where he chose to target Christine. But smoke-pit chats weren't the only reason the janitor knew of Jorgensen, not the only reason why he stood out.

One evening, shortly after starting his residency at the hospital and arriving early for a night shift, Jorgensen lured the custodian into an empty wardroom under the auspices of showing him something. Like a giddy schoolchild eager to reveal a secret, Jorgensen apparently saw something in this regular middle-aged man that he trusted. Whether he thought he was a kindred spirit of sorts, or whether he simply couldn't stop himself from boasting in keeping with his narcissistic nature will never be known.

For whatever reason, Jorgensen at that particular time and place pulled from his white coat a pair of old Polaroids—images depicting two grotesque black-and-white scenes snapped and printed on location. Each photo revealed a pile of mutilated bodies composed of a man, a woman, and three children. The woman and kids—dark complexions, genders unknown—were too horribly hacked up to discern any identifying features. The man in the images had been dismembered and eviscerated, his eyes still intact and wide open. In furnishing the appalling images, Jorgensen boasted that the gore depicted therein was his handiwork, that he'd sedated the family for extermination and then cut them to pieces while serving—or more accurately posing—as a mission doctor. He confided that he had more snaps back at his place if his new mop-wielding confidante was interested. He explained that, since they were taken in South Africa ten years earlier, the decennial anniversary of the massacre was fast approaching and would require celebrating.

Linda would indeed later discover that Jorgensen had been, a decade earlier, a recently graduated GP without a designated medical specialty. While floating aimlessly around the United States, he'd ultimately been snatched up by a Christian mission and sent to the remote regions of the, at that time, segregated nation of South Africa. The family in the photographs had been one of an anonymous series of victims Jorgensen had in turn butchered with his issued surgical field instruments and a machete while also honing his killing skills during his time spent abroad, cloaked in anonymity and exploiting American white privilege. He later posed the bodies of his murdered victims in such a fashion that everyone would blame the local tribal factions if and when the victims were ever discovered—should the deaths end up even being properly investigated. If the crimes had, in fact, been investigated, the national police service would have no doubt chalked them up to cases of what he explained was *muti-murder*, the slaying and mutilation of victims to obtain body parts and organs for folk medicine rituals—still such an occurrence in South Africa that it has its own area of investigative and forensic expertise today.

Later, the story changed when Jorgensen, endlessly eager, it seemed, for the custodian's approval of the horrific images, would follow up with other versions. To pique the man's curiosity further, Jorgensen would then refer to the images as "Māori justice," a curious reference to New Zealand and not South Africa. Later, he claimed the victims were massacred members of the Zulu tribe, again setting the location back in South Africa. Amid the fluctuating accounts and Jorgensen's obsession with the gore of the photos, the custodian figured the doctor was just another garden-variety Mad City nutcase, a guy who, given the significant age difference between him and other residents, had taken a few too many acid trips back in his day and was trying to play grown-up while still clinging to some fictive past—an attention seeker who, like most attention seekers, could never seem to keep his version of events straight. After several weeks of back and forth, the custodian never took Jorgensen up on the offer to view more of the grotesque Polaroids that he later came to convince himself, perhaps as a coping mechanism, were fakes. He did, however, remember where Jorgensen told the man to find him if he ever changed his mind—the nearby medical resident housing where Jorgensen lived with a roommate named George.

At last Linda had more than conjecture. At last she had more to follow up on than mere anecdotal confirmation. She had what appeared to be corroboration of the fact that Christine's instincts were right, that Jorgensen was some kind of dangerous sexual psychopath using the campus as his proverbial candy store. She now had a general hit on a last-known Madison address for him, the first name of a roommate. She also had a sketchy story of a murderous holiday on the Catholic Church's dime a decade earlier during which time Jorgensen, such was his psychopathic taste for murder, chose to stage scenes to read like tribal genocides and muti-murders. Although the hospital custodian instinctively felt he had good reason to doubt the veracity of the images and Jorgensen's stories, he still should have known, false images or not, that they meant trouble—*big* trouble. Big trouble, especially in the hands of a doctor with an apparent erotic fixation on the subject of murder. Sure enough, fifteen years later, the nexus between mutilation photographs and necrophilic sexual homicide would be cemented in a case that began in eerily similar fashion to Jorgensen's misdeeds at UW.

In the early 1980s, a malnourished and strung-out sexual sadist and avowed Satanist named Richard Ramirez went from being a nocturnal burglar and sleepwatcher while working as a Holiday Inn night clerk to a terrorizing predator in greater Los Angeles. Earning the lurid moniker the "Night Stalker," Ramirez went on to murder fourteen victims between 1984 and 1985 after first having been groomed with similar atrocity photos. Ramirez's down-and-out cousin had been a decorated Green Beret in the same Vietnam War that, by the time of Christine's murder, was already the epicenter of daily life at UW. Soon after his return from combat, "Cousin Mike," by sharing his Polaroids with a teenaged Ramirez, showed how he had mutilated the "enemy"—mostly female civilians in villages his rogue unit had overrun. These included pictures of severed heads and flayed corpses of the women he had raped before killing—sometimes after. Before long, Ramirez, so engrossed by these images, was a budding necrophile, sleeping in cemeteries and experimenting with a hodgepodge of drugs. He would later claim a nine-year-old girl as his first victim during nearly a yearlong string of home invasion sexual murders that horrified the world and essentially held America's second largest city under house arrest. The difference between Ramirez and Jorgensen, however, was that the latter-day doctor was a remarkable multitasker. He was not only a murderer, but apparently also a photographer, raconteur, and sleepwatcher all in one. Again, no one sounded the alarm. Surely a trained physician, the custodian had reasoned, undoubtedly a bizarre boaster and teller of tall tales, would not also be a killer himself.

"Nice Day for a Murder"

It took Linda until the winter of '69 to track down "George" and put a face to the name—it had taken the entire preceding autumn to even locate the specific university apartment where Jorgensen had lived during his murder holiday in Madison. It turned out that George was a senior medical resident named Dr. George Johnston who, like everyone else at UW, was simply in the wrong place at the wrong time when Jorgensen came to town. Before long, Johnston, like Linda, would be the real-life iteration of the cursed seaman depicted in Samuel Coleridge's poem, *The Rime of the Ancient Mariner*. In this eerie eighteenth-century poem, the mariner, forever condemned to retell the same story time and again, is forced to wander the earth for eternity as the lone survivor of his encounter with the emissary of death. All the while, he is haunted by what he has seen—by what he now knows about the cruelty of the world. George and Linda, shortchanged of what should have been happier times in Madison and beyond, ended up inheriting a one-way ticket to that same nightmare. Soon, they would together become the mariner, the emissary of death being Jorgensen himself.

For their brief time as impromptu roomies, Jorgensen and Johnston couldn't have been more dissimilar, the veritable odd couple in the Felix and Oscar sense. The two fledgling doctors had been paired ad hoc by the university hospital's administration and shoehorned into a walk-up garden apartment on the campus earmarked for medical residents. Nearly twenty years his junior, Johnston had already been living in the spartan efficiency style two-bedroom unit for several months and enjoying his privacy when Jorgensen showed up. He told George he'd come from Carson City via Las Vegas and that he had completed his MD back home in California—where and when unstated. Particulars of his first two years of medical residency were equally—and suspiciously—vague. Jorgensen also recounted the usual war stories from the Battle of the Bulge, the fact that he was a certified blue-ribbon Nazi slayer on one hand and a medical humanitarian and mission doctor on the other. Referring to work abroad, he would cite his countless field hospital and missionary roles in Africa—tall tales of his genius and heroism never in short supply. But supporting evidence was always scant at best.

Jorgensen later told George that he'd gone to med school on the GI bill in the fall of '45, enrolling within a week of V-J Day and the emperor throwing in the towel on September 2, 1945. He also claimed that his kid brother hadn't been so lucky—KIA at the Battle of Midway, June 7, 1942, after going down with the *Yorktown*. An ocean away, his war bride to be was dead in Cherbourg—last seen pinned under a collapsed tenement following a Luftwaffe blitzkrieg. With nothing left, Jorgensen wandered the earth with MD degree in hand in search of adventure, or so the story went. True to form, George had also been shown the Polaroids of Māori justice and a few other items he would come to wish he hadn't seen—all of it an insight into what "adventure" apparently meant for Jorgensen. His roommate also told George that he would go to the library reading rooms to check out undergraduate females, particularly the blonde, pretty, preppy-looking ones. Once again no official alarm was sounded. By the spring of '69, however, George, as did Linda, had Jorgensen permanently rattling around inside his head, forever wondering where and when he'd surface again—forever haunting him. The mariner's lot.

George's time with Jorgensen as a roommate went beyond just an assemblage of disquieting stories. One night George also found himself staring down the barrel of Jorgensen's snub-nosed .38—an old-school revolver of the Sam Spade flavor apparently brought by Jorgensen to UW. The gun had been displayed and pointed on a single occasion when George let his girlfriend sleep over. As Jorgensen—ever the sleep-watcher—hid in the shadows of the room to spy on them, George apparently woke up earlier than expected to find Jorgensen reaching in to cop a feel. Following a verbal confrontation, Jorgensen, obsessively needing to assert his dominance, left and returned with the handgun, pointing it, and then leaving again. Occurring only a week before Christine's murder, it was obvious that Jorgensen's fixations and level of risk tolerance were both by that time quickly escalating—his ten-year celebration of Māori justice fast approaching. For the next six days, George quite literally slept with one eye open while keeping another eye on Jorgensen's activities at the hospital during any shift they shared, remaining vigilant to observe his interaction with patients.

On the other hand, George was equally concerned that complaining about Jorgensen's nocturnal prowling and unstable behavior in the apartment might be dismissed as a personality conflict, that it might cause damage of a collateral nature and possibly even jeopardize his own employment at the hospital. Before long, George occupied that precarious place in a "don't rock the boat" status-quo university hospital world where rational self-interest reigned supreme. It was a world where it might be easier to simply watch Jorgensen crash and burn—to initiate his own self-destruct sequence—rather than to be the instigator of his demise and become some kind of martyr in the process. Unfortunately, damage of a collateral nature was already inevitable.

On Sunday, May 26, early on the morning of Christine's murder, Johnston would later tell Linda that he recalled seeing Jorgensen leave the apartment dressed in army fatigues. He described it as a US Army Rangers' jacket—khaki, weathered, and emblazoned with chevrons and regimental patches. This was the first time Johnston had ever seen him in such clothing, the outfit that apparently went with Jorgensen's story of seeing combat in the European Theater in World War II. While on the one hand it might have been the first tangible evidence of Jorgensen's purported time at Battle of the Bulge at age eighteen, George also knew that such jackets were highly coveted and comparatively easy to come by both as keepsakes for collectors and as props for posers. Although the location and time of day, George thought, were both curious, he also well knew he had been saddled with a very strange roommate in Jorgensen. Whatever the reason for the chosen apparel that morning, Johnston—in part due to their opposite rotation schedules, and in part because of what would happen next—never laid eyes on Jorgensen again after he walked out into the rain and vanished amid the morning fog. His military attire also blended in among the other uniforms coming and going from Sterling Hall, state headquarters for the US Army Mathematics Research Center. It was there and then that Johnston last saw his soon-to-be ex-roommate, and where a new mystery began.

Jorgensen coolly kept his commitment to work his shift in surgery that day despite having just killed Christine some time before—in fact, it would turn out to be part of the larger MO. On one occasion during that same shift, according to both George and a nurse at the UW hospital whose name George had reluctantly provided to Linda for corroboration, while passing the nurse's triage station just beyond the public area, Jorgensen—now in his regular hospital attire, the clothes from the murder secreted somewhere in the hospital—looked out on the gray and drizzly spring morning with an oddly gleeful demeanor. Then, knowingly within earshot of a nearby nurse, he casually remarked, "It's a nice day for a murder." Perhaps dismissing the utterance as yet another one of Jorgensen's macabre and eccentric quips for which the strange new surgical resident was known, the young nurse apparently offered no comeback. Although never interviewed by the police, more inexplicable is that she did not voluntarily come forward with this valuable information after Christine's death. It was only years after the murder that she provided these jarring details, still not to the police, but to Linda.

When this late disclosure came to Linda's attention, she was left to wonder how Jorgensen, despite all his hubris and narcissistic grandiosity, his perversions and penchant for fibbing, could have been so overt that day—how he could have been so smug in leaving this same oral postscript to his crime. She wondered why he would make such a comment and tacitly reveal what any other killer would have inevitably kept concealed. She also questioned why he would make such a cryptically damning statement for a nurse to potentially report to others. The words uttered, however, spoke for themselves—there was simply no other interpretation to be made. Linda knew as well that the myth about killers, especially serial killers, secretly *wanting* to be caught was little more than nonsense. But she also knew that Jorgensen was a killer who broke the mold.

In her subsequent interviews with George Johnston, Linda had learned that, because he and Jorgensen worked different shifts, they would often have limited contact with each other day in and day out. This was also the case immediately following Christine's murder. After Jorgensen completed his shift on the evening of the twenty-sixth, it appears he returned to his shared apartment. He would be gone, however, very quickly, gone out of Madison for good by the end of that same week, possibly even as early as Tuesday the twenty-eighth. Although the precise date and time remain unclear, Johnston recalled returning from a night shift within that time to find the aftermath of a mad dash, the telltale signs of a man who left in a hurry with what he could throw into a go bag while his roommate was on shift.

Between his antics at the hospital and his flight from the city, Jorgensen had already become a person of interest in the Rothschild job by the fall of '68. Disturbingly, when later interviewed by police, however,

Linda would learn that Johnston chose only to tell them that his roommate was something of a loner and a little on the strange side, leaving out the part about the voyeurism, the groping, and, of course, the .38 caliber Roscoe. Even though by that time Johnston himself apparently believed that Jorgensen had probably killed Christine, police learned nothing of the suspect's prior activity in the days leading up to the murder, including the donning of army fatigues. It was all relevant and then some in terms of suspectology, directly probative to the investigation, and ought to have been provided as background information if nothing else. An eighteen-year-old had been brutally murdered at the hands of a sexual psychopath, but not only did Johnston as a key witness want nothing to do with his erstwhile roommate, he wanted nothing to do with his murder. Self-interest trumped all. For Linda, it was all becoming boringly repetitive—and infuriating.

Linda had been diligent about sharing any information she uncovered with UWPD investigators as her freelance investigation progressed. Her first such tip was provided in the days immediately after the murder when she'd urged the detectives on the case to check with the UW med school about an over-the-hill surgical resident who'd been giving her the creeps and loitering around the Memorial reading room. Later, she would also share with them the disturbing revelations made by Johnston. Once again she had corroboration that Christine had been right all along in seeing Jorgensen for who and what he was—right in her suspicion to report him to UW officers Golemb and Frey.

Armed with the latest information gleaned from Johnston, Linda soon placed a follow-up call to Dick Josephson, the lead detective on Christine's case. Although she had not been kept in the loop, she would learn for the first time that the police, despite the significant early missteps, had actually followed up on that same tip, especially upon getting wind from others about what a lecher he was, and that he'd blown town within two days of the murder. Linda, by that time herself aware that Jorgensen was no longer on campus, nonetheless played dumb. She would soon discover even more from Josephson—she'd learn where to start looking next.

After initially receiving the pat and sometimes necessary "the investigation is ongoing" platitudes from the circumspect plainclothesman,

Josephson let something slip. The previous fall, it turned out, Josephson and Detective Charlie Lulling took a trip to New York City to interview Jorgensen, who was now living there following a brief stint in Detroit immediately after Christine's murder. In addition to her own tip and the circumstances of Jorgensen's sudden departure, police had also received information from a senior administrator and chief physician at the campus hospital, a Dr. Sandy Mackman. Jorgensen had been hired out of rotation by Mackman on a three-month probationary contract due to expire June 30, 1968.

At some point in the week immediately preceding the murder at Sterling Hall, Jorgensen had been called in for a meeting at which Mackman had the unpleasant duty of telling him he had failed his probation period and was due to be fired. Jorgensen, perhaps having anticipated the purpose of the meeting, had come with a deadly offering. Armed with the same .38 caliber revolver he'd brandished in front of his roommate, concealed under his white coat, upon hearing the bad news, Jorgensen pointed the barrel of the weapon at Mackman's face. Just as he had done with George weeks earlier, Jorgensen paused for a moment, looked around, and then simply retracted the weapon before quickly exiting the room. This, perhaps as early as three days before Christine's murder, spoke to Jorgensen's increasingly erratic downward spiral—a descent into madness reminiscent of a Gothic horror story. In terms of suspectology, few murder investigations offer behavior this telltale, this incriminating. The trouble is that no one was looking for it—the cops and hospital administration alike had been actually too busy *not* looking. It was more, it seems, than they wanted to know.

Like George Johnston, Sandy Mackman reportedly sat on this information about Jorgensen, not coming forward to police until September 6, 1968, well over three months after the murder. When he finally piped up, however, it wasn't to press charges or even offer Jorgensen as a suspect in the murder; he opted instead to file a restraining order—the justice system's flimsiest of paper tigers. It was as if the entire medical community at UW campus hospital had been gripped by some paralytic fear about coming forward in a timely manner with information of obvious use to the police. To this day, no one knows why. Sadly, UW was, however, the rule and not the exception in such cases.

The truth is that universities are notoriously effectual at burying problem issues and people along with them when it suits their agendas, seldom discriminating between offender, victim, or witness in terms of vigorously whitewashing potential bad press. Consider for one the remarkably still-unsolved murder of twenty-two-year-old Betsy Aardsma at Penn State in November of '69. Like Christine Rothschild, she was a young coed also stalked at a campus library. She was later found stabbed to death in the stacks of that same library while it was packed with students and staff on a Friday afternoon—yet no one, it seems, saw anything. Quickly suppressed, the Aardsma case is today a matter of American esoterica and little else. Similarly, the home-invasion murders and Rothschild-like posing of four young women at the University of Florida in Gainesville in 1990 by Danny Rolling is, these days, largely unheard of. These two cases, of course, only scratch the surface of campus murders across America that, it seems, are easier to tidy up when they go unsolved, and the tide washes over them after a few years as new cohorts come and go.

But one might have expected better at UW. Given that Johnston and Mackman were both physicians—educated men whom one would expect to feel obligated to report such things—they might have at least tried to report Jorgensen and get the matter on official record sometime *before* Christine's murder. To his credit, Mackman finally did come forward, as did Johnston—albeit belatedly. Others with material knowledge never did at all. Many had suspicions but these were left unvoiced. Distancing oneself from Jorgensen and anything remotely relevant to the murder was the unofficial order of the day—a groupthink consensus. The hospital, like the campus proper, was something of an echo chamber.

Within two days of Christine's murder, Jorgensen grabbed a bag from his apartment closet and disappeared with what he could carry in it. For all he knew, the police were hot on his tail not only for the murder but also for the Mackman incident, an incident even Jorgensen himself assumed would have been reported with charges filed. In due course, once the cops received a hit on Jorgensen's name when he tried to transfer to the hospital at Columbia University—the same New York university Christine had once hoped to attend—detectives Josephson and Lulling flew east and sought him out at his rented Harlem townhouse. They had dropped in for a surprise visit, showing up at his door after first notifying the local NYPD 28th Precinct that they'd need to borrow an interview room and a polygraph examiner for a few hours. They were getting their ducks in a row for an arrest.

Jorgensen made Lulling and Josephson as cops through the spyhole of his front door as soon as they arrived. Creepy as ever and speaking with them through a narrow opening with the night chain strung across it, Jorgensen kept his cool and shot them his usual glib smile. He stick-handled their questions with precision, telling all kinds of fibs and fatiguing lies. He offered up potential alibis without committing to a single one, saying it was all still "a bit foggy." Josephson and Lulling, suits wrinkled to the max from their express flight to LaGuardia, stood stone-faced at Jorgensen's door while he talked himself in circles. On counterpoint, they offered him a chance to clear it all up—to clear the air—by coming with them to the local precinct and taking a polygraph, a quick drive there and back in the rental vehicle parked at the curb. They even managed to receive his preliminary agreement and talked him into their car when Jorgensen suddenly balked.

Claiming that he wasn't feeling well because of a dreadful summer cold, Jorgensen told the duo he was concerned that his fluctuating blood pressure would throw off the instrument's readings. He was, after all, a doctor and knew about these things—or so he reminded them. It wasn't hard for Jorgensen to bushwhack the cops with all sorts of anatomical and physiological mumbo jumbo. That was quite apart from the fact that Jorgensen was under no obligation to take the test, and the cops, though suspicious, had no probable cause to make an arrest—not yet anyway.

It was accordingly agreed to postpone the polygraph examination until the next day after a good night's rest. Jorgensen promised to attend the precinct at nine o'clock the next morning and then shut the door. The following morning came and went. Josephson and Lulling, flanked by an NYPD polygraph examiner and a uniformed lieutenant, waited in vain at the precinct as 9:00 a.m. became 10:30 a.m. and the doctor on the lam was a predictable no-show. No one had bothered to stake out his townhouse overnight, to keep him under surveillance in the event he blew town a second time. The lie detector test they hoped would allow them to lead Jorgensen by the hand into a full confession soon dissolved before their eyes. By 10:30 a.m., Josephson and Lulling were back in the rental vehicle heading to the tenement where they had located Jorgensen the previous day, only to find him gone again—another dash move to destinations unknown. The Harlem townhouse visit the day before would end up being the last time a law enforcement officer ever officially laid eyes on Christine's killer—by then an already seasoned serial murderer.

The Love Pirate

Over nine hundred miles from the crime scene at Sterling Hall, Jorgensen's decision to blow town a second time would have a future ripple effect on the Mad City. It was a decision that would set into motion new events, bring new victims and their killers together, and subsume the city in folklore for the foreseeable future. It was at that time and place, having been denied an opportunity to successfully interrogate and potentially collar the killer of Christine Rothschild, that the lore of the Capital City Killer was born. In hearing Josephson's story about the one that got away, Linda's instinct was that innocent men don't skip out on lie detector tests—much less med school residencies—if test results might help clear their name. She also knew that the campus PD, not the Mad City PD, would maintain control of the case for the foreseeable future, part of the typical factionalism, turf guarding, and empire building that defined police work both then and now.

In so doing, Linda also knew that the well would eventually run dry, that as long as Jorgensen kept on the move, the police would never have the money or resources to keep up with him. If they had the evidence to make an arrest, they would have already drawn up an arrest warrant, issued an all-points want, canceled his passport. With Jorgensen remaining a "person of interest," forever languishing in the purgatory of being not quite an arrestable suspect, trying to persuade other law enforcement agencies to pitch in—when they had their own wanted suspects and persons of interest to track down—would be the epitome of a fool's errand. Linda knew by the time she hung up the phone on Josephson that, after only a few months, the Christine Rothschild murder investigation was already played out.

If Sandy Mackman, the old-school doctor who had stared down the barrel of Jorgensen's .38, had been willing to press charges, the UWPD might very well have had a reason to arrest and hold Jorgensen with an "armed and dangerous" coast-to-coast felony arrest warrant. It would have been enough to ensure that Jorgensen's movements could be tracked, that he'd be arrested in the next town he arrived in to complete his studies, and that he would be returned to Madison for arraignment while cops worked actively behind the scenes to finally solve Christine's murder. Unfortunately, both then and now, some people just didn't want to get involved in the judicial process. There are a variety of reasons why, an array of justifications for opting out of reporting matters to the police. These reasons are suspected to account for two-thirds of all actual felony events not being properly reported, documented, and followed through with police—what criminologists call the *dark figure of crime*.

In this case, pressing charges for the gun incident would have meant that Mackman would be subpoenaed to testify for any required trial and that the incident would hit the papers and play badly for a campus already shrouded in macabre curiosity and lurid reportage since Christine's grisly murder. Knowing that Jorgensen had left town and wasn't coming back—that he was now somebody else's problem—was good enough of an ending for Mackman and his cronies in the UW medical department. By not even bothering to alert the state regulator or the American Medical Association, this omission essentially gave Jorgensen carte blanche to start over again in the next town on the map. And that's precisely what he did.

As it turned out, however, it wasn't what the fledgling general surgeon took with him as much as what he left behind that ultimately proved to be the most revealing—the most startling clue. In clearing out Jorgensen's old room, George Johnston popped a dresser drawer and came across a curious and unsettling find. It wasn't additional massacre Polaroids like the ones Jorgensen always proudly toted around, nor was it the souvenirs taken from Christine's body that might have proven to be the smoking gun Linda and the cops had been looking for. Rather, it was something more elusive—but just as sinister. In an old, waterlogged cardboard box too big for Jorgensen to take with him in a rush, George stumbled across a cache of old books, all of them similar with one exception. At the bottom of the box was a loosely bound copy of a typewritten manuscript, roughly two hundred or so pages, double-sided. The title on the front page, all in block letters, read *The Love Pirate*, by Heidi B. Jorgensen. Neither George nor Linda knew at that time that Heidi was Jorgensen's mother, and the unpublished manuscript Jorgensen had taken with him to Madison had been a map of his madness penned by her in an act of catharsis, a need to warn others about her son—a veiled literary depiction of the monster she'd unwittingly created.

When George later turned over the newly discovered manuscript to Linda, she dug into the story and soon realized it was more cryptogram than it was a conventional book aimed, from what she could gather, at preteens—what her English prof might refer to as a "young reader" adventure novel. The plot itself was also strangely lurid for a story written for children, the moral of the story puzzling to say the least. Equally puzzling was why Jorgensen brought the story with him to Madison. Although Linda recognized it as a carefully disguised recitation of tragedies and evil deeds past, it seems that Jorgensen was also using it as a guidebook about where to go next, using it to make the more fictive elements of the story a reality. The novel was a window into the future as much as to the past—a portent of things yet to come. But now that it was in Linda's hands, it would serve as the decoder ring that would allow her to understand the monster she was chasing as his own mother knew him.

The protagonist of *The Love Pirate*, a Dr. Francis Corcoran, is in reality Dr. Niels Jorgensen, his "immaculate white coat" described in the book serving as his uniform whenever he is "going hunting." In other words, it seems Heidi Jorgensen understood long before her son arrived in Madison that his profession as a doctor was little more than a façade used to hide his true self—an inveterate predator who in the book actually hunts his prey while dressed in his doctor's coat. It was the character's camouflage, just as it was for Jorgensen. The doctor in the book as the literary analog of Jorgensen has everything he desires, or so he thinks, until he meets a girl named Annabel. Soon he becomes obsessed and "must have her." After being rebuffed, Dr. Corcoran kidnaps the girl and takes her to a remote cabin in the Pacific Northwest where he intends to "make" her love him. He sees the girl as "pitiful"; she sees only his "black eyes."

Though it was disguised as a children's book, Linda recognized the story for what it was. It amounted to what's known as a roman à clef, or a true biographical piece disguised as fiction. Most of the better known examples of the roman à clef written in English—Lauren Weisberger's *The Devil Wears Prada*, Hunter S. Thompson's *Fear and Loathing in Las Vegas*, Tim O'Brien's *The Things They Carried*—are thinly veiled works of fiction written by the authors about themselves as pseudo autobiographies penned with great creative license. Heidi Jorgensen's *The Love Pirate*, however, was the story of her son, an unusual choice for any writer, and one that Linda knew had to symbolize something bigger. In analyzing the text page by page, dissecting it passage by passage and word for word, Linda would in time be able to reverse engineer Jorgensen's psychopathology and the trail of destruction he'd left over the previous ten years. It would serve as a cipher for what he had done and what he might do next. His mother knew the things he'd done and soon so would Linda. But there were also new questions to emerge, the most salient of which was *who was Annabel*?

While it was evident that Dr. Corcoran was Jorgensen, a duplicitous man of "violent tenderness," the specificity of his chance meeting—and subsequent abduction—of Annabel in the unpublished novel suggested it was an exposition of a confirmed past and not a speculative future. The beautiful Annabel—same spelling and general description as the equally doomed Annabel Lee of Edgar Allan Poe's last complete poem published in 1849—is found by Dr. Corcoran in San Francisco. *Why San Francisco?* Linda pondered the significance of the locale, the connection between the book and real life, and whether San Francisco was actually San Francisco or whether it was yet another fictionalized stand in for somewhere or something else. Annabel is later taken against her will by Dr. Corcoran to a place—a secondary crime scene—known as Paradise Valley. *Where was the real Paradise Valley?* Linda read on. She found repeated mention of another remote hiding place within a hiding place—of water, a boat landing, of secret "experiments" being conducted in a "laboratory"—and of a servile assistant named Quong Sha who serves the doctor and does his bidding. She found references to the doctor's unlikely ownership of a revolver just like the one Jorgensen brought to UW and pointed at doctors Johnston and Mackman. Linda noodled the meaning of it all, what the places and names *really* signified—which references were literal and which ones were metaphorical.

What was clear was that Annabel, for reasons beyond her control, was doomed to belong to the doctor one way or another. It was also clear that, in spite of his being depicted as "superior," Dr. Corcoran was actually a monster in disguise. As the manuscript was to become increasingly dark and lurid while encompassing obviously adult themes, Linda also wondered who the intended readership of the story might be. Or if it was ever meant to be read at all. As she began her second pass of the story, it dawned on her that *The Love Pirate* might be less a novel than it was a confession—an admission, committed to writing, by Jorgensen's mother as to what she knew, the things she'd seen and heard and failed to stop. As Linda later realized upon finding references to Dr. Corcoran's mysterious family background in the story, it might also have been Heidi Jorgensen's insurance policy on her own life. As Linda would discover in the coming months, Heidi had reason to fear her own son as much as any other woman did.

Now armed with the unsettling manuscript, Linda's new priority was to uncover where Jorgensen had fled to after bailing on the NYPD polygraph and leaving Lulling and Josephson twisting in the wind. She also needed to figure out what else he might have been up to before fleeing from the Mad City shortly after Christine's murder. Her search led her back to the campus hospital, back to the same ER department where the deviant doctor had stuck a snub-nosed revolver in the face of his boss, his last known activity before fleeing east to the Big Apple. Maybe he was on edge and feeling the cops ratcheting up the pressure; maybe he had started to snap. If so, he need not have worried. Jorgensen, although on the police radar as a person of interest, did not appear, at least to Linda, to be a subject of any urgent pursuit—of any real efforts by police to corral him. For months on from the New York visit, it was a matter of file number 68-78994 officially still being a who- and *why*-dunit for the UWPD. Unofficially, however, Linda's own freelance parallel investigation was picking up speed, soon to take her due west.

Boiling Point

Tracking down, interviewing, and debriefing George Johnston, and digesting the enormity of the clues and ciphers left by Jorgensen's mother in the puerile prose of *The Love Pirate*, took the better part of Linda's sophomore and even her junior year at UW. All the while, she would venture back to that same fateful spot at the foot of the Sterling Hall hedgerow to mark anniversaries that ranged from respectfully somber to outright macabre. Each new lead—each new window into Jorgensen's grotesque predilections and the extent to which he terrified his own mother—brought Linda back to the scene of the crime to look for what else might have been missed. In time, she was the only one who showed any lasting interest in the symbolic significance of Sterling Hall. But that was all about to change.

Unlike the fall term of '68, by the summer of '70 as Linda prepared for her senior year and put the finishing touches on her grad school application, forever determined to remain at UW until Christine's case was solved—and also to be on the watch for Jorgensen possibly resurfacing there—the murder at Sterling Hall had become yesterday's news. It had the ring of an Agatha Christie cozy mystery to it, but was forgotten nonetheless. Christine's slaying had thrust both UW and Sterling Hall under an unwanted microscope and, within two years, previously simmering issues had taken over and come to a rolling boil. As people began to wonder what else was going on at Sterling Hall, before long there were new topics to enrage UW students who were otherwise running out of things to rebel against, matters that had nothing to do with Christine Rothschild. By 1970, protesters were descending on the building en masse once it was revealed that it was essentially a war laboratory. As the Midwestern headquarters for US Army mathematics and physics research, the hall was a place some saw as a facility to reconfigure genius math minds to help Uncle Sam build a better bomb—how to more efficiently napalm the Vietcong and Agent Orange the jungles of Southeast Asia. On a campus replete with conscientious objectors who saw disavowal of the war in 'Nam as their raison d'être, this latest revelation was a new disaster in waiting, one that the university administration should have seen coming but didn't.

Before long, campus cops stood in formation with batons at port arms—zero training, zero clue, zero tolerance—to hold back and as necessary beat down protesters caught between acid trips and high ideals. Soon those students were joined by profs from the lunatic left, self-proclaimed "student combatants," and garden-variety agitators, all of whom were held back by johnny law to clear the way for military brass and brainiacs threading their way through the police cordon. It was a campus dancing on a precipice. Things were getting ready to boil over. To scald. To scar.

UW campus police in paltry riot gear hold back an angry student mob outside of Sterling Hall in the spring of 1970, the crowd gathering to protest the secret use of the building for US Army research related to the war in Vietnam. Courtesy: Wisconsin Historical Society.

Linda made her final trip to Sterling Hall as she remembered it to hold a vigil upon returning from Milwaukee in August of 1970, just prior to fall classes starting for her penultimate semester as an undergrad. A little over two days following Linda's final visit to the spot, and just under twenty months to the day after the atrocities committed upon Christine's body there, Sterling Hall would claim its next innocent victim before the campus had time to catch its breath. It didn't matter that Jorgensen was some fifteen hundred miles away at the time, the first unofficial reports in the press and the equally *official* word on campus was that the killer had returned after a two-year respite—that he'd come back to UW for revenge. Revenge for what exactly no one dared to ask, but in the years before splatter films like the *Halloween*, *Friday the 13th*, and *Nightmare on Elm Street* franchises popularized the idea of serial killers hell-bent on revenge and punishing the inhabitants of cursed places, the concept of a campus killer playing the long game—the Capital City Killer—already had a certain cultural currency in Madison and its surrounding regions.

Of course, those who started and later propagated such rumors didn't know what Linda already knew about who had actually killed Christine Rothschild—much less why. What they also didn't know was that the next Sterling Hall victim wasn't intentional. He was a civilian casualty in a war that had come to the Mad City and would soon attract other wartime criminals. Like British serial killer Gordon Cummings, better known as the "Blackout Ripper" who used the chaos of the German Luftwaffe's relentless bombing raids on London in 1942 to kill at least four women while disguised in a gas mask, the wartime chaos and social upheaval on campus and across the whole of Madison would provide the perfect distracting backdrop for the killers who would later follow in Jorgensen's footsteps. As Cummings's crimes revealed in England nearly three decades earlier, the existing social disorganization along with the panicked and primal nature of the wartime environment provide easy access to victims and permit horrific crimes to otherwise go unnoticed, or at least not get properly investigated. In some cases, killers won't bother to wait for chaos to come to them as Cummings did, they'll seek it out themselves. They will pursue occupations and opportunities that allow them to find those same target-rich environments on their own terms.

Consider, for instance, serial killer, peeper, and underwear pilferer "Killer Colonel" Russell Williams murdered two women—including an armed forces colleague—while stationed in a small Canadian town in 2009. While Williams's regimental records are clear and his whereabouts known while stationed in Canada, he also served in a peacekeeping capacity in war-torn regions—including the Balkans in the 1990s—with essentially zero supervision and no standing law enforcement or record keeping. One can only wonder if the specificity of his sexual murders committed upon his return to Canada in the following years is not perhaps the predictable aftermath of rehearsal crimes never reported, much less ever investigated in the war-torn former Yugoslavia—Williams's own version of Jorgensen's Māori justice. The truth is that certain people and circumstances will always attract sexual predators, while certain occupations also tend to attract psychopaths. Sometimes they're mutually inclusive, sometimes not. Civil service military occupations like Williams's are actually the tenth most common among psychopaths, statistically speaking. Surgeons like Jorgensen the third most common. Go figure.

The New Year's Gang

It was August 24, 1970, shortly after 3:00 a.m. when a foursome of disaffected reprobates wheeled a stolen Ford Econoline toward the east wing of Sterling Hall. With the keys for the van somehow lifted from an absent-minded chemistry professor the previous day, during the intervening hours the modest vehicle had been transformed by the group into a Trojan horse set to change history—set to put the Mad City on the front page of every Midwestern newspaper and the four young men responsible on the FBI's Most Wanted List. Their actions that day would also ensure that Christine's case went to the back burner indefinitely. As if by eerie coincidence, of all the places to ditch the vehicle, it was precisely ten paces between where the van was curbed—from where the Ford's transmission was left in "P"—and where Christine's black umbrella was found just over two years earlier. It was just a five-second jaunt from where the four mooks hopped out with the van rigged to blow and where Christine had been posed by Jorgensen nearly two years earlier. For all intents and purposes, it was the *same* spot. Within an hour, Sterling Hall would go down in the archives as the only known campus building in America to claim not one but two victims of murder in separate incidents. It's a piece of macabre trivia not found in any campus literature or in any daily double question. It is, however, a dark reminder of things past—a reminder of the contagious and mimetic nature of criminal violence both then and now.

It was exactly 3:42 a.m. when the fuse burned to its terminus and detonated a cobbled array of primary and secondary explosives which, given the soft-target nature of Sterling Hall, bordered on overkill to the point of the absurd: a dozen sticks of TNT, a hundred gallons of fuel oil, and 1,700 pounds of ammonium nitrate fertilizer as the coup de grâce. When it blew, the bombers—David Fine, Leo Burt, and brothers Dwight and Karleton Armstrong—were long gone, not present to see a molten and seismic BLEVE swallow the classrooms, offices, and laboratories of Sterling Hall whole. It was while celebrating the "success" of that message to Uncle Sam, while tailgating to the sounds of a local AM station at a shuttered gas station just beyond the city limits, that the four first learned from an overnight DJ that they were murderers.

Left: Parked cars located hundreds of feet from Sterling Hall still managed to fall within the blast radius and sustain heavy damage once the time-delay bomb left by a foursome of radicals calling themselves the "the New Year's Gang" was detonated. Right: A police officer stands guard over the most badly damaged section of Sterling Hall where a university physics researcher was killed by the blast. Courtesy: UW–Madison Archives & Wisconsin Historical Society.

Prior to cutting the engine, lighting the wick, and running for it—their getaway car left near the campus hospital Jorgensen had only recently called home—the four bombers had made a quick, cursory survey through the windows to make sure no one was inside Sterling Hall. Or so they claimed. They would later insist that it was never their intention to hurt anyone, only to cause property damage and obliterate the army assets inside what had become a predominantly military think tank. They would cite the timing of the attack as proof positive of this. It had been just before 4:00 a.m. at the tail end of a weekend and before classes were set to begin for the year. It was a day and time when they guessed that neither faculty nor students should have been on campus, when no researchers—army or otherwise—should have been inside Sterling Hall. Just like the mistaken quantities used in their recipe for the fertilizer bomb, they guessed wrong.

As it turned out, there were, in fact, four people inside the building at the time. These four included three researchers burning the midnight oil and the building's hapless security guard pulling the graveyard shift. The three occupants, horribly injured, included an international student from South Africa who was permanently deafened by the blast and left for dead in the rubble before being discovered by city firefighters hours later. Then there was Robert Fassnacht. The thirty-three-year-old physicist, finishing some postdoctoral research on superconductivity, had been working alone in the physics laboratory. He had been observing the final stages of an experiment in the wee hours of the morning so that he could take his three children on a family vacation to California before the fall term kicked off. The physics department where he was based at the time was never the intended target of the group but the myopic overzealousness with which the bomb was crafted ensured that the scale of the explosion was guaranteed to cause damage of a collateral nature—that the bomb would destroy not only the building's Army Mathematics Research Center but the *whole* building. In addition to the three others injured, Robert Fassnacht—found facedown in a foot of water after having his internal organs liquefied by the sheer force of the explosion—was a senseless casualty of an act that was itself senseless from start to finish. As an innocent victim unrelated to anything the bombers hoped to achieve, he paid with his life for their act of "resistance."

After upping the ante following at least three earlier gaffes, the Sterling Hall bombing as a purported act of righteous revolution was in reality little more than an act of domestic terrorism—murder and mayhem under a false flag. Despite having been consistently looked upon with comparative forgiveness by popular history, the bombing was also strangely similar in MO and bomb construction to both the first World Trade Center bombing in 1993 and, later, Timothy McVeigh's use of a rented Ryder cargo van to destroy the Alfred P. Murrah Federal Building in Oklahoma City in April '95. Like in the destruction of Sterling Hall, the Oklahoma City bomb also consisted primarily of an ammonium-nitrate/fuel-oil mix, an inevitably catastrophic recipe that ATF agents and other explosives experts call an ANFO bomb for short. McVeigh's barbarism killed a total of 168 people and earned him a much-lauded rig in the arm—execution by lethal injection—in Terre Haute in 2001. This was, of course, after first spending a few years, along with his chief coconspirator Terry Nichols, in the so-called "Bomber's Row" of the infamous and impenetrable ADX Florence supermax prison in the Colorado Rockies. Nichols is still there while McVeigh has gone on to become a leading case study in what are known as *set-and-run killers*, mass murderers who—through time-delay explosives, product tampering, or other acts of deadly sabotage—put time and distance between their depraved handiwork and their subsequent hideouts. In the summer of '70, no one knew the term "set-and-run" or even really considered the concept of domestic terrorism, much less that it might have come to UW. It would be another twelve years before the Chicago Tylenol mass poisonings put the reality of set-and-run killers as a new breed of domestic terrorist on the national radar. In fact, not since the work of anarchist carriage bombings in New York—most notably the Wall Street bombing of 1920—had Americans conceived of specific buildings and locales as political targets by other Americans. But at UW in the late '60s and now on into the '70s, anarchism, like that at Sterling Hall, had been repurposed against the backdrop of the Vietnam War. These new radicals called themselves "the New Year's Gang."

The New Year's Gang, as with many self-styled revolutionary groups to emerge at the tail end of the turbulent '60s, both foreign and domestic, from SLA to IRA, Black Panthers to Black September, was a mash up of ideological agendas and personalities commingled for the purpose of starting trouble. Having begun their destructive high jinks in earnest on the previous December 31—hence the name—the group of student combatants started by stealing a prop plane from the nearby Middleton Municipal Airport. Once airborne, the bomb-making Armstrong brothers, Dwight and Karleton, dropped homemade grenades and other improvised explosive devices, or IEDs, onto the roof of the Badger Army Ammunition Plant located in the neighboring town of Baraboo and closed for the New Year holiday. During the Second World War, the plant had been the largest arms manufacturing facility in the world and was the epitome of the American industrial might that helped cripple the Nazi war machine. It was a distinction which, during less popular wars like Vietnam, also made the facility a prime target for leftist militants looking to make a name for themselves. The problem was that the New Year's Eve bombs didn't detonate on impact, leaving the group to plot additional attacks on any installation in the area deemed to be military in nature, even if only in the academic sense. These follow-up offensives included the firebombing of the so-called Red Gym, a nineteenth-century armory-turned-gymnasium on the UW campus. Once again, the attack missed its mark, as did Karleton Armstrong's private attack against the Badger Plant, his attempt to bomb the electrical substation having been thwarted by the overnight caretaker. Very quickly, it seemed, the New Year's Gang's tactics weren't measuring up to its bravado. That was when the decision was made to escalate—to hit a target with great symbolic value. Sterling Hall was moved to the top of the list.

At the time of the bombing at Sterling Hall, only Fine and Burt were actually students at UW. Fine, born and raised as a Quaker, was still riding a near-perfect GPA from his freshman year and working for the school newspaper, *The Daily Cardinal*. Burt fancied himself something of an activist-journalist fixated on 'Nam, having become radicalized in his views on the war, the draft, and student politics—so his story went—after he took a police baton to the head while covering the Kent State protest and shootings earlier that same summer. It was that same incident in which four unarmed student protesters were gunned down by the Ohio National Guard, which had almost single-handedly galvanized the two UW students and the bomb-making Armstrong brothers, both Mad City locals. They would join forces to send a message that the US Army and its mathematics research project were entirely unwelcome in the Mad City, much less at left-leaning, Bohemian UW.

Today, aside from the plaque on the wall of a restored Sterling Hall mentioning Robert Fassnacht as a tragic footnote to the whole affair, a historical marker on the same Bascom Hill where Linda last set eyes on Christine Rothschild cites the 1970 New Year's Gang bombing as something that brought the campus's long-running "period of protest to a tragic end." Although Fassnacht's death and the ensuing FBI manhunt put the New Year's Gang out of business and perhaps served to neuter potential imitators, the bombing would set in motion a new era of violence that would pull the campus—and the entirety of Madison—even further down the rabbit hole.

Folklore

In the wake of the bombing and their landing on the FBI's Most Wanted List, the New Year's Gang headed due north to hole up in one of the Vietnam Era's preferred dumping grounds for American draft dodgers, felons, fugitives, and general detritus: Toronto, Canada. From there, they split up and went their separate ways. Bomb-maker Karleton Armstrong was the first to get collared in 1972, while his brother—by then using the Zodiac Killer-esque pseudonym "Virgo"—later fled Toronto for San Francisco to hook up with the SLA at the height of the Patty Hearst affair; by that time, he apparently developed a taste for self-righteous violence in the name of peace.

After later being cashiered by the militant group for reasons unknown, "Virgo" made his way back to Toronto where he was arrested in 1977, less than a year after David Fine was scooped by the cops back in Northern California. Today, no one has seen or heard from Leo Burt. He remains at large, walking the streets under an assumed name, likely still somewhere in Canada. Law enforcement's appetite for chasing him down has no doubt waned as the years have gone by, especially given that the three other bombers were paroled in no time flat, released to the great adulation of disordered fans and like-minded *Anarchist Cookbook* types within the following decade.

A remarkable beneficiary of revisionist history, Karleton Armstrong served just seven years and then managed to open a lemonade stand catering to students and situated near the gates of the same campus that had, upon initial importuning by Linda back in the summer of '68, denied Christine Rothschild a memorial—whether permanent or makeshift—at the same building and on the same campus where Karleton had killed and maimed staff and students while causing tens of millions of dollars in damage. Later, he and his brother Dwight—paroled a second time for the production of crystal meth—acquired a sandwich shop aptly named Radical Rye on State Street near the library mall.

But back in the early '70s, when the New Year's Gang save Burt was still locked up, other gangs of a similarly cross-border composition soon emerged, seemingly created in their likeness. Soon these same groups were no longer feigning any political or moral agenda, and were instead simply fighting "The Man" for the money. By the mid-1970s, with the FBI now investigating upward of one thousand bombings a year in the United States alone, the most notable of these syndicates was known as the Stopwatch Gang. Breaking away from the new '70s tradition of bombings, skyjackings, and other forms of mayhem, the Stopwatch Gang was a Canuck trio and precision stick-up crew who—as the inverse of the New Year's Gang—assembled first in Canada and then moved stateside. In time, they would go on to commit what would become some of the largest and most expertly executed bank jobs of all time. They also occasionally returned to Canada to take down additional scores. The name assigned to the group was actually coined not by the gang itself but by the FBI after investigation revealed that they could rob banks and airports of as much as $750,000 and be gone in under ninety seconds. Eyewitness accounts additionally confirmed that the leader in each robbery would actually be keeping time with a stopwatch, a theme later played on in countless caper films, with the Stopwatch Gang being fictionalized as the "Ex-Presidents" in the 1991 film *Point Break*, later remade—and made worse—in 2015.

But the Stopwatch Gang as a bank-robbing iteration of the New Year's Gang isn't where the events of the summer of '70 would come to an end. In fact, the reprise of Sterling Hall as a murder site—a place some would later describe as hexed, a place to forever serve as a lightning rod for violence and tragedy—connects the lore of Christine Rothschild's murder with what current criminological data suggests about the importance and recurrence of specific places as magnets for crime. New areas of research known as microgeography and psychogeography actually suggest that certain locales are particularly susceptible, often for symbolic reasons, to being enshrined as places for criminal activities. This doesn't mean sizeable and period-specific criminal hot spots—like Central Park in the 1980s, as the Big Apple rotted—so much as it refers to a phenomenon criminologists call *place-specific crime*.

The term in criminology describes why otherwise unremarkable places such as the Big Otter Creek, located in a Canadian town of only a few thousand people about an hour from Toronto, has had a total of eight people either murdered there or killed elsewhere and dumped there over the last fifty years. The creek doesn't offer an improved means of escape or disposal—it offers killers no instrumental or tactical advantage. In fact, on the contrary, all but one of the killers who have found themselves drawn to the creek either have been arrested or have committed suicide there. Yet there's something about its location, its design, and its snowballing lore that consistently draws killers back there time and again, generation after generation. Ditto for a specific stretch of Gilgo Beach on Long Island, New York, and a drainage ditch off of Black Horse Pike in Atlantic City, both of which have proven to be instrumental and signature-related disposal locations for one or more serial killers who remain at large. In fact, the symbolic and fantasy significance of specific kill sites and body dumpsites—once again the specialization known as psychogeography—is only now gaining significant attention.

But when Robert Fassnacht was killed at Sterling Hall within two years of Christine Rothschild's murder, despite the term "psychogeography" not pinging on anyone's radar, people were already talking about the academic building being precisely such a symbolic place—maybe even a hexed place. Within a day or two, the four members of the New Year's

Gang were all over every newspaper and television screen in the Midwest and on every screen in the nation within another week once the feds ratcheted up the pressure. There was no great mystery about who was responsible, who'd pilfered the van, loaded it with explosives, and left it to blow at the eastside of the structure—the spot where the blast would cause the greatest devastation.

Yet, by the fall of '70, as Linda made her way back to campus following a summer-long layover in Jorgensen's native California in a bid to track his movements, there was already talk that a Capital City Killer was behind the now two deaths at Sterling Hall. It was the antecedent of a local boogeyman tale in the Mad City, one that made as little sense in 1970 as it would a decade later when even some cops were buying into the theory. After all, as is often said, never let the truth get in the way of a good story.

That truth includes the fact that Niels Jorgensen had stalked and murdered Christine Rothschild back in May of '68—her best friend Linda knew it and, by 1970, so did nearly everyone who'd come to know him. The cops knew it too but were waylaid by a lack of resources and interest on one side, outmaneuvered by Jorgensen on the other. They had bigger fish to fry—or so they thought. These fish included four fugitive bombers who the student body at UW already and irrationally thought might have had at least *some* connection to Christine's murder. It was in that symbolic link to Sterling Hall as the unlikeliest of common ground for two separate killings that the construct of a mythical Capital City Killer was hatched. The horrific mutilation murder of Christine—what's known as an act of *lust murder*, where the sadistic and brutal nature of the crime serves a sexual purpose in the absence of an obvious rape—and the subsequent politically motivated bombing couldn't have been more different, aside from the common location.

And while no one for a minute suspected that the New Year's Gang had actually killed Christine, the Capital City Killer mythos was initially less about a person than an idea—an unseen and intangible force. It was something in the ether that compelled people to come to UW, and more specifically, Sterling Hall, to murder. When people say the Devil comes to town, they don't actually mean Satan incarnate, they're talking about everything the Devil carries with him—something that ensures the town is soon consumed by something bigger and more sinister. Such was the case in the Mad City when the 1970s dawned. In later years, however, the myth of a nebulous and elusive force would take on a more tangible dimension, a more human form. Some came to believe that one man might very well be walking the streets of the Mad City, venturing on to its pristine college campus to claim young lives.

Today, many still believe that myth. There will be no convincing them otherwise. With as many as 75 percent of Americans today believing that Lee Harvey Oswald was actually framed by the CIA, the FBI, or the Mob—and maybe all of them at once—and nearly that same number believing that Earth is currently under observation by extraterrestrial spacecraft, there is simply no disabusing people of a version of events they want to believe. There is no talking them out of a story they will forever cling to in spite of all cogent evidence to the contrary. Decades on, some even claimed to have seen the Capital City Killer—as though he were perhaps Bigfoot, the Loch Ness Monster, or some other fixture of cryptozoology—while others claimed to know his true identity. All the while, as the story gained momentum, it became little more than an impediment to catching Christine's real killer—Jorgensen—and the killers, plural, who came to Madison afterward. As Linda continued her search for Jorgensen and bounced around from place to place in later years as part of an elusive and thankless pilgrimage for justice, the lore of the Capital City Killer was already destined to become fact for men who, like Jorgensen, would find their way to the Mad City to hunt—to emulate his methods. Indeed, if after the Sterling Hall bombing the Capital City Killer was still little more than supposition and a local spook story, there were those prepared to make it reality. Those ready to claim the title for themselves.

Chapter 4

Postage Paid

The criminal is the creative artist; the detective only the critic.

—G. K. Chesterton, *The Blue Cross*

Book of Revelations

In the summer of '70, as the New Year's Gang put the finishing touches on its sinister plot to level Sterling Hall, the American League expansion franchise known as the Seattle Pilots was transplanted to Linda's hometown of Milwaukee and, with a turn of the screw, became the Brewers. For Linda, there was still precious time during those first few years of the search for Jorgensen to ponder what had happened and the turn life had taken—to contemplate what to do and where to go next. Some weekend afternoons when taking in a game at County Stadium on South 46th, she even pondered what might have been but never could be—what the future might have held had Christine made it out of the Mad City alive.

But the real nagging question by that point was the story told by Jorgensen's mother in the unedited mess of papers that was the unpublished manuscript titled *The Love Pirate*. That compendium of blemished old photostat pages, while seemingly pandering to Jorgensen's ego, was also a carefully veiled hit piece on his manhood and mental stability—something that Linda recognized for what it was. She knew that there was, quite simply, more to the story. The text was in actuality a deceptively innocent and inviting veneer pulled tight across a darkened recess, the flimsy manuscript a map to a place no one was ever meant to venture. In reality, it was a coded message detailing what had actually happened in the Jorgensen family's North Hollywood home some decades earlier, a four-bedroom on Toluca Estates Drive hand built by the old man, Dr. Niels Jorgensen Senior. It was a dressed-up confessional of what they had since realized their son was—*what* he had become. It was Heidi's warning to the world about what the family had unleashed. Like Victor Frankenstein, she, at once obsessed by and terrified of her creation, chose to provide a written record of her observations.

Some of the connections in the book were self-evident. Others were less so; the names had been changed to protect both the innocent and ignominious alike. Jorgensen had been remade as Dr. Corcoran—after the state prison of the same name, sometimes referred to as the *COR* and located just two hours north of the Jorgensen homestead in King's County. A veritable gladiator school considered by watchdog journalists to be the most dangerous state prison in America, notable future inmates would include Charles Manson and Robert Kennedy's assassin Sirhan Sirhan. At the time Heidi penned her infantile confessional, Corcoran prison also housed any number of LA area sex creeps and coed killers, which made Dr. Corcoran—the eponymous "Love Pirate"—and his treatment of young Annabel in the story all the more unsettling. The story, written in the years before Christine's murder, also begged the question of the identity of the purportedly fictional person whom Annabel was standing in for. Like Poe's Annabel Lee, a beautiful woman condemned to death for reasons beyond her control, the Annabel described by Jorgensen's mother might have been one woman or a surrogate for many. She might have been a young woman who had already met her death as a result of Jorgensen's past misdeeds, or one in imminent danger because of what Heidi Jorgensen believed to be inevitable once her son made his way to any destination where women of such an appearance were plentiful—and vulnerable.

To Linda, Heidi Jorgensen's ostensible children's book amounted to a series of cryptic clues daisy-chained together over the course of two hundred or so typed pages. Clues about the past. Clues about the present and future at once. Clues about what Niels had done and would do again—and again. One of those clues was what really happened to Niels's brother, Søren. The grandiose yarn told by Jorgensen during his time at UW was that Søren—his *younger* brother—drowned at Midway at age twenty. He had been, just like Niels, a war hero bar none, but unlike Niels, he never had the good fortune to make it back to the States. Linda knew the arithmetic didn't add up—the fib didn't compute. If Niels was at the Bulge at age eighteen or nineteen, his younger brother couldn't have been twenty a full two years earlier. Even if he had lied about his age to recruiters, he would have been only fifteen or sixteen when the draft age was reduced to age eighteen in November '42. The detail about his brother drowning also bothered Linda upon reading and rereading *The Love Pirate*, in particular, the repeated mention of Dr. Corcoran as a "strong swimmer," among other arcane nautical references. On the surface they read like non sequiturs, but beneath that surface something seemed to align at varying points with Jorgensen's stories about his brother's death at sea. She needed to find out more.

As Jorgensen remained off the grid, Linda did some digging into a web of lies that she knew would provide a clue about Niels's origins and why he'd come to UW of all places. It would offer a window into why he'd killed, why he'd chosen Christine, and where he'd be next. Linda's time at the *Sentinel* had taught her a thing or two about muckraking—about turning over stones, beating the bushes, and just about every other nature metaphor that might fit in terms of uncovering a concealed truth. She knew exactly where to go next, and she would use *The Love Pirate* manuscript as her sextant. Although it was a ledger of carefully concealed names and dates, Linda had enough experience as a result of her now-burgeoning freelance investigation to fill in the blanks where the cops could not—or more accurately, perhaps, would not.

Linda started with the Census Bureau. Then the American Medical Association. Then the obits and birth notices—glad tidings—published back in the Jorgensen family's home state of California and which she could access through Associated Press records held in the archives back at the *Sentinel*. Even the expansive UW library with seemingly interminable repositories of microfilm and its redheaded stepchild—microfiche—came in handy as Linda, now a master's student, began her research in earnest. She was to stay forever on campus, she vowed, keeping watch over the UW and the Mad City as a whole in case Jorgensen or his like showed up again. In case he showed up, as he had last time, when no one seemed to be watching. Linda also knew, as with all lies, that there had to be some verisimilitude to Jorgensen's charade that had prefaced his slaughter of Christine and his present life on the lam. She knew that, beneath it all, there was some kernel of truth around which the more elaborate affectation was constructed. It turned out, using the book as a starting point for that truth, it was even worse than she thought.

Open Water

As 1971 became 1972, the hits kept on coming, information rolling in as "official copies" from various government agencies and medical regulators, or as seen by Linda through the looking glass of a microfiche reader at various libraries. Niels Bjorn Jorgensen, born August 28, 1925. Graduated UC Berkeley with a BS in zoology on June 16, 1950. Graduated Loma Linda Med School sometime in '55—the same medical school, conveniently enough, where his father taught at the time, specializing foremost in conscious sedation in dental procedures. Following his father's death from natural causes in August of '74, the family name was bestowed on the med school library, now the Jorgensen Memorial Library. In contradiction, Niels Jr. had grown up as a low roller—a theta male in a family of alphas. His medical career, if one could even call it that, wasn't as stalwart as that of Niels Sr. It never could be, not so long as his younger brother Søren, a preeminent scientist in the tradition of his father, stayed in the picture. Not so long as he remained the heir apparent and Niels little more than the mimic—the renowned surgeon manqué. When his father died, his mother, Heidi, told him not to bother coming to the funeral. Jorgensen took the advicc—he figured the cops would have staked it out and would be waiting for him anyway. He gave them too much credit. They didn't even know the old man was dead.

Although Linda turned Jorgensen's medical licensing history upside down to see what might fall out, she was still left with more questions and fewer answers—questions that would only lead her farther into darkness. It turned out that Jorgensen was originally issued medical license number A17049 on July 2, 1956—more than twelve years before landing at UW hospital as a fortysomething resident making his third kick at the can in completing his required residency. For a number of years, his license history actually showed him as being inactive, totally off the grid, with dues to the AMA never paid over 1955 through 1958, '60 and '61, and '63 through '67. *Where* was he? *What* was he doing? *Why* didn't he surface? Linda was troubled by these questions that no one else had, it seems, ever bothered to ask. His mother, Heidi—Danish-born Harriett Warberg—had married Niels Sr. in Copenhagen in 1919. They had moved to the United States in 1923, settling in Los Angeles at the height of the silent film era when land magnates and news barons like Harry Chandler ruled the day—just after the ribbon was cut on the Hollywood Bowl and just before the **HOLLYWOODLAND** sign rose from the hills. First born was Niels Jr., followed by his brother Søren, when Niels Jr. was four and whatever was wrong with him was already beginning to take hold—the plaster starting to set. Søren was born April 23, 1929, and would have a short life; he died September 6, 1949, barely over the age of twenty, seven years after the Battle of Midway where Niels later told people his brother had been killed. Then there was the kicker. Cause of death on the coroner's certificate for a Robin Claude Søren Bjorn Jorgensen—his full birth name—was officially listed as drowning, but not at Midway due to the actions of a kamikaze pilot or Imperial Japanese U-boat commander as the tale had been. The real story was far more sinister. By the fall of '72, Linda at last had confirmation who it was she was chasing and what he was capable of.

An obituary entry later pulled from the *Los Angeles Times* on September 7, 1949, and found on microfiche at UW revealed that a memorial service for Søren was to be held at Steen's Chapel in North Hollywood on Friday, September 7. The obituary, as sometimes was the case, had not provided any circumstances of death. An afternoon edition of the *Examiner* that same day did, however, have a blotter item—an accompanying eyewitness account—from which she could glean some details of Søren's mysterious drowning. The headline, "Abalone Diver Dies in Sea," told, however, only part of the story. Søren, only age twenty but a natural outdoorsman with nearly a decade of abalone diving experience, had been in only fifty feet of water in Little Harbor on the west side of Santa Catalina Island, part of a larger archipelago of nearby small islands within the jurisdiction of LA County, when things suddenly went bad. It was in an area not known to be especially rough or perilous, even for beginners—something Søren most certainly wasn't. He had even taken steps to have a spotter before he headed out—what's known as a line tender—a man named Jim Luntzel, also twenty years old. As Luntzel later told the press and police, Søren had just started to scour for mollusks when, as the paper quoted it, his forty-pound lead diving belt had somehow become "fouled" and he was unable to loosen it. A horrific death at the bottom of the bay soon followed. The article went on to hail Luntzel's heroic efforts to save his friend as being "futile." The circumstances had from the beginning ensured the defect was fatal.

The brevity of the piece, not hinting at the involvement of any police or regulatory investigation, all pointed to a death that would likely end up in the dustbin of LA history. In a city consumed by systemic corruption and a torrent of violent crime at the time—the Black Dahlia torture murder, the Sleepy Lagoon slayings, the Bloody Christmas affair, the Chief Clemence Horrall and Brenda Allen sex scandal—the greater Los Angeles area was in investigative disarray that same autumn. Given that diving accidents, even today, don't follow any standardized scientific investigative protocol at either the local or state level in California, someone with a motive had an ideal constellation of circumstances—legal loopholes and institutional indifference mostly—with which to work in sabotaging the otherwise carefully maintained diving belt. When Søren ventured out into open water that morning, he had been the Jorgensen family golden boy. But he soon would forfeit his life and that status, his diving belt sabotaged to the point that his death was certain in spite of Luntzel's efforts to save him. Linda pondered the significance. Although he was an experienced diver with proper safety measures in place, Søren's skill set was no match for his older brother's avarice—his psychopathic bent and malignant narcissism. Between the clues left in *The Love Pirate* by a bereaved Heidi Jorgensen, the phony stories of Midway told by Niels to conceal the truth, and the fact that only members of the Jorgensen family had access to Søren's diving belt, the circumstantial case was just that—circumstantial—but it was significant. It brought Linda to the same conclusion it seemed that Heidi did in burying her youngest son. "Fouled" in this case could only mean sabotage and murder—fratricide no less—by design.

The Jorgensen family in an undated photograph, from left to right: Niels Sr., Heidi, and Niels Jr. A young Søren stands behind his parents and brother in happier times, entirely unaware of the tragic scheme that awaits him. Courtesy: Linda Schulko

By the summer of '76, it was becoming increasingly obvious to Linda that Jorgensen's first victim was likely his own brother Søren, his inaugural murder having been committed as far back as the autumn of '49. While the precise motive wasn't yet entirely clear, Jorgensen was not unlike many other notorious serial killers, also often documented necrophiles, who first begin with the murder of a blood relative. As a true psychopath prepared to claim an array of victims for an equally wide range of reasons as his delinquent career evolved, it seemed that Jorgensen's first kill amounted to what the FBI classify as a *personal cause homicide*. Later, perhaps during those years for which he was MIA overseas, he began to cultivate aberrant libidinous impulses and an erotic fascination with death, experimenting with a variety of criminal paraphilias that ensured his subsequent murders were *sexual homicides* by definition.

It was an evolution that would allow Jorgensen's willingness to kill for what he saw as a matter of rational self-interest to progress into an actual *desire* to kill for very different reasons. Linda was now satisfied that by the time he had arrived in the Mad City, having claimed even more victims, Jorgensen's constitution had changed into something his own mother felt compelled to fictionalize. Either way, there was no turning back. Heidi Jorgensen knew it then and Linda knew it too by the time she graduated from UW with her master's degree in the summer of '72. Linda remained on campus an extra two and a half years to audit courses into the winter of '75 and to get to the bottom of the true identity of Annabel in *The Love Pirate*—likely one of Jorgensen's victims after Søren. Alternatively, Annabel may have been a composite of several women—what is known among serial killers as a *preferred victim type* and the exemplar of their twisted fantasies. By late '75, however, Linda knew she couldn't continue to be a professional student languishing at UW, guarding it, in her mind at least, against the return of Jorgensen, or others like him, for years on end. It would instead require going at it full-time—full bore. Within the next six months, by June of '76, she'd left Madison and signed up to join the Milwaukee PD—the fall academy class. She'd caught the cop bug.

High Wire

Back in the Mad City, in the wake of Linda's departure for Milwaukee and just after the fanfare of the Independence Day holiday had subsided, a woman named Debra "Debbie" Bennett, age twenty, walked into the old Cardinal Hotel on East Wilson Street. The Cardinal at the time was a four-story throwback to when the Madison downtown was a true drifter's delight, at once a port city, railway city, and military community. Perched just outside the UW campus bubble in terms of surrounding geography, the old-style hotel was worlds away in terms of demography. It was a place steeped in history and human tragedy, for many the end of the line where rooms were let mostly to down-and-outers, parole absconders, and others who didn't want to—or more accurately couldn't—rent at places such as the Edgewater, the Hill Inn, or even the Ruby Marie right down the street. Following its brief golden era as a Mad City hot spot, like many downtown businesses in Great Lakes industrial cities, the Cardinal as a period hotel was also one of Madison's first casualties of twentieth-century mass suburbanization.

Once a legitimate destination for businessmen and tourists alike, the Cardinal had, by the mid-1970s, devolved into a "weekly rates" firetrap that also sported an old-school roughneck kick-n-stab saloon on the main floor. By the time Debbie Bennett checked in, the bar proper—one that was shuttered for nearly fifteen years during Prohibition—had begun playing host to a motley array of both daytime and nighttime regulars. During the workweek, these regulars included mostly local teamsters on their lunch breaks and sometimes Oscar Mayer factory workers needing a belt of something after punching out early. As daylight died, the occasional Mad City greaser or UW hippie hailing from one of the student ghettos in the 500 blocks of Mifflin, Dayton, or West Washington might stop by to score Mary Jane or angel dust. Juvie punks would come there to meet their fences and those who peddled goods stolen from daytime residential burglaries. The occasional prostitute might even show up to meet a trick. Two years earlier, the place had received a roughshod makeover, the original dining room dating to the building's 1908 construction renovated to become the Mad City's inaugural discotheque. In time, as the area gentrified on through the 1990s, the Cardinal dropped the "hotel" and, as the Cardinal Café & Bar, went on to become a destination for a more eclectic and multicultural clientele. The place evolved to epitomize Mark Twain's adage that with age even politicians and old tawdry buildings can become respectable. But in the summer of '76, the Cardinal was still a hotel and was still rough trade—not a venue for the light drinker or the faint of heart. It was also about to become the next morbid curiosity in the city's expanding reign in murder.

The evening of Thursday, July 8, 1976, marked the official countdown to the summertime blues in the Mad City—the start of the summer blockbusters being screened beneath the twilight at Madison's iconic Big Sky Drive-In—when young Debbie showed up at the Cardinal out of luck and out of money. Originally hailing from the village of Ridgeway about an hour to the west, whatever had led Debbie to the Cardinal as a last resort for weekly lodging and devoid of belongings spoke to a narrowing world that had been shaped by pain and despair—a pain that was about to get worse. As one of five children in a tight-knit cheese-making and farming community, Debbie's biographical details chillingly reflect what research in victimology has already confirmed with respect to the correlation between family size, birth order, childhood geography, and the risk of victimization. With Debbie's small-town life seemingly played out back at home, she relocated from Ridgeway with a friend shortly after graduating high school about a year earlier. An all-too-familiar tale, she'd longed to live the big-city life while completely unprepared for the world into which she soon found herself being hurled headlong.

By the time Debbie landed in the Mad City in the fall of '75, her life was already something of a contradiction. Her family would later describe her as someone who was naïve and overly trusting while at the same time irrationally and unremittingly paranoid about death. Debbie was so afraid of dying that she avoided any activity that offered any hint of danger—direct or indirect. Risk averse to the max, she even forewent getting a driver's license for fear that it might increase her chances of dying in a car wreck one day. Perhaps paradoxically, she also believed in the kindness of strangers—certainly more than she should have. She also, mixing with the wrong crowd in Madison, became hooked on one or more of the many drugs that were in generous supply at the time. It was that element of her life that seemed to lead her, time and again, into the clutches of one of those countless opportunistic strangers who—as Jorgensen had—knew that Madison was a target-rich environment.

In the week or so before turning up at the Cardinal, Debbie, for reasons unknown, had been summarily evicted from her low-rent apartment on Loftsgordon Avenue in the city's east end. Having only been in Madison for a short while, Debbie's life had quickly turned into a high-wire act without a safety net. Popped for felony breaking and entering by Madison cops back in June, she was keeping company with an undesirable assortment of dope fiends and petty crooks while largely estranged from her father Bill, by that time in palliative care back in Ridgeway in the final stages of terminal cancer. Debbie, on the street without money, had nonetheless somehow—perhaps through the kindness of strangers upon which she had come to depend, perhaps by some other more nefarious means that would foretell what came next—managed to scrounge enough cash to secure a room for a week's stay at the Cardinal.

Debbie's meager possessions still locked inside her apartment back on Loftsgordon, she took the room key from the hotel manager and barkeep, a man named Luther Getty, and was gone again that same afternoon—July 8. Although she had checked into the Cardinal as her next stop in an apparent downward spiral, Debbie would actually never spend a single night there. It was the first of a series of mysteries to dog a case that would never get past square one. If closing the lust murder of a Sunday School–going Chicago socialite like Christine Rothschild proved to be too much wood to chop for local law enforcement eight years earlier, the case of Debbie Bennett—a troubled young woman who other than her immediate family had few advocates in either life or death—was effectively relegated to the unsolved column before it even happened.

One of the chief problems in what would become known as the Bennett "big sea" case—a nautical reference later made by a quick-rigged task-force detective that suggested, presumably, that the investigation was either underwater or listlessly adrift—was that, all preconceived notions about Debbie's lifestyle and habits aside, piecing together her final movements proved even trickier than one would expect. While the psychological autopsy in Christine Rothschild's murder was comparatively well established, albeit with some pieces of the timeline missing, Debbie's final forty-eight hours were a matter of pure guesswork—a combination of several delays and missteps in the investigation based on wrong assumptions. Her last verified whereabouts weren't in fact at the Cardinal as some first speculated or as the *Capital Times* erroneously first reported.

Rather, the place Debbie was last seen was back on Loftsgordon Avenue, in the 1400 block. As was later confirmed by an eight-year-old child who had been playing in the street at the time, Debbie was last seen walking barefoot down a sun-parched sidewalk away from her old apartment, looking dazed and slinging a brown purse. That was the afternoon of July 10—a Saturday—and a full two days after renting a room at the Cardinal from Luther Getty. Debbie Bennett was never seen alive again. From then on, exactly how, where, and when she fell off her precarious high wire remained a mystery. That is, until the afternoon of July 21, nearly two weeks later, when the horror of her brief life's end was unveiled.

"Beyond Recognition"

On that afternoon of Wednesday the twenty-first, two Dane County land surveyors walking along Old Sauk Pass Road, about twenty miles from where Debbie was last seen alive, happened upon a grisly discovery in a culvert near the former Wilkie Farm—today a protected Ice Age scientific reserve. Initially unsure of what they were looking at, the indiscernible mass in the gulley soon revealed itself to be a human form, twisted and charred as black as the rural Wisconsin soil that surrounded it. The Dane County Sheriff's Office and local coroner, Dr. Clyde Chamberlain, soon arrived and estimated the remains to be those of a woman in her twenties and the body, "burned beyond recognition" as was later publicly stated, to have been there for at most two weeks. No one in Dane County—where Madison serves as the county seat—knew Debbie Bennett, and would have had any reason to assume that she was the Jane Doe in the ditch. Further, no one back in Madison or elsewhere even considered that Debbie was missing. In the intervening two weeks since she was last seen walking alone down the street, no one was even looking for her save a couple of social workers stopping into the Cardinal hoping to find her and persuade her to return to Ridgeway where her father lay on his deathbed. Cardinal manager Luther Getty later confirmed to *Capital Times* reporters that Debbie never spent a single night at the Cardinal in spite of checking in two days before her disappearance. She also "never even checked out" he told reporters once it was revealed, nearly a week later through dental records, that the scorched body found out in Dane County was in fact Debbie. Two days after that revelation, Debbie's father died. A joint funeral was held for the two—father and daughter—in the nearby town of Dodgeville.

As July became August, a task force consisting of some thirty full-time detectives known as the Intra County Investigative Squad combined the resources of Madison PD and the Dane County Sheriff's Office in a bid to crack the Mad City's latest whodunit. Much to the surprise of many, given that victims on the margins didn't typically garner such massive investigative resources, the team even enlisted outside experts—including the anthropology department at UW—as they dug into the case for answers about the wayward farm girl's final days and hours. For a couple of months at least, the multijurisdictional and unequivocally brutal nature of the murder earned a greater commitment from police brass trying to solve the case than was ever afforded to Christine Rothschild—killed solely within campus police jurisdiction. But in spite of their best efforts, the task force quickly came up empty. There was no verifiable timeline, no witnesses, and no cause of death established given the state of the body. Although Debbie had been identified by way of a missing lower molar and previously fractured collarbone after investigators compared X-rays and dental charts, absent those individuating details the charred corpse might well have stayed a Jane Doe forever.

Whoever brought Debbie, likely already dead, to that fateful spot on Sauk Pass knew the ditch where she was set ablaze and knew it well. A grave about three feet deep and nearly thirty feet off the road, the killer knew it would provide the isolation needed to set a fire without attracting attention. So intense were the flames of that same fire, in fact, created with the use of an unknown accelerant, that they scorched the branches of trees hanging up to twenty-five feet above where the body was immolated. While investigators were never able to verify the fuel source used, few widely available accelerants other than gasoline allow for such rapid and intense combustion. That would mean that the Sauk Pass location was in all likelihood what's known as the *secondary crime scene*, strategically selected by the killer as an ideal location for disposing of—and destroying—the victim's body. Debbie's murderer knew this because he'd been to that same spot before. Killers, even the most reckless and confident of killers, don't simply load a body into a car and hit the road at night without some semblance of a plan. A mobile killer with access to a car is required to make a series of calculated decisions regarding locations, routes, and post-offense behavior under intense pressure and with a victim on board. Such decisions are thus among some of the best indicators as to whom the police should be looking for—a means of vetting what in Debbie's case was a seemingly endless list of potential suspects. Notwithstanding that the primary crime scene, wherever it was that Debbie was actually held and killed, could never be determined, the postmortem activity with her body, based on what we know today about offender behavior, speaks volumes about the murderer—who today is likely still at large.

Anytime a killer elects to transport a body and create a secondary crime scene—a significant behavioral marker in its own right—no decision with respect to location is ever arbitrary. The decision to move a body and conceal it, in this case by removing it from public view and destroying the remains, would require extraordinary risk on behalf of the killer, both prolonging his time with the body and also running the risk of being seen or caught in the act at either the secondary crime scene or in its vicinity. The decision to select the Old Sauk Pass Road dump site indicates that the killer had been to that location and knew it well enough to realize that, at night and under cover of absolute rural darkness, the likelihood of his being interrupted or seen, even after starting a raging fire, was slim to none. What risk it did pose would have been rationalized on the basis that it was still less risky than if the body were to be found quickly and identified as Debbie Bennett equally quickly. Her killer felt compelled to drive the county roads surrounding Madison's bedroom village of Cross Plains—a dead body on board and a jerry can of gasoline at the ready—because, had Debbie been left at the primary scene or merely transported and dumped to be found and identified within a day or two, his sense was that this would have led the police straight to him. The killer presumed, rightly or wrongly, that city cops would immediately find some obvious connection between Debbie, the crime scene, or the cause of death—or all three—to do some basic arithmetic and link her murder to him. The decision to transport and conceal the body, the decision to essentially make Debbie disappear, was therefore a strategy to place time and distance between the killer and the eventual discovery and identification of the body. By the time the charred remains were positively identified as Debbie Bennett, a mere two weeks it seems provided more than enough time.

Today the FBI's National Center for the Analysis of Violent Crime actively monitors trends with respect to this very specific—and risky—post-offense behavior among offenders, what the Bureau calls Disposal Pathway #1, and has found overwhelming commonalities that might have been useful in the early days of the Bennett investigation to help cops narrow their focus. In just under half of such documented cases in the United States involving this disposal pathway, the victim is known to the killer, the primary crime scene is the killer's own home, and the most common cause of death is strangulation. These figures tend to align with the autopsy of Debbie's burned body, which, while inconclusive, suggested she was neither stabbed nor shot when killed roughly ten days earlier. In nearly all similar cases, the killer is also employed full-time and owns the car used to transport the body. In all solved cases where this same disposal method is used, the motive for the murder is also paraphilic in nature—a sexual homicide. That would no doubt also account for the fact that, in nearly 80 percent of these occurrences, the killer kills again, in most cases two to four additional victims. It means that in eight of every ten such cases involving this same disposal pathway, once a killer does this successfully, he gets a taste for it. He goes serial.

Fan Fiction

While the Bennett task force had an army of thirty plainclothes cops chasing a budding or perhaps an existing serial killer without so much as a clue to work with, Linda was single-handedly chasing another. By the end of the summer of '76, she was confident, based on the available evidence and his own statements recounted by witnesses, that Jorgensen had started his homicidal career by murdering his own brother before moving on to kill one or more families in Africa and then finally coming to Madison where he murdered Christine. In between these events, she was also satisfied—and no doubt correct—that there had to be more in the intervening years. By the time he arrived at UW, Jorgensen's growing sadistic and necrophilic impulses were impossible to contain. He'd been at it and escalating for more than a while. Maybe his transformation to homicidal necrophile and sexual murderer began back in Africa, she thought, but the attack on Christine was too specific for it to have been his first of its kind. It once again took her back to *The Love Pirate* as Jorgensen's disguised biography—his roman à clef. It took her back to the same nagging question: *Who is Annabel?*

Soon, as two investigations, one official, one unofficial, moved in opposite directions in pursuit of two different killers, one unknown and the other one known—at least to Linda and a small handful of cops—the cases of Debbie Bennett and Christine Rothschild managed to start blending together in the local rumor mill. Given that both women were so brutalized postmortem and that, more notably, both cases had a tangential connection to UW—Christine murdered while renting a room on campus and Debbie while renting a room near the campus—people started speculating that the slayings were the work of a common offender.

Talk of the Capital City Killer escalating his behavior made its way through the streets of Madison along with the parallel rumor that he was becoming increasingly fixated on toying with local law enforcement. The Bennett job, people speculated, was an indication that the killer was miring the murders in predictable police bureaucracy and factionalism by involving as many different agencies as possible—that he was standing back and watching the mayhem of his work carry on for months and years later, always enjoying the fact that muddled and multijurisdictional investigations were going nowhere. All the while, the Rothschild case remained the closely guarded property of the campus police—the tiny UWPD—and not the Madison city cops. The MO in the Bennett murder had taken what should have been one case and divided it into two, a city case on one hand and a county case on another. He was dividing and conquering. He knew the task force was a perishable veneer—a PR smoke screen. Although police politicians were masters at maintaining appearances, interagency cooperation, he knew, would be short-lived and soon fizzle, each agency predictably hoarding its own information and leaving the sandbox.

The Capital City Killer, though a figment of the collective local imagination, provided for many an effective explanation as to why a second murder had now summarily gone cold in what seemed like record time, even by Mad City standards. Someone, it was thought, had to be masterminding the whole affair and outsmarting the police in Professor Moriarty-like fashion. As terrifying a prospect as it was, Madisonians wanted to believe in the Capital City Killer. They wanted to believe that he was the new "Napoleon of crime," Sir Arthur Conan Doyle's one-time description of Moriarty and Scotland Yard's characterization of master criminal Adam Worth, the real-life inspiration for Doyle's villain. The idea of a single and comparatively ingenious Capital City Killer was, for many, a notably less terrifying prospect than the idea of the Rothschild and Bennett murders being separate random events—less terrifying than the thought that three different police forces were now simultaneously out of their depths and two separate sexual murderers still on the loose. The machinations of a single calculating master criminal being behind it all—that there was only one killer to be caught—for whatever reason, allowed people to sleep a little easier.

By the fall of '76, anything in the Mad City, it seemed, was possible. That same year, Wisconsin body snatcher and necrophilic serial killer Ed Gein was still languishing in a Madison insane asylum. Known as the "Plainfield Ghoul" among other monstrous pseudonyms, Gein murdered two people in Waushara County, an hour north of the Mad City in the 1950s following a decade of trolling rural cemeteries and robbing graves of body parts he later fashioned into decorative items and clothing. When the police searched his dilapidated Waushara County shanty after arresting him for the 1957 murder of a local hardware store owner, they found a veritable house of horrors that shocked the world. Among other items, sheriff's deputies discovered masks and lamp shades made from human skin, bowls made from human skulls, and even a corset crudely fabbed from a dismembered, decaying torso.

Gein was later charged with the shopkeeper's murder and declared criminally insane, spending the rest of his life in the Central State Hospital in Madison where he died in the summer of '84. The car Gein used to haul the disinterred corpses was then sold at auction to a sleazy traveling carnival showman who charged admission for a quick gander inside and out, an early example of a murderabilia item that would later spawn an industry sustained both by and for the sad and disordered. Although Gein was safely locked away in the summer of '76, the Capital City Killer soon emerged as the state's next conceptual public enemy and necrophilic supervillain—the Plainfield Ghoul's heir apparent—but in a more cunning and intelligent form. Soon, with Gein still recent history and by then the subject of Hollywood movie magic, the existence of a Capital City Killer emerged as an entirely plausible theory that even some in law enforcement were prepared to buy in to. What had happened in the Bennett case therefore seemed to lend credence for many to the idea that the killer was himself some kind of twisted theater impresario. Like the debased roadside promoter now selling tickets to Gein's deathmobile, the killer was himself putting on a show while he terrorized the Mad City and mocked its law enforcement officials.

As leads dwindled and rumors swelled, on the morning of August 12, 1976—a muggy Thursday in the Mad City—members of the emaciating Intra County Investigative Squad watched graphic Debbie Bennett crime-scene and autopsy slides on a pull screen in a darkened boardroom. They sipped soluble coffee out of Styrofoam and kicked around some suspect names, most of which had been coughed up by their various stoolies and jailhouse snitches. The names were all reruns from earlier briefings, all since cleared and alibied. Less than a month in and the investigation was already running on fumes—gridlocked for the foreseeable future. At that same time, Cardinal manager and barkeep Luther Getty was back on East Wilson Street taking delivery of the day's mail when he made a chilling discovery.

Checkout

Amid the various letters and parcels that made their way to Cardinal that day, including the usual bills from Ma Bell, mailers from liquor purveyors, and Dear Johns sent to upstairs tenants both past and present, was something entirely unexpected. A single room key affixed to a plastic Cardinal Hotel tag lay loose among the items dropped on the bar by the mail carrier, a "Please Return to 418 E. Wilson" request, along with a "Postage Paid" guarantee, etched on the back. Confounded, Getty, studying the key and checking the registry, suddenly realized that it was *the* key—Debbie Bennett's room key. It was the key she'd taken after checking in and making a small deposit back on July 8. It was the key to the room she'd never slept in, never so much as entered, before vanishing. It was the key to a room she'd never checked out of—until now.

As investigators headed down to the Cardinal yet again, they contemplated the meaning of Debbie's room key having been returned through the mail. True, some Good Samaritan may have stumbled across the key discarded in the street and done the right thing by dropping it in the next mailbox he or she saw and ensuring it made its way back to its rightful owner. Then again, the key might also have been taken by the killer as a sadistic keepsake—just like the many souvenirs stripped from Christine Rothschild's corpse by Jorgensen—before being dropped in the mail to taunt police, to keep the case above the fold in the area papers, and to stoke the flames of the Capital City Killer lore. To go public with this latest development in the case might very well bring forward that Good Samaritan to reveal where the key was found. It might allow cops to glean the precise spot on the map where it was dropped, the site, perhaps, where Debbie was snatched by her killer—maybe at or near the still-unknown primary crime scene. It might also very well bring the false confessors, kooks, and agitators out of the woodwork. On the other hand, if the sender was in fact the killer, it might empower him further, leading to additional attempts to upstage the task force by mailing more items or even providing him with inspiration to kill again and collect additional souvenirs, the mementos of his work. It was a catch-22—damned either way.

Knowing in part that Getty at the Cardinal would likely not be able to keep this latest development quiet, the decision was made the next morning to go public rather than deep-six the key as holdback evidence and lose control of the narrative once again. In short order, Madison PD detective Ted Mell, the latest in a series of local spokescops straight out of central casting and the task force's new mouthpiece, made a public plea in the *Capital Times*. He implored the finder of the key to contact police, stressing that the person might be unknowingly holding an additional key—one that might very well unlock the mystery of Debbie Bennett's murder. Other area papers picked up and ran the story for a few days, making hay of the mysteriously returned room key and speculating as to its meaning. The same appeal also received regular top-of-the-hour play on most AM radio stations, including in nearby Milwaukee where conservative talk radio dominated. Yet nothing materialized. The call never came. Not even from the kooks.

Before long, time got away from Madison. Soon August became September and, with that, the students trickled back into town—back to UW. Their return brought an eerie anticipation of what might come next as the autumn air and unanswered questions both hung heavy in the Mad City. Two of the four Sterling Hall bombers were still on the lam, and the murderers of Christine Rothschild and Debbie Bennett were now both also at large. The Capital City Killer theorists of course preferred to think the latter two were in fact the same person—a single and increasingly emboldened sex slayer. In the following years, as the body count on or near the campus climbed, more and more Madisonians started to cling to that same idea. Single serial killer or not, by the end of 1976 it was evident that the identity of the person who found and returned the Cardinal Hotel room key last in Debbie Bennett's possession—in her possession at or just before the time she was murdered, driven to Cross Plains, and then set on fire—was bound to remain unanswered. There might well have been many reasons, whether rational or irrational, why whoever found the key might not have read or heard the appeal to come forward, even why that person might have chosen not to come forward if aware of the appeal. The chilling possibility also remained that the key might have been thrown in the mail by the murderer himself.

The brown purse Debbie was sporting when she was last seen alive was not with the charred clothing debris found with her body and has never been found. Had the key been in her purse as one might expect, it would have still been there once she met her killer. If it was the killer who had mailed the key back to the hotel, the question remains why. Returning it to the hotel to play cat and mouse and assert his self-perceived power is one possibility. Another possibility, given that he could have simply tossed it in the trash, is that he wanted to be rid of it—that any sadistically erotic souvenir value it offered was outweighed by its identifiable and incriminating nature, its ability to link him to Debbie. By the time the key had been through the rigmarole of US Postal Service sorting, had made its way to the carrier's bag, and had been retrieved by Luther Getty, the shiny plastic key tag—a smooth surface normally ideal for yielding fingerprints—bore only an array of indiscernible smudges, none of which could be used to identify either the killer or the finder. Whether to stick his thumb in the eye of the local cops or simply divest himself of any remaining physical evidence, if the killer was indeed the one who sent the key back to the Cardinal on the hotel's dime, he'd won.

Linda was completing her final background check forms for the Milwaukee PD when she learned of the Debbie Bennett murder. It then dawned on her that, whether killed on or off campus, whether hailing from the boondocks or big-city Chicago, or whether living between addresses and on the margins of society or in Ann Emery Hall and armed with a sterling-plated trust fund, class differences in Madison offered no protection from motivated killers—or police apathy at the time. The MOs between the Rothschild and Bennett murders couldn't have been more disparate—chalk and cheese—but what took Linda back to the spring of '68 when she heard of the ghastly discovery on Old Sauk Pass Road was the willingness of senior police brass to monitor the case, if only to call balls and strikes. The county task force that had been cobbled together was mostly sizzle and no real steak, but a mere eight years after Christine's murder, Linda was surprised to see how criminal investigations appeared to be modernizing—how there was less of a cold war between police departments in terms of information sharing, at least in the early days of investigations. It both frustrated and inspired her, gave her pause to think just how random death, and more so its ensuing investigation in the case of murder, could be. As the current data compiled from cities such as Baltimore, actually a famed locale in the annals of television crime drama, and "Big Easy" New Orleans suggest—with their police departments' clearance rates for murders hovering around 40 percent annually—it's equally random whether a murder gets solved. In fact, it may simply be a matter of luck—whether good or bad.

The contrasts between the Christine Rothschild and Debbie Bennett murders that also stuck out in Linda's mind weren't only what a difference eight years made; nor was it limited to the expanse between an isolated makeshift grave and burn pit in rural Dane County and the hedgerow outside of Sterling Hall on a marquee college campus. Instead, Linda wondered how one victim being found on university property with countless prying eyes and the other on a remote private property where no one seemed to pay much attention ultimately altered the course of how the investigations were handled as discrete undertakings. Neither investigation, as was clear from the outset in both cases, at least after the New York snafu in Christine's case, was going anywhere. Meanwhile, Linda wondered, *What if*?

What if Christine had been killed somewhere else—anywhere but the UW campus—and cops from outside UWPD, effectively lapdogs for the university's senior administration, had been allowed to investigate? What then? This was of course years before similar questions would be raised not only with respect to how serious felonies on campus are either investigated or not investigated by university cops in the interest of publicity and reputation but also how campus police services are managed altogether. Most notable in recent times would be the 2011 attack on protesting students at the University of California at Davis—what's become known as the UC Davis pepper-spray incident. As described, a group of otherwise passive students sitting passively—albeit disruptively—on the university grounds were pepper sprayed at close range with a tactical "Mark 9" canister, a weapon normally reserved for violent mobs. It was later revealed that the entire police operation was deployed—and was being controlled—not by an experienced police manager trained in crowd de-escalation, negotiation, and use of force, but by a civilian university paper pusher who had assumed executive power over the police and ordered the cops to move in. Whether in 1968 or today, the reality is that campus police work is closely and precariously tethered to corporate interests, with even senior officers from the chief on down having their strings pulled by puppeteers sitting safely up in the ivory tower.

As Linda ruminated the Debbie-Christine dichotomy, she completed the "Educational Background" component of the police department's questionnaire, filling in "UW–Madison" under the header asking for the name of the institution from which her latest degree had been conferred. In this case, said degree was a master of arts in Spanish, a degree that she was already preparing herself to be questioned about by recruiters, academy instructors, and her field-training officers. She was certain she'd be asked why she went to grad school and what the degree meant—how that helped her in *police work* and what she would really "bring to the table" once through the academy.

But Linda knew the masters was a voucher that, in 1976, would help her make, at the very least, captain or lieutenant one day, still believing that police departments actually allowed the cream to rise. If nothing else, her background would all but ensure a fast track to detective, allow her to parlay her freelance investigation and research experience into something with bigger chops. She had made it this far on her instincts and her anger over what had happened to her freshman friend and confidante—what had happened and would happen to women all over the Mad City and every other city in America for that matter. But if she could pair that anger and those instincts with actual field training, backup, and PD resources, there would be no limit to how far she could pursue Jorgensen, to the good she might be able to do in other cases sitting idle in bankers' boxes and growing colder by the day. If asked what she brought to the table by a cynical senior cop who didn't like the cut of her jib, too bad for him. In other words, her response would speak for itself—she *was* the table.

Chapter 5

Permafrost

> The larger crimes are more apt to be simpler, for the bigger the crime, the more obvious, as a rule, is the motive.
>
> —Sir Arthur Conan Doyle, "A Case of Identity"

Old Milwaukee

By the first Wisconsin snowfall of '76, the dust had settled on the Debbie Bennett case for good—an open/unsolved to add to the growing pile of Madison mayhem. Meanwhile, about eighty miles east on I-94 in Linda's hometown of Milwaukee, it was the second of two consecutive decades known as the Breier years. Chief Harold Breier was an old-school cop in the best and worst senses, a brass knuckles–tough Polish immigrant who had a twenty-year reign as the city's top cop, a run largely unrivaled even among America's other better-known police leaders, from August Vollmer to Raymond Kelly. Old Chief Breier swung a big enough stick, going back to his rise to power in '64, that had Christine Rothschild been from the Brew City herself, it would have meant fingers on the throats of investigators, results demanded—the case put down lickety-split. It would have meant hell and high water being moved until the killer—Jorgensen as a few Madison PD cops knew by the end of '68—was in cuffs. Either in cuffs, that is, or dead himself—eminent bullet bait for every cop under Breier's thumb almost statewide.

But as a Windy City transplant, Christine might as well have been from Neptune. She was an out-of-towner—an interloper on Wisconsin soil and, moreover, squarely within the jurisdiction of a small police force with limited resources for an occurrence of such magnitude. Although a horrific case, it was also a case that would become a lingering nuisance without any vigorous pursuit of Jorgensen after the first year and that failed ground game in New York. As Christine's case soon became colder, it also seemed to be enveloped in an incremental disinterest in trying to locate Jorgensen at all, even though still a prime suspect. As the case faded away into the distance, the Rothschild job ceased to be a news item as well—out of sight, out of mind. Bit by bit people would forget. But part of Linda's promise to Christine was not only to make sure her killer got caught, but also that no one forgot. No one. Ever.

With Breier at the helm back in Milwaukee, Poles ruled. With a distinctly Polish accent that made his background obvious, Breier actively recruited Poles, and they eventually made up a large part of the police department—from rank and file to brass buttons. Linda, of Polish descent herself, had her application to the academy rubber-stamped and, her rock-solid credentials notwithstanding, a welcome mat was rolled out from day one. It was also clear that she would be an asset to the department as a polyglot, a multilingual woman with a master's degree and an investigative intuition that eluded even some of Breier's best case men. Given her newspaper background at the *Sentinel*, she might also be useful in dealing with the press—one day. But that same background would additionally be useful to Linda in her personal quest, something she would leverage in later years to get Christine's murder back on the front page—back above the fold. In an age when college grads and women represented a small sliver of city cops, Linda was a poster child for reform and progress. It wasn't, of course, only the police work that appealed to Linda, at least not the type of police work that drew the other applicants. By '76 she also knew that the UW campus cops—some well-intentioned, others dangerously inept—could never cultivate the underworld contacts necessary to keep tabs on Jorgensen as he trekked with impunity across the Lower

48 using various schemes and pseudonyms. Her status as a member of the police force, she thought, would provide access not only to a variety of records and resources but also contacts. Access to people no one else seemed to be mining, people who knew a thing or two about disappearing, and people who might find themselves crossing Jorgensen's path. In the end, however, Linda would need to pass on committing herself to a cop's life.

By early '77 she also had a few sources passed to her through old crime-beat contacts at the *Sentinel*, contacts brokered by Bill Share, Linda's beloved boss from the summer of '68. From there she worked her way up—or perhaps down—the ladder of local ne'er-do-wells who claimed to have seen Jorgensen over the course of their travels. Linda knew that his malignant narcissism and need to spin tall tales would give him away every time—in every city he slipped in and out of—and that he no doubt would indiscriminately make himself known to anyone who would listen. He would impose on every social situation as a self-proclaimed cognoscente on every topic even when in theory he should have been lying low.

The best tip from Share's contact list came from a disgraced day-drinking croupier from Binion's Horseshoe on old Fremont in Vegas, a man who by the spring thaw of '77 had moved to Milwaukee to open a bookie mill for the local sports scene. He soon also had to begin a new gig as a paid snitch for city cops and reporters after most of that same gambling scene he tried to get in on turned out to be already mobbed up, and he got muscled out before even starting. Desperate, the croupier took to diming out old clients, friends, and even family for the equivalent of chump change as a confidential informer, or "CI" in police circles, who unapologetically played both sides. After an initial intro, he offered a new lead to Linda on the cheap—information in exchange for a case of Linda's parents' homemade wine. After the deal was made and as shaky hands uncorked a bottle right there in Linda's car, the snitch went on to describe a doctor, claiming to have worked ringside at Caesar's Palace for the Foreman-Lyle bout in January of '76, who seemed to fit the bill. The man went on to describe the doctor, coming into the Horseshoe the night after the bout, boozy breathed and with a sweet roll of hundreds burning a hole in his pocket. All the while, the doctor was rambling on about his time back in the Mad City—in Africa before that. The story had the ring of truth.

Linda knew, since she was dealing with a grifter and a boozer, that the info also could be pure bunk. Although she'd heard make-believe tips before and would again, she also knew that no one but a few, maybe only two, people had ever known of the Africa missions and Jorgensen's so-called Māori justice pictorials. She knew of only two people—George Johnston and the campus hospital relief custodian—who had actually seen the Polaroids of the anonymous maimed family, butchered by a machete, for whose deaths Jorgensen had gleefully taken credit. He had killed his brother, after ensuring he would drown, by tampering with his diving belt—a textbook case of homicidal sibling rivalry, of set-and-run deadly sabotage. This next stage in his killing in Africa seemed to have been his experimental foray into what forensic psychologists call *necromutilimania* after he'd killed Søren with comparative cleanliness and a more personal motive. The unnamed African village had been the undocumented dress rehearsal for Christine and likely others before her—it was where lust murder became his oeuvre. Linda had to buy in to what she was being told by the tipster, had to take the info at face value. If Jorgensen was in fact in Vegas—Sin City, the perfect cover for his dark perversions and the ideal backdrop for his various bogus identities—he was potentially more dangerous than ever. If he'd come to Madison to up his game, he'd go to Vegas to turn pro. He'd kill again—and soon. It was time to make a U-turn.

Due South

It was Valentine's Day '77—a Monday—when Linda let the Milwaukee PD recruiters know that she'd need to take a pass on the new job, that some lesser qualified applicant would have to take her seat at the academy to hit a city beat for a little better than the state minimum wage. With the tip most recently received from the croupier, Linda's personal investigation was taking her on the road. After years of starvation rations in terms of information and making progress at a snail's pace in her bid to locate Jorgensen, it was the most timely and actionable of leads she'd come across in nearly a decade. That same road, however, led not immediately to Vegas but first to Dallas, the city she thought would be ideal as her base. It was to serve as a hub for any needed regional branching out that her pursuit of Jorgensen and the truth might later require—her new home and an ideal jump-off point to anywhere and everywhere, whether by plane, train, or automobile. If Jorgensen wasn't still freelancing as a ringside physician at Caesar's Palace—assuming he ever had been—then the strategically situated Dallas-Fort Worth area would make any next stop on the map easier to get to. The weather was also consistent—hot, dry, and seldom changing—which made for minimal disruptions to travel plans. More pragmatically, the city's proximity to Mexico made it an ideal place for her to teach and translate Spanish while making use of her master's from UW. If Jorgensen also happened to run out of places to hide stateside and make a run for the border she'd be there too—knowing the language, knowing the customs.

Linda arrived in Vegas via Dallas on March 3, 1977. She soon found that no one she talked to could corroborate the croupier's story. The ringside docs at Caesar's—several on staff at the time—were hand-picked men tapped specifically by the World Boxing Council or Nevada Athletic Commission for the job, not random walk-ins and residency washouts like Jorgensen. Linda knew that this in itself didn't necessarily mean that Jorgensen wasn't in Vegas that same winter, but more likely that his cover story for being there—as he spun yarns when playing the tables—was once again pure fiction. Yet the grandiosity and specificity of the story, just like his bravado back in Madison in '67 to '68, suggested that his presence in Nevada was more than an excursion of indulgence, not exactly a "what happens in Vegas" weekend. Jorgensen just wasn't the type. Instead, he'd have more sinister intentions upon his arrival. Although he'd come to the city to hunt, something pushed him out—Linda wasn't sure what. Or perhaps, she thought, something somewhere else pulled him in.

Linda scoured news reports. She later charmed a pair of over-the-hill sheriff's deputies doing radio runs along the strip to make a quick check of open murders and reports of endangered missing women in the metro area. To do so, she posed as a girl dispatched to Sin City by her parents to look for her degenerate gambler runaway sister. The well-intentioned swindle worked but turned out to be for naught. Nothing since early '76 in the police files and when Jorgensen was seen at the Horseshoe seemed to fit. If it was indeed Jorgensen the fink had spoken with at the Horseshoe the previous January, he hadn't stayed, at least not long enough to find his next Annabel. He'd moved on to some other place by now.

With that, Linda returned to Dallas and placed a call to Bill Share back at the *Sentinel*. It was a Hail Mary throw, but Linda gambled that the casino-boxing-bout-doctor account had not been an entirely improvised ruse. Like all of Jorgensen's past lies, there was no doubt some element of truth to this one too. One possibility, she thought, was that Jorgensen had prizefight or ringside doctor experience somewhere else before January '76—or experience in the gambling world since disappearing from NYC back in the summer of '68 and before landing in Vegas. Another possibility was that he had been planning to do something in that vein and also had a new murderous scheme in the offing. Either way, the lie had been rehearsed—vetted and tested. It was the yield of yet another depraved fantasy that he soon would act upon—if he had not already—with his usual deadly efficiency.

Casino. Doctor. Prizefight. Murder. Endangered. Missing. They were peculiar keywords as Bill Share searched for AP images filed by category back in Milwaukee. Unlike a laborious search of entire articles, Linda knew that the *Sentinel*'s image cataloguing system was brass-tacks efficient. It was an alphabetized system that allowed file photos to be located on the quick by relying on bursts of representative descriptors, images often recycled as stock photos for similarly themed pieces under insanely tight deadlines. So it came as little surprise when, within the hour, Linda received a call back from old Bill. Although it wasn't exactly what she was looking for, it was close; it was a better chance than not of explaining what the possible Jorgensen sighting in Vegas meant. Filed under Casino/Nurse/Missing Persons/Nevada was the case of a Donna Ann Lass, a twenty-five-year-old infirmary nurse at the Sahara Hotel-Casino in South Lake Tahoe, California. Since Share didn't have more to tell her without access to the article proper, within the hour Linda was on the phone to a retired *Daily Tribune* reporter who was still living in South Lake Tahoe—his number was quickly coughed up by directory assistance. He'd been one of the newsmen who covered the initial story and quickly helped fill in the blanks as best he could remember when Linda dredged up the town's seldom talked-about past after calling him long-distance. It turned out that Lass, a registered nurse at the local casino—which had a small skeleton-crew medical staff running a first-aid station catering to the largely inebriated and geriatric clientele—had gone missing just before 2:00 a.m. on September 6, 1970. But that was only the beginning of the story.

Christmas Past

Donna Ann Lass had worked as a nurse in South Lake but lived out of state—in neighboring Nevada. Her apartment was located in the town of Stateline, southwest of Carson City, and only a day's drive from Vegas. Following a September 8 search of her apartment by local cops within forty-eight hours of when she was reported missing, the interior of the modest dwelling suggested that she'd never made it home from work in the wee hours of Sunday the sixth. Linda also learned that on the morning of the seventh, a mystery male caller had rung the manager's office back at the Sahara. The call was placed in order to apparently alert Donna Ann's boss that, due to an unspecified family emergency, she'd have to miss her scheduled 6:00 p.m. to 2:00 a.m. shift that day. It was the same shift she'd worked the night before and a fact mentioned by the caller who clearly knew her schedule. But the call turned out to be a ruse, a delay tactic used to buy time for whoever had taken and was holding—or had already killed—Donna Ann, to give him precious hours to extend the distance between her last known whereabouts and where he was going to hide her, or bury her. Although the caller was never identified, it wasn't the last time he'd surface. He would reappear as part of a cruel and twisted ploy to taunt Donna Ann's family four years later.

A little over four years later, in December of '74, a macabre Christmas card landed in the mailbox of Mary Pilker, Donna Ann's sister. The card, not to mention its timing and message, clearly reveals a person with a peculiar fixation on writing to his victims' families. It was highly individuating post-offense behavior and an accompanying set of high-risk actions eerily reminiscent of the behavior of infamous child killer Albert Fish, the so-called "Brooklyn Vampire."

Fish was a geriatric serial murderer and cannibal who rode the lightning at Sing Sing in the winter of '36 at age sixty-five—he was one of the most senior men ever put to death in America, and the oldest to get strapped into the electric chair. A set of autopsy X-rays later confirmed that he had, presumably between his grotesque and unspeakable crimes, inserted at least twenty-nine rusty needles into his own scrotum as part of his ongoing self-mutilation. His masochism aside, Fish endures today principally as a foundational case study in what's known as *coprographia*, or an erotic fixation on the often repetitive creation of obscene or offensive writings intended to shock or frighten. It's among the rarest and least studied of psychosexual disorders—paraphilias—and is linked with any number of violent behaviors, typically also sexual in nature. It is theoretically also a root cause of a great deal of online harassment and cyberbullying content authored today. While the writing medium has modernized, the underlying paraphilia remains largely unchanged. However, the fact that Fish limited his crass handwritten correspondences to the families of his victims, as well as a final statement intended to be read aloud following his death in the electric chair, is additionally unusual, even for an already unusual and rare disorder. The reappearance of interpersonal correspondence sent from the killer of Donna Ann Lass to her kin is equally unusual—perhaps more so.

No one who didn't know or work with Donna would have known that Mary—with a different surname and in irregular contact with the victim—was her sister. Featured on the front, the unsettling card received by Mary in December of '74, her sister still missing and by then presumed dead, was a starving-artist vista of some snow-covered pine trees; the image was actually an advertisement for the Forest Pines condominiums in Lake Tahoe. On the backside, a generic preprinted caption in cursive title case read, "Happy Holidays and Best Wishes for a Happy New Year." Beneath it, in ballpoint scratch, a more ominous handwritten inscription: "Best Wishes, St. Donna & Guardian of the Pines." The officially unidentified Zodiac Killer, who terrorized the San Francisco Bay Area between 1968 and 1969, killing five and claiming to have slain nearly forty, would actually later try to take responsibility for the Lass murder and this subsequent communiqué to her sister. A print advertisement for the Forest Pines condominium development was also sent four hours away to the *San Francisco Chronicle*, one of the past recipients of the Zodiac Killer's missives. Although the communiqué to Mary brought back memories of the taunting cryptograms sent by the real Zodiac Killer five years prior, that was all. In fact, neither the penmanship nor the MO matched the Zodiac's handwriting exemplars already on file with police. Both sets of mailings had also been posted in Nevada, not California.

By late '74, the Zodiac Killer was thought by many to, in all likelihood, be a low-functioning creep named Arthur Leigh Allen, who later died in 1992. Since then, conjecture and half-baked theories have yielded as many suspects as Jack the Ripper and more potential scenarios than the JFK assassination. He's also seen countless imitators intent on emulating his theatrics, including a New York version named Eddie Seda and copycat letters still being received by the San Francisco press as recently as 2007.

Imitations aside, Donna Ann's disappearance spelled an organized stalker relying on—much as had happened in Madison—the cops making false linkages to the earlier Bay Area slayings on the strength of the postcard alone, and despite the fact that the crime had no apparent connection to the area. The disappearance clearly had a Nevada connection: Donna Ann's abandoned car was reportedly found near but not *at* her apartment in the town of Stateline, though versions vary in part due to a baffling lack of police cooperation with the press on the matter. In learning all of this, Linda wondered about the symbolism of the message sent to Mary Pilker as the sister of the victim and what the "Saint" prefacing Donna might mean. While it might have represented innocence and altruism, it might also have represented sainthood in the more literal sense, perhaps even horrific death as a martyr. The theme of innocence, as Linda already knew, is found on page 11 of *The Love Pirate* when Annabel is described by Dr. Corcoran as "chaste" and "virtuous." It is in part for that reason that she is considered to be the right choice as his captive in Paradise Valley. It is a place where no one will find her, a place where the gentle serene setting will inspire her—where it will *make* her love him.

As a nurse, Donna Ann Lass was in a vocation now recognized in the field of victimology as one of the top three at-risk occupations for targeted stranger attacks. Today, the body or remains of Donna Ann Lass have never been found; the case remains open, unsolved, and predictably inactive, yet there has been no additional correspondence and no suspect has ever been identified. And while what exactly happened to Donna Ann and where it happened remains unknown, there was something about the inscription on the postcard that took Linda back to *The Love Pirate* as the codex of what Jorgensen had done and would do again. Signing the card "St. Donna" *and* "The Guardian of the Pines" was effectively a message sent by two different personalities occupying a single disordered mind. While the reference to "the Pines" might have been a convenient image borrowed from the tacky corporate postcard, little more than subterfuge, she pondered the significance of the "guardian" reference. She'd seen it before in Heidi Jorgensen's ominous manuscript where Dr. Corcoran is described as both guardian and protector of Paradise Valley and Annabel alike. It's also while reading the *San Francisco Examiner* that Annabel first begs Dr. Corcoran, her guardian—and captor—to take her home. Forest Pines and Paradise Valley; the *San Francisco Chronicle* and the *San Francisco Examiner*; Saint Donna and the equally righteous—and virginal—young Annabel. It was an unsettling interplay; it was a nexus in wordings and setting between the postcard and *The Love Pirate*. It was also a coincidence that Linda simply couldn't reconcile.

After hanging up the phone with the old reporter in Nevada, Linda knew, even if she could never prove it, that Jorgensen's reported mysterious presence in that state in January of '76 was key. His claim of being a casino prizefight doctor and the disappearance of a casino nurse during that blackout period after NYC—after dodging Detectives Lulling and Josephson, subsequent whereabouts unknown—all *had* to be connected. Donna Ann had vanished from Jorgensen's home state of California while her car had been found in Nevada, the same state where Jorgensen later turned up with his polished cover story suggesting that he'd been working as a casino doc in the intervening years. The taunting and twisted content of the Christmas card sent to Lass's sister over four years later evinced a level of fantasy role-playing that also fit Jorgensen's psychopathology and his compulsive need to get paraphilic mileage out of souvenirs from his crime scenes. It fit his penchant for narcissistic grandiosity, his need to have some kind of physical or imagistic record of his work and to boast of it. Of greatest significance was likely that the penmanship on the postcard matched, at many points, the handwriting Linda subsequently managed to get from Jorgensen as she refined her tactics in later years—as she began to dupe him just as he duped his victims.

By 1977, it was all starting to add up; however, as usual, it seemed that Linda was the only one doing the arithmetic. To put two and two together would mean that cops back east would need to get on the same page and share their findings with cops out west. Aside from the Zodiac Killer being falsely credited for the Lass disappearance, his earlier crimes had managed to expose the fact that cops even in the same state and separated by only a hundred miles wouldn't cooperate on cases, much less when the crime scenes are thousands of miles apart. Without the FBI's involvement, there would be no one else to follow Jorgensen's trail—the trail of dubious sightings and potentially related killings. But without someone else in law enforcement making and reporting on those links, the FBI could and would never get involved and invoke its mandate. It was an obstacle that left Linda no way out, nowhere to go—nothing to do but to chase ghosts.

Winning Numbers

The remainder of 1977 saw Linda largely marooned back in Dallas, using the monies obtained through teaching and tutoring Spanish part-time to fund her ongoing and increasingly risky freelance investigation and skip trace of Jorgensen. But with no new leads and no other potential matches to Jorgensen as best as she could determine from press clippings and news reports, back in Madison, the balmy autumn of that same year, another young woman destined for UW—exactly a decade after Christine Rothschild arrived in town—was, it seems, just as quickly marked for death. Like Christine, Julie Ann Hall was only eighteen when she completed an application for a state-sponsored job at the UW Historical Society. Unlike Christine who'd been sent there against her will to a safe campus—or so her parents believed—Julie Ann proactively and quite enthusiastically seized the internship position offered as a way of tunneling out of an idle life in the small village of North Freedom located in Sauk County. Like Debbie Bennett's arrival in Madison in the summer of '75, Julie Ann also hailed from a large family with seven other siblings. For as long as she could remember, she forever pined to make her way in the big city—the Capital City.

Since ten years had passed, Julie Ann, like most other eighteen-year-olds destined for Madison that year, likely never knew the story of Christine Rothschild. The turmoil of the war in Vietnam and the accompanying destruction of Sterling Hall in the intervening decade, not to mention the more recent Debbie Bennett slaying, ensured that the tide had washed over the shock of the Rothschild case that at one time had seized both city and state. In 1968, university administrators had even discussed disbanding the UWPD as part of what became known as Bill 299. They thought that Madison police could just as easily deploy from a satellite station on campus for major crimes, with day-to-day gofer work being delegated to rent-a-cops. But by 1977, with Sterling Hall rebuilt and Christine's case in cold storage, that plan had been abandoned. The campus police had been given an indefinite stay of execution. The 1976 off-campus murder of Debbie Bennett had no doubt also led some to believe that the campus was likely the safest place to be after dark in the Mad City. Memories, like the hemlines on campus, were growing shorter; only ten years on and it was already Christine *who*? What happened a decade prior was, however, destined to repeat itself. The close of the school year brought events that would change everything—a second time.

By the end of '78 spring exams at UW, Julie Ann had filed the paperwork for the entry-level job she hoped would open up a world of options for her. That paperwork, having made its way through the bureaucracy of the state's Comprehensive Employment and Training Act (CETA) program for women, allowed Julie Ann to pack her bags for the Mad City. It had been a competitive placement to land what was supposed to be a built-to-suit sinecure created with state dollars. A Joe job created to supposedly help women transition to the professional workforce, in the end the position offered little in the way of professional development and transferable skills—even less in terms of real responsibilities for the money. In other words, a plum gig. It wasn't the first time the Hall family rolled the dice only to have the Fates look kindly upon them, not the first time the gods of state-level administration threw them a bone. In March of '75, Julie Ann's parents Donne and Betty Hall struck it rich when their regular numbers won them a $300,000 jackpot—nearly $1.5 million in present dollars—from the Illinois State Lottery. But the windfall, like many lottery prize purses, did little other than to send the overgrown family with improvident parents careening over the edge.

The Halls, like many lotto jackpot winners, were right back where they started within a matter of years. After the mandatory IRS skim off, they were then fleeced by an assortment of characters ranging from long-lost acquisitive cousins to fair-weather friends who ultimately helped contribute to their decadence and overspending. By the fall of '77, before filing for bankruptcy, the couple first filed for divorce, Donne moving to the town of Fennimore in Grant County while Betty was relegated to moving with a handful of the kids to a trailer park on state Highway 12. The park was located outside the town of Baraboo and just a short drive from where the desecrated body of Debbie Bennett was set ablaze a year prior. It was, in fact, while sequestered in her mother's Sauk County double-wide trailer that Julie Ann instinctively penned a letter to CETA and sought a way out via the Mad City. By then, a series of events had been placed in motion, events that seemed to foretell what happened next. Julie Ann Hall would in a sense cross paths with Debbie Bennett as two young women with Madison in their sights and condemned to take a one-way trip there.

By May of '78, when Julie Ann started her first day at UW as a "file clerk" at the old UW Historical Society, things were starting to look up.

In short order, she had found herself a modest apartment on Woodview Court by subletting a couch off the books from an older brother who had arrived in Madison ahead of her, and who'd landed the place with a one-year lease. Despite the pastoral name, the location was and remains a transitional neighborhood pervaded by flaking paint and security glass. Perched near the infamous South Transfer Point, one of Madison's dodgier metro stations, the area was also relied on by newcomers to the city as they went to and fro while trying to scratch out an honest living. Julie Ann was one such newcomer. The Park Village Apartments she called home were the conceptual and aesthetic opposite of her new job at UW; the historical society was also a world away from the trailer park back near Baraboo. Julie Ann had landed a cushy, state-subsidized gig in a palatial building constructed in the Greek Doric style on the Library Mall, so named for the same Memorial Library where Jorgensen first set eyes on Christine—where he first set his devious plan into motion. As Julie Ann stared out at that same library day after day—still never knowing the story of Christine Rothschild—she soon found the job was easy, the setting regal, and for a while it seemed as though, like her parents before her, she'd won the lottery.

Happy Hour

By the end of work on Friday, June 16, Julie Ann Hall had been exactly six weeks into that new life. It was also payday. With a little prompting, she chose to join her brother and some friends at the Main King Tap—since rebranded—just east of the city's Capitol Square, and generally beyond the inner sanctum of UW hangouts. It was happy hour in both the literal and figurative senses. But as the festivities carried on into the evening and the sun set on Madison, Julie Ann's brother left the bar as the country-girl transplant hung around to finish dinner with some other newfound acquaintances. Unfortunately, she was completely oblivious to just how dangerous the city had become by that time for young women. Julie Ann Hall was never seen alive again.

The following Monday when Julie Ann didn't turn up for work at the historical society, no one thought much of it. The job was, after all, an invented and largely extraneous position, meaning that no one was really affected by her absence. The system for documenting absences also wasn't clear. Although Julie Ann was working at UW, she wasn't *technically* a university employee, but rather one of several CETA placements sprinkled throughout the state. When she didn't show up Tuesday or again on Wednesday, people probably thought that she had simply been transferred or the position had been rescinded. That no one thought it odd enough to report her missing or call home to her brother is therefore to some limited extent understandable. What is less understandable is that her same brother never reported his sister missing to police—the sister he was living with at the time and had left at a watering hole just this side of respectable. Giving him the benefit of the doubt, perhaps he figured that she'd met someone at the bar and gone home with that person. In a roundabout sense he was right. It seems that Julie Ann most certainly left the Main King with the wrong man that Friday, as was later confirmed by Madison area contractor John Wagner. It was he who, while clearing a vacant lot on Woodland Road in the neighboring town of Waunakee on the afternoon of June 21, made a gruesome discovery. It was a place eerily reminiscent of where Debbie Bennett was discovered and almost precisely the same distance out of town in the other direction.

As Wagner that Wednesday walked the expansive property primed for development, he stumbled across what he initially thought to be a shop-window mannequin—like the mannequin Christine's body was once mistaken for—lying amid a pile of brush. Anyone who has ever seen a corpse has usually done so under fairly manicured conditions, such as embalmed bodies in funeral parlors. To come across one in the open, much less a murdered and ravaged corpse, is the reason that the human brain so often seems to default to the most rational of explanations, the mind initially seeming to prevent the observer from acknowledging the obvious horror that lays before him or her. Most people in such circumstances know it's a human form they're looking at, but simply can't resign themselves to the idea that a *real* body could or would be in the location where they first lay eyes on it. Within a matter of seconds, however,

Wagner had come to terms with what he was looking at—the nude and battered body of a young woman, haphazardly concealed beneath some dirt and leaves—what's known as a *surface burial*—her skull crushed in but devoid of blood and brain matter. She'd been killed elsewhere, once again at an unknown primary crime scene. It was another Jane Doe dump job—Debbie Bennett redux.

For nearly two days the body remained unidentified. The attending coroner, once again Dr. Clyde Chamberlain, could only describe the victim as being eighteen to twenty-five years of age with long brown hair tinted with shades of red. The local sheriff's department with jurisdiction over the Woodland Road property, comparing the biometric data—height, weight, and other characteristics—to about forty women listed as missing in the county, came up empty. A check of the victim's fingerprints with the FBI also proved to be a strikeout. Finally, word of the grisly find hit the state newswire on Thursday the twenty-second, and by Friday evening—exactly one week after she was last seen eating her final meal at the Main King Tap—the body was officially ID'd as Julie Ann Hall. The cause of death was given as blunt-force trauma to the head, death almost instantaneously following a sexual assault. No suspects, no witnesses, no forensic evidence, and no known crime scene. No clue yet—again.

As in the case of Debbie Bennett, the dump site selected by Julie Ann's killer was and remains, in the absence of other investigative indicators, the best starting point with which to connect suspectology with victimology, doing so with a view to building a general offender profile. Certain deductions can immediately be made to narrow the field. It can be deduced, for instance, that the killer is a male with his own car or direct and consistent access to a reliable vehicle. It can be deduced that the motive was sexual and that the crime scene would be covered in copious blood in light of the severity of the head wound. Although this in all likelihood rules out a public place, it also means that the privacy or security of that place was both ephemeral and unpredictable, such as a shared home or other semiprivate space, requiring that there was some urgency to remove the body to the secondary scene almost immediately.

The transportation of the body by vehicle—and subsequent carriage of the body to the burial site—suggests that the killer once again perceived these associated risks as being preferable to disposing the body in plain sight, such as by the roadside. Body transportation and concealment on land is also almost exclusively seen in younger white male offenders and female victims under the age of thirty. It is also exclusive to sexual homicides versus other motive types. This method is also strongly correlated with prior military service and minor criminal records, typically records for theft or misdemeanor property crimes. In nearly all cases, the offender, intimately familiar with one or both of the contact site or disposal site, has used some type of ruse to calmly lure the victim, frequently the offer of a ride. While much of this data was not available to law enforcement in 1977, even then it should have generally been known that in all likelihood police were dealing with a young white male. At the time it had been identified that sexual murderers—and by extension serial killers, even if not using that precise term—typically killed within their own ethnicity, seldom if ever jumping the racial boundary. With this knowledge and the obvious access to a motor vehicle, and with the Main King Tap venue as the probable contact point along with the specificity of the dump site as locations of obvious connection, this should have immediately pointed police to a workable short list of persons of interest. Once again, however, the killer knew how to lead the police into an administrative labyrinth and leave them there.

Gag Order

The Julie Ann Hall slaying was Debbie Bennett part two, though in all likelihood a different offender. They nonetheless shared more than a few points in common. Julie Ann's killer had divided and conquered, taking the young woman from Madison, holding and killing her at a mystery location—statistically likely to be the offender's own home or a semiprivate neutral space based on the MO—and then disposing of the body in another jurisdiction to delay both discovery and identification. In so doing, he would entangle the case in predictable police infighting. He knew, whether from experience or simply watching the local news, that the recipe for an instant unsolved and all-but-guaranteed cold case was to do as Debbie Bennett's killer did. Although the additional desecration by fire, as in the Bennett case, might have been effective, it was overkill—and an unnecessary risk. In both cases, no evidence was found at the dump sites, in Debbie Bennett's case because she and any of her combustible possessions were burned in the pit into which she was thrown, and in Julie Ann Hall's case because the killer had kept them for himself, playing the odds that the police would never come looking for them. He was right. Although Julie Ann's brother and her colleagues at UW were able to offer very clear descriptions of what she was wearing and also of the handbag she was carrying that fateful Friday, there is no evidence that police actively searched for the items at all. Curiously, there was also no press release ever drawn up to ask the public to keep an eye open for similar items turning up in the trash or elsewhere. Logical avenues of investigation were not traveled—opportunities were missed. The intrastate task force investigating Debbie Bennett's death had already come up empty-handed, had packed up their tent, and gone home. Julie Ann Hall's death didn't have a task force at all. It had been all hands on deck two summers earlier, but now, even as talk of a serial killer had veteran cops nodding, the case was run by only a small handful of Madison's major crime detectives juggling other files.

The reality is that Julie Ann's murder marked the start of a new beginning in the Mad City. The first of a now rapid succession of women to be murdered at or near UW, it was a storm that no one could imagine coming—a harbinger of what was to follow. But by 1978, as the early indicators of a public panic were starting to take hold, no one who should have been concerned seemed to give it much thought at all. Tone-deaf leaders abounded. If there was any vestige of concern, it was buried. A decade prior, Christine Rothschild's murder had been a comparatively easy one to stickhandle by UW and city stakeholders after going through the usual public motions: a paltry reward for information was offered by UW president Fred Harrington, to be drawn from the university's gift fund. Later, an anonymous benefactor added an extra thousand bucks to the pot. Later still, UWPD chief Ralph Hanson offered a paid month's vacation to any detective who could solve it. Translation: find, interview, arrest, and return Jorgensen. On Hanson's watch and after dodging the Bill 299 axe, a total of three thousand people eventually were interviewed and cleared for Christine's murder by the time 1978 came around. But good intentions—however short-lived—don't collar suspects. Not one of those three thousand interviewees would turn out to be Jorgensen.

After the tip about his probable presence in Vegas and equally probable involvement in the Lass vanishing, Linda began a regular routine of updating the UWPD—especially during Hanson's tenure as chief—on Jorgensen's whereabouts, whether known or suspected. No one ever followed up; this, in spite of cops having tailed him to New York in the weeks after the murder. This, in spite of the fact that within a year of Jorgensen's hightailing it out of the Big Apple, Sandy Mackman had also come forward to report the gun incident as having punctuated Jorgensen's time at the hospital, even taking out a restraining order for fear that he might return one day to Madison. It was the same fear Linda had—the fear that kept her at UW when all signs indicated that Jorgensen would likely jump ship to another university. But at the end of the day, Christine Rothschild was an out-of-state student, her parents didn't make a fuss or file suit as some rightfully expected, and her murder came and went at the tail end of the school year—the year 1968 no less, when the country was in crisis and the world itself already upside-down. Its timing left a whole summer for a whole lot of people to forget—to *make* themselves forget—what had happened amid the background noise of the era. The university's stance was in a sense similar, or at least helped with the process of forgetting. It prohibited the placement of items at the crime scene to memorialize the tragedy, and it generally shooed away any remembrance activities organized by Linda off the campus proper. Christine's story was later erased almost entirely by the Sterling Hall bombing and the continuing distraction of Vietnam activism and student radicalism on campus—and across America. But now, with the successive deaths of Bennett and Hall, matters were getting tougher to cover up—events in Madison harder to dismiss as one-offs.

As speculation fanned the flames of the Capital City Killer mythos, it seems that city officials and senior cops were more concerned with censoring statements—acting as the Thought Police from Orwell's dystopian super state—than they were actually working murder files. Suppressing the rumors through proscriptive gag orders imposed on Mad City officers and UW personnel alike—that they not mention a word of the ongoing investigations, that they neither confirm nor deny the possible existence of any serial killer—was the top priority among the powers that be. Whatever the motive, it almost seemed to be a public relations survival and local security strategy rolled into one, a necessary measure in order to keep the city running on the status quo and also to keep people coming to UW. In the end, however, information follows the same path as any commodity in a prohibited market—people will always find a way of getting it. As the narrative of what was happening to the Mad City and its young coeds was driven underground, a black market in gossip and conjecture sprung up. It was one that ultimately ensured the code of silence and myopic campaign of censorship imposed by the Madison chief of police, mayor, and UW chancellor. It also had the effect of creating a host of new problems. Big problems, in fact.

With three unsolved campus and area murders in a decade, Madison and UW officials still had failed to learn from the mistakes of the past about containing the flow of disinformation—whether wrongly reported details or confusions of fact taken at face value, or false rumors regarding the more recent criminal investigations. By pussyfooting around the issue, they completely asphyxiated any and all talk of investigative progress—or more accurately the lack of progress—concerning the murders. They neither confirmed nor denied any connection between the cases, much less the existence of a Capital City Killer. The predicament Madison found itself in by the end of 1978 was not dissimilar to that of the 1947 case of Elizabeth Short in volatile postwar Los Angeles, better known as the Black Dahlia murder.

Like the very real Whitechapel murders credited to a very fictional Jack the Ripper, the Dahlia slaying went on to create its own cottage industry in murder tourism. The Dahlia was Elizabeth Short, an enigmatic would-be Hollywood starlet both in life and in death. *Who* she really was, *why* she was killed, *what* the grotesque severance of her body and ghoulish "Glasgow Smile" carved into her face, ear to ear, were supposed to symbolize no one really ever knew for certain—but it consumed the public. Some people, mostly armchair sleuths, have at varying points also seemed desperate to link the Dahlia murder perpetrator to other murders—a sort of LA Ripper for America to call its own. Ridiculously, as some amateurs have posited—and various published screeds have even suggested in writing—the Dahlia killer and Jack the Ripper might have even been the same person. The reality is that the modern-day chaos and mishmash of theories about the murder serves more as an indicator that the LAPD immediately lost control of the dominant narrative of the case.

It was a problem additionally compounded by the fact that they also lost control of the investigation by way of an official blackout on media updates leading to wildfire speculation. Having spent the previous seven years devoting resources to curtailing vice and rousting subversives—an "alien" squad to round up Japanese expats and even American citizens of Japanese ancestry for internment, and a second "red" squad to ferret out Commies—LA cops were completely unprepared to properly investigate the murder and to deal with the insatiable public interest that followed. Since they, for the most part, also didn't have much experience with such complex and intricately paraphilic lust murders, nor did even some of the largest American police departments of the day, in time the investigation was a veritable mess.

With the left and right hand within the department forever parted, many cops themselves came to rely on the newspapers for updates, following the leads of legitimate reporters and scandal-rag peddlers alike. Even the name by which history has come to call Short following the killing—the Black Dahlia—was a media invention after detailed victim information had been initially withheld by police and was instead cobbled together by enterprising reporters through interviews with sketchy associates. Inspired by the 1946 film noir crime thriller written by Raymond Chandler, *The Blue Dahlia*, the macabre pseudonym given to Short seemed in the public mind to capture her femme-fatale nature and strikingly dark features—also her even darker and tragic brief life. It satisfied a public appetite for lurid details otherwise black boxed by police.

Today, the most cogent theory about Short's killer's true identity is offered by a retired LAPD detective who has implicated his own father, George Hill Hodel—Hollywood physician to the stars, psychopath, and inveterate sexual deviant—as the real killer. After fleeing to the Philippines in 1950 and later being linked to a similar 1967 murder there, unsealed LAPD wiretap transcripts confirm that not only was Dr. Hodel the prime suspect in 1947 but that he also made various statements that could be interpreted as roundabout confessions. As well, Hodel's secretary, a material witness able to confirm that Short had been his patient and probable sexual partner, died under mysterious circumstances when the investigation was at its height—and immediately before Hodel fled the United States to a non-extradition treaty country. Possible linkages to Short by way of supporting documents and records, including that Short was Hodel's patient, would later mysteriously disappear.

Over the years, these details have been drowned out by a chorus of various theories running the gamut from the vaguely plausible to the ludicrous, another example of how the public expects reasonable police disclosure and frankness about investigative progress. In the absence of such details, people will invent—and will often later cling to—the myth instead of the truth. Fast-forward thirty years from 1947 to 1977 and the song remained the same. By year's end, whether the Capital City Killer was fact or fiction no longer mattered. The tail was now wagging the dog.

Boulder Creek

As the calendar flipped over from 1977 to 1978, nearly a thousand miles away, back in Dallas, the erroneous link to the Zodiac Killer by virtue of the Christmas postcard had Linda scouring the microfiche archives at Texas Wesleyan U looking for any and all newspaper reports of other California murders with crime-scene behaviors that matched Christine's. Where there was smoke, she thought, there would be the proverbial fire. Common denominators matching those within Jorgensen's paraphilic wheelhouse—hospitals, college campuses, elaborate or torturous deaths, the posing of bodies, the collecting of souvenirs—would no doubt turn up cases in his home state of California. It was, after all, Linda had theorized, where he'd claimed his own brother as his first victim—where he no doubt claimed others. The question was how to separate Jorgensen's crime-scene behaviors from those other killers who also roamed the state.

By the winter of '78, drawing on her grad-school research acumen, Linda had discovered that any number of killings were being credited to the Zodiac Killer, whether a rational inference or not. They were being wrongly connected in much the same way that the Ripper and the Boston Strangler—like the Capital City Killer back in Madison—had themselves become convenient targets for false linkages. She knew that back in the Mad City, the damming of all information by PD brass had led to poetic license being taken by the press but that in California, the lessons learned from the past, including those from the Black Dahlia case, had engendered a system of transparency that meant details would still be made public, even if the cops had it wrong. Then Linda found something.

Published April 10, 1966, in the *San Francisco Examiner*, Linda located the story of Judith Williamson, age eighteen and a freshman at UC Berkeley when she disappeared three years earlier, on October 29, 1963. Later identified by dental records, the skeletonized remains of the young coed from the nearby town of Albany were ultimately located in a ravine within the Santa Cruz Mountains. Discovered just north of a secluded spot on the map known as Boulder Creek, the remains had been found by a foursome of woodcarvers collecting redwood tree burls. Found on its back out in the open, the skeleton was missing its lower half, presumably hauled away by scavengers in the intervening years. The remaining torso, however, was found fully clothed along a debris-strewn ledge running parallel to a nearby rural route—to Waterman Gap Road.

While no definitive cause of death could be confirmed, given the advanced decomposition and missing lower half of the skeleton, the local sheriff confirmed that the breastbone had been pierced with what the attending forensic pathologist could only describe as an unusually "narrow-bladed instrument." The same weapon was believed responsible for another fifteen "rents" from a finely edged instrument that had left discernible holes in the girl's black cardigan sweater and also chipped her ribs. While the sweater remained intact on the skeleton, Judith's bra was found to have been removed and was never recovered. It was apparently taken as a souvenir after she was either already dead, or before she was re-dressed following some sexual assault—bodies disposed of in undressed, semidressed, or re-dressed states constituting sexual homicides by definition, especially when souvenirs are taken. The details jarred Linda as she read them, particularly the specificity of the weapon, the posing of the body, and the apparent souvenir collection. The weapon hadn't been a regular knife but something more precise like a scalpel used to make the frenzied stab wounds—a total of sixteen punctures to the chest. Christine had suffered fourteen such wounds to the same area with a similar weapon. But the similarities didn't end there.

In reading on about the Williamson slaying, Linda found the usual array of absurd links made by many, yet again, to the Zodiac Killer in later years simply because it was a California murder. Such connections may have been made inferentially in many cases given that the Berkeley coed's murder was also regularly written about by *Chronicle* crime reporter Paul Avery, the same newsman who later played a key role in the Zodiac investigation. But amid the reportage on public speculation, Linda stumbled upon what was likely the most startling and verifiable similarity to Christine.

When Judith was last seen alive, she was carrying a white umbrella—one not recovered with the body, one apparently kept by the killer, at least for a while. Within two weeks, on the afternoon of November 12, that same white umbrella—the handle broken and the stretchers snapped in a manner that eerily recalled the damage to Christine's black umbrella—turned up in a trash can in El Cerrito Plaza, a shopping mall only a mile from Judith's family home back in Albany. The killer *knew* where she lived. The umbrella was deposited there, nearly two hours from the crime scene, to prove it—to showcase this knowledge to others. Well after the murder at a time when the killer should have crawled back into his hole, he was still getting paraphilic mileage out of the souvenir umbrella he'd taken, toying with authorities and the girl's grieving family alike. The next day, November 13, Judith's blood-smeared textbooks were found in a trash can on the UC Berkley campus—again, two hours from the crime scene and dumped only after the body had been discovered and the investigation was running full tilt. The killer *knew* the campus.

Left: A path carved into the landscape of the Santz Cruz Mountains leads to the clearing where the bisected skeleton of Judith Williamson was discovered in the spring of '66. Right: A composite sketch of the Zodiac Killer created with the assistance of a survivor of a subsequent knife attack at nearby Lake Berryessa in autumn of '69. Given the bucolic setting in both Northern California cases, many would later surmise that the Williamson slaying was also the work of the Zodiac.

By the winter of '66, three years later, police, having interviewed and cleared nearly four hundred UC Berkeley students, had discovered what they thought was the probable primary crime scene. A massive pool of dried blood had been discovered in a campus parking garage that Judith would often cut through when traveling to and from class. The killer knew her routine. The cops had also managed to locate a couple of reluctant witnesses who reported seeing a man in a convertible sports car—make and model unknown, color likely white, plate number and state unknown—driving suspiciously in the area of the parking structure on the night Judith vanished.

Some would-be witnesses reported a nondescript lone male driver possibly even coaxing Judith into the car that same morning she disappeared—a classic homicidal ruse. The lead on the car also prompted police to reveal that they had not one but four suspects in mind, all of whom had by then been questioned and intermittently rousted by detectives to no avail. The police even played with the theory that there were two killers working in tandem, investigative and analytical techniques at the time not having the benefit of today's evolved knowledge in this area of team killers. Organized lust murders involving long-distance transportation and the collection of souvenirs—a full inventory of items had determined that Judith's brassiere, shoes, and pantyhose had all been taken—reflect the work of someone whose highly nuanced paraphilias and twisted fixation almost always necessitate that he act alone, not with an accomplice.

The police in California, despite a valiant effort and working the case hard, didn't seem to recognize that the killing had all the telltale indicators of a serial offender honing his craft, a midcareer murder committed by an offender with psychopathic proclivities and a penchant for theatrics. He was a needs-driven but high-functioning offender with a bizarre fixation on specific objects—clothing items, an umbrella—and an offender defined by *expressive violence*, or acts that went well beyond what was necessary to simply dispatch and dispose of the victim. It wasn't his first murder and certainly wouldn't be his last. It certainly wasn't the work of an erratically behaved acquaintance whose sexual advances went awry in a public parking garage as the early theory suggested. Nonetheless, that's the theory they ended up following. It's the theory they would make into reality years later when opportunity knocked, as Linda ultimately discovered in perusing the most recent stories on the murder—the latest developments having occurred only a couple of months earlier.

In November '77, as first reported in the *Oakland Tribune*, Linda learned that a former classmate of Williamson at UC Berkeley named Joseph Otto Eggenberger Jr. had "confessed" to Judith's murder after walking into the office of the Alameda County district attorney following the fourteen-year anniversary of the brutal crime and spilling his guts. Showing up to see the DA on the morning of November 30, 1977, without a lawyer, Eggenberger explained that his recently excavated suppressed memories indicated that it was he who killed Williamson after she'd rejected his repeated advances during their time at UC Berkeley.

As the former chief in Oakland would later admit, he had "always suspected" Eggenberger—the son of the former Albany mayor—who had also gone to high school with Williamson and who had been pulled over for speeding, in a white convertible, by the California Highway Patrol one afternoon in the immediate aftermath of her disappearance. Described as being in a state of emotional distress and possibly even under the influence of an unknown narcotic, Eggenberger's behavior in the aftermath of the murder tweaked the instincts of investigators, but they never followed up. A search of that same convertible, the one later thought to have been used in the murder, ultimately yielded evidence of stains on and in the trunk, but none could be positively identified as blood so many years later. Also, none of the items taken from the body were ever recovered and, in fact, there was no physical evidence at all to support Eggenberger's confession. That may be why he later changed his mind. Pleading not guilty at a subsequent trial and recanting the earlier confession, the prosecution forged ahead on the flimsiest of evidence and in spite of Eggenberger's mental state—one that seemed to have only worsened and become more erratic since police first took note of his acting strangely back in 1963.

Following the Williamson murder, Eggenberger dropped out of UC Berkeley on the heels of a mental breakdown that had actually started months prior to the murder, one that seemed to have had little to nothing to do with Judith. He later drifted around the San Francisco-Oakland area for the next few years, working odd jobs before returning to school at a community college and obtaining a diploma in computer programming. He subsequently relocated to Chicago and, after attending a self-improvement seminar, a seed seems to have been planted. He eventually went to see a psychiatrist about a sense of guilt he was feeling about the murder and was convinced by the shrink that, if he believed the memories to be accurate, he should just turn himself in and confess. He then quit his job as a data analyst with US Steel and returned to the Bay Area to surrender to authorities. The reason he surrendered to police in November of '77 was and remained for several years a point of legal and psychological debate; it was seen as a key case study in recovered memories and questionable confessions for years to come. It would eventually become little more than an obscure footnote in the history of California crime.

The problem was, as Linda saw it and as a California judge also later seemed to, that the stated motive for the murder didn't square with the paraphilic specificity and expressive acts of violence committed against Judith during and after the slaying. Crimes of passion, whether the result of jealous rage or some kind of mental break—as Eggenberger claimed to have had—typically lead to murders where the body is either left at the scene "as is" or is instead transported and concealed with the hope that it is never located, such as through burying or burning. This is because the nature of the murder, even if rooted in a real, perceived, or intended romantic affiliation, is personal rather than sexual in nature. Personal-cause homicides thus cannot, by definition, involve the erotic removal and collection of souvenirs from the body, much less the surface disposal and posing of a body to suit some existing fantasy. Personal-cause killers are purely instrumental in their use of violence, just as they are instrumental and pragmatic in what they do next. They don't leave morbid trails of clues like umbrellas and bloody textbooks to be found later—they don't hang on to items that can link them to the crime, and they don't revel in the prolonged media attention and public fear that these actions stir up. In fact, they go out of their way to avoid it all.

The actions taken in Judith's case are instead indicative of post-offense behaviors of a much different breed of killer—one who is organized and psychopathic, and who will not be dogged by guilt after having gotten away with it. It's certainly not someone who would be prepared to forfeit his life and career over a decade later as part of some moral or spiritual obligation to "make things right." On the contrary, the actions suggest—if not demand—that he continue killing. Such glaring contradictions might also explain why, after later being found guilty of second-degree murder in April of '78, a judge sentenced Eggenberger to serve a mere *five years* in prison for the murder of Judith Williamson. At the time, the paltry sentence not surprisingly caused outrage, but, in retrospect, it reflects the equally paltry nature of the case against Eggenberger. It's unclear exactly how much time he did end up serving before being later released and disappearing once more into the breach. It's also unclear why he chose to confess before later reneging—whether the confession was genuine at all or the result of other underlying emotional or psychological issues. Either Eggenberger is the most notable exception to every rule of sexual homicide documented over the course of the last century—findings that in both clinical and forensic settings are informed by interviews and analyses of literally thousands of murderers—or, as is statistically more likely, he falsely confessed.

A *voluntary false confession*, more rare and less understood than a *compliant false confession* resulting from police interrogation or coercion, describes a set of circumstances in which a person comes forward to confess to a crime without police prompting or external pressure, and is thought to have a variety of causes. Many of these causes relate to a combination of diminished mental capacity and what's known as *confirmation bias*, meaning that a person may believe or be led to believe a certain set of events occurred and will then look for evidence to support that conclusion—to confirm what he or she believes, whether it's accurate or not. In the United States, a consistent average of about fifty people come forward to confess to each high-profile murder case. They are later ruled out once their confessions are revealed to be filled with factual errors relating to the signature or other holdback evidence that would only be known by the killer and a handful of cops. Over two hundred false confessors came forward in the "crime of the century" kidnapping and murder of the Lindbergh baby in 1932.

In Judith's case, in the fourteen years between the murder and when Eggenberger ultimately fell on the sword for it, most or all of the holdback information had been made public—whether leaked or intentionally released with the passage of time to help generate tips. Everything else Eggenberger shared as part of his confession could be neither proven nor disproven—an account of events that had no other witnesses or physical evidence.

In the winter of '77, while Linda didn't know that Eggenberger would later recant his confession, she certainly knew the latter-day solving of the Williamson slaying seemed a little too convenient. The umbrella, the unusual murder weapon, the souvenir taking, the early-morning ambush, the fact that Jorgensen was a Berkeley alumnus and had been to the campus for homecoming just a month prior to the murder—it simply doesn't compute, either then or now, that whoever did these things could later be turned inside out by guilt and remorse. Linda later realized she had just one item to double-check as part of her theory—the car that Jorgensen had driven to the Mad City the year after the murder. With a single call to George Johnston, Jorgensen's one-time Madison roomie, Linda had her answer. True, Eggenberger might have owned a convertible while in the Bay Area in the fall of '63. But so did Jorgensen.

George Johnston recalled that Jorgensen had arrived at UW and moved into their shared apartment after unloading a couple of bags from the trunk of a two-door drop-top. Although George couldn't recall the make, model, or color, he knew it had been a car previously kept in the family's garage back in California. The car stayed parked outside their walk-up building until Jorgensen blew town and drove to NYC and onward from there after absconding from his date with the polygraph. Linda reasoned that he would have driven the convertible back west, eventually turning up in Vegas. If she could only find Jorgensen, she knew she might find the car—the car that might help confirm what he had been up to both before and after UW. In the meantime, the similarities between Judith Williamson and Linda's friend Christine haunted her. Both were freshmen attacked on relatively peaceful university campuses after first having been stalked, their habitual movements memorized. Both were attacked in public campus locations; both were stabbed over a dozen times in the chest with particular—and atypical—attention paid to avoiding the face and throat; both were stabbed with an equally atypical-edged weapon rather than a conventional knife such as is used in over 90 percent of other fatal stabbings; both had garments taken as souvenirs; both had their umbrellas taken, bent, and deposited in either a symbolic position or at a symbolic location. The victimology, MO, and even the signature were all nearly identical. With this information, Linda considered it likely that the antecedents of what was done to Christine started much earlier, years before Jorgensen came to UW. By the spring of '68 when Jorgensen arrived at UW, his methods had been tried and tested. Christine never had a chance.

But the enduring question, assuming Judith Williamson was indeed an early prototype of Jorgensen's MO and a pattern-setting crime that would establish his preferred victim type moving forward: What was he doing as far north as Berkeley while still living in LA's Toluca Estates with his parents—his brother Søren dead, his mother in self-exile and locked in her bedroom typing *The Love Pirate*? Linda then checked her notes. Jorgensen graduated from UC Berkeley in June of '50. He *knew* the campus. After calling the toll-free number for the alumni association, she learned that the homecoming weekend for former grads, including the class of 1950, was September 27 through 29, a month to the day before Judith's abduction. Linda wondered if Jorgensen attended—if he was there that weekend and had honed in on Judith at his alma mater just as he later did Christine at UW. She didn't know it at the time, but Jorgensen would return there again forty years later to the day—in 2003—for yet another "reunion" of sorts, his staying in the same International House dormitory where he'd lived from '46 to '50. It was strangely close to the same spot and on the same campus where Judith's bloodied books were dumped in November '66.

Judith Williamson and Christine Rothschild were two young women—naïve, headstrong, good-looking—whose paths in death would refuse to diverge. Two names, forever soldered together by linkages no one else would ever make, forever together in a state of mutual permafrost—cold cases that could and would never be fully thawed. In *The Love Pirate* manuscript, Linda could now finally make the connections. Annabel had been crafted as a literary archetype of Jorgensen's preferred victim type, the book created in the aftermath of the Williamson murder and with Judith as the muse. It explained the San Francisco connection in the book—UC Berkeley—and the Crater Lake creek in the fictive Paradise Valley where Annabel is taken—Boulder Creek. The spurned advances, the obsessive stalking by Dr. Corcoran, it was all real. *The Love Pirate* was at once untold history and a window into the future. Annabel was at once Judith Williamson and Christine Rothschild. She was every woman—past, present, and future—who might find herself in the wrong place at the wrong time once Jorgensen took notice and formulated his plans. Heidi knew of the past murders. She knew of Judith Williamson, she knew of the murders yet to come—that there would be a familiar refrain to them all. She *knew* her son.

Chapter 6

The Vanishing Hitchhiker

The true mystery of the world is the visible, not the invisible.

—Oscar Wilde, *The Picture of Dorian Gray*

Thin Air

Beginning sometime in the 1870s, in a cold and foreboding czarist Russia, there emerged a legend of a phantom traveler who, after obtaining passage from carriages traveling along country roads, would mysteriously vanish. Sometimes the driver would turn to find the passenger already gone, other times the mystery traveler was said to dissolve into thin air before the very eyes of the driver—and even other passengers. Those dabbling in the fledgling field of psychology at the time dismissed the sightings as hallucinations and the product of exhaustion, starvation, or simply the power of hypnotic suggestion following long and arduous days on the road—in effect a human mirage. During the 1940s, however, Midwest and Southern United States college students began experiencing a similar phenomenon, recycled for the modern age and blacktop highways. The difference this time was that the silent passenger was not some wandering soul in the frozen hinterland of Russia, but rather, a modern-day hitchhiker. Although the nomadic culture of improvised vehicular travel and a thumbed ride might have dated back to the affordability of Henry Ford's Model T, the hitchhiker as a fixture on the lonely road only became even more so after World War II with the newly conceived interstate system—not to mention the American love affair with the automobile.

Whether as hitchhiker or driver, this mode of travel came into its own, emerging as a rite of passage for those seeking adventure, camaraderie, and a free lift from A to B. It was a travel system built upon the kindness of strangers, yet, like all things spawned from good intentions, before long hitchhiking became a fool's errand. As the public service campaigns of the day would have one believe, it was a deadly game of chance in which your luck would eventually run dry—neither a hitchhiker nor sympathetic driver be. Hollywood soon followed suit, and, before long, a volley of films playing on the fears that drivers had of hitchers and hitchers had of drivers fanned the flames of paranoia, depicting the open road as a dangerous and wanton place. Between the Freeway Killer case—actually three separate serial killers sharing the same mantra who simultaneously targeted teenaged hitchhikers in California—and a host of other stories about murderous drifters ripped from the headlines, there was certainly enough lurid and real-life material for film producers to work with. Yet, amid the public blowback against this increasingly perilous pastime, the urban legend of the vanishing hitchhiker—one who posed no harm but whose presence was uncanny, perhaps a harbinger of death—pervaded both campfire stories and textbooks on American folklore.

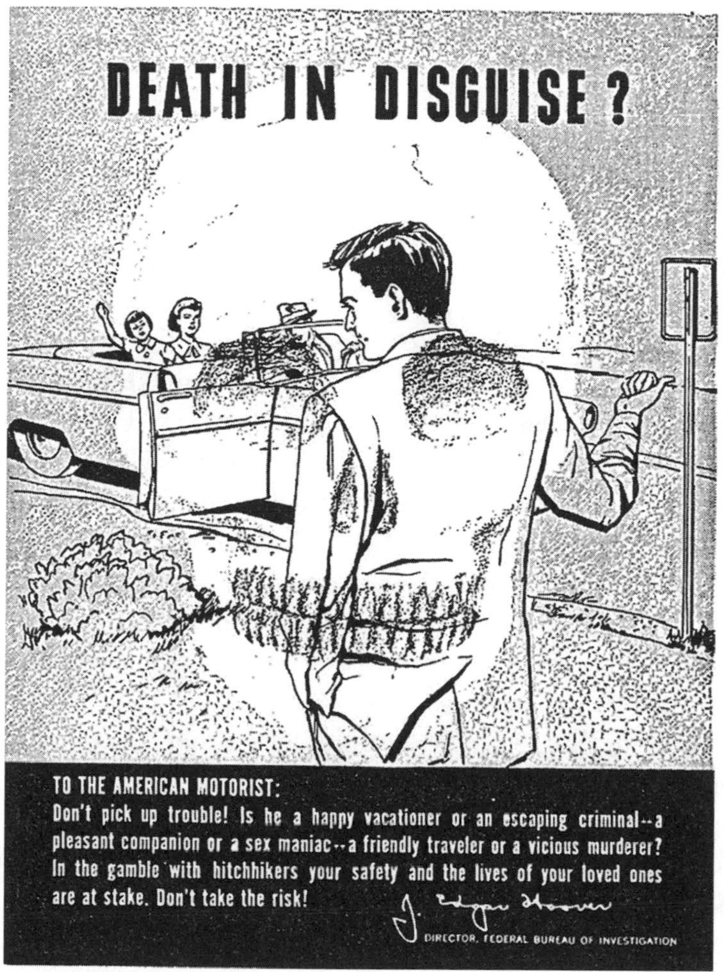

A public service announcment, signed by FBI director J. Edgar Hoover, appeared on highway billboards from the late 1950s through the 1970s along various interstate routes across the United States. The message: never pick up hitchhikers, the latest murderous threat to American public safety. It was a safety campaign rooted in fearmongering that did little more than to create a new cultural fascination with the danger and intrigue of the open road, spawning a new era of urban legends about hitchhiking.

First thought to have been committed to writing and collected in South Carolina during the 1940s, by the 1960s and 1970s the story of the "vanishing hitchhiker," a taciturn hitcher who disappears into thin air, only to be later seen silhouetted by headlights again and again during that same driver's journey, had become one of America's best known urban legends. A 1960 installment of Rod Serling's iconic paranormal anthology series *The Twilight Zone* titled "The Hitch-Hiker" only added to the public's fascination with the legend. The episode featured a diminutive hitcher whose continuous reappearances haunt the long journey of a woman driving alone from New York to Los Angeles. It's later revealed that the hitcher is death incarnate and that the woman died in a car wreck at the outset of her journey, that she had been dead for the entire drive and just didn't know it. Because the hitchhiker needs to be picked up in order to ferry the woman's soul to the next life, her drive has been nothing more than a drifting between two worlds—a turnpike through purgatory. Then, in 1981, University of Utah folklorist Jan Harold Brunvand published an academic treatise titled *The Vanishing Hitchhiker*, which not only summarized variations of the same legend and its evolving cultural significance, but also aggregated all of the best-known hitchhiker folktales in American history and what they symbolized. All the while, the original story that started it all still has its most significant telling back in the Mad City. It's one that remains more horrific than any commercially scripted spin-off—and it's no legend.

The start of the '78 school year at UW was one marked by a "don't ask, don't tell" policy of its own urban legend. It was at once the legend of the Capital City Killer, the Mad City Slayer, the Campus Ripper, and the handful of other names that were used to try to link a single mystery perp to all Madison murders going back to Christine Rothschild. But by that same fall season, the first name circulating through Madison for who the Capital City Killer *might* be was a local creep named William Zamastil. At first blush, he certainly seemed to fit the part.

Like Charles Manson and a number of other notable serial killers, Zamastil started out as a small time car thief but soon graduated to murder to satiate his need for thrills. He was arrested by Dane County Sherriff's detectives in August of '78 for the execution-style slaying of twenty-four-year-old Mary Johnson in nearby Sauk City. He'd shot the victim—due to be married in two days—at point-blank range in the head after kidnapping her from a Madison department store parking lot. It turned out to only be his latest murder. Earlier that same year, while living in California, he'd bludgeoned a teenaged brother and sister to death in the Mojave Desert after he found them hitchhiking near San Bernardino. Five years before that, he kidnapped an Arizona woman—the daughter of an FBI agent who was en route to the Tucson airport—and then raped and murdered her before burying her in a shallow grave and stealing her car. None of these earlier crimes, however, would be linked to Zamastil for another twenty years.

In the meantime, the fact that Zamastil hailed from the Mad City and had returned there at age twenty-six to carry on killing had people wondering if he might have been back and forth over the years. It all had Madisonians speculating what *else* he might have done. It didn't matter that his MO didn't match any of the Madison sex slayings or that he would have been barely eighteen at the time of the Christine Rothschild murder—a crime whose specificity and paraphilic complexity all but defied its being anything other than the work of an older more experienced sex killer. For the time being at least, Zamastil would be a plausible placeholder—a tentative stand-in—for the Capital City Killer.

The police being circumspect to a fault about all the unsolved cases certainly didn't help. The blackout on providing timely updates only exacerbated matters; it kept the rumor mill running at full capacity. The various police forces involved failed to recognize that even the well-intentioned withholding of information could not excuse the need to protect and that they had the obligation to provide information that might prevent future victims. Two decades later, the Toronto Metropolitan Police Department, one of the largest police agencies in North America, was successfully sued by a rape victim used as bait for a serial attacker entering through apartment balconies. The police in that case had held off on issuing press releases or warning the public about the attacker's MO and customary manner of entry until the theory about a lone suspect was firmed up, and probable future target locations were identified and staked out. Similarly, in Madison of 1979, not only was there no active official public dialogue about the successive murders of young women, but the rumor mill was already running full tilt. In short order, two concurrent urban legends, both fictitious and yet also dangerously real, would collide head-on as the lore of the

Capital City Killer and the vanishing hitchhiker became entangled. With that, a new wave of violence would wash over the Mad City and its beloved campus.

But that same fall of '78, at least on the surface, it seemed like business as usual at UW. There was a predictable new influx of moneyed east coasters, Greek-life "legacy" types, and the hodgepodge of other students drawn to the university's sanded-down version of activism from the decade prior. But beneath that veneer, there loomed the unanswered questions about the accumulating deaths—students, employees, and visitors at either UW or places nearby—one left posed gruesomely at the scene, others transported out to remote locations to be torched or otherwise defiled postmortem. While today a student gets mugged near a campus and warnings go out by e-mail or Twitter feed lickety-split, as 1978 became 1979, the rule of the day still was to maintain a posture of silence, in essence to bury the whole sordid affair—Plausible Deniability 101.

True to recent history, by the time twenty-year-old Julie Speerschneider landed her first waitressing gig at Tony's Chop Suey Restaurant on S. Park Street—just under a mile due south from UW—she, like most other young women in the area, was oblivious to how perilous the outwardly bohemian area surrounding campus had become. Known to hitchhike in the area surrounding UW either to reach the restaurant from her second job at Red Caboose Day Care on Williamson Street—a little over a mile due east from the campus—or to return to her home on S. Dickinson Street just a little farther northeast, Julie relied on thumbing a ride anywhere she went that winter to abate her exposure to the cold. With one of the longest freezing spells in recent memory, that same Wisconsin winter had seen a number of people hitchhiking and, with that, trollers knowing where and how to find them. Around this same time, the Madison PD, the UW Five-O, and the Dane County Sheriff—a pared-down version, if you will, of the defunct Intra County Investigative Squad—were all spitballing and checking records from the past ten years for unchecked leads, anything—or anyone—they could hang the serial killer theory on. Meanwhile, another madman was already walking the streets of the Mad City, hiding—and driving—in plain sight.

Defiance

That same winter, February '79, Linda made her way to Virginia and later to Michigan chasing Jorgensen's ghost—the places where the barren threads of evidence suggested he might have been both before and after UW. Linda had fastened on to the Judith Williamson case in Berkeley—the presumed basis for *The Love Pirate*—the Lass disappearance in South Lake Tahoe, Jorgensen's time supposedly dispensing "Māori justice" in South Africa, and his fake army backstory to possibly alibi himself for his real movements during the dying days of World War II. It mandated that she expand her timeline and list of locations where he'd been—where he'd likely be again. Her trek took her first to the city of Lynchburg where, on April 16, 1973, at the end of her freshman year and immediately before final exams, another freshman, Cynthia Hellman of Houston, had been found murdered on the campus of Randolph-Macon Women's College. She'd been found posed beside the Martin Science Building, the small liberal arts college's equivalent of Sterling Hall. Like Christine, she had also been killed in the morning while on a regular walking route. Her face had been left against a hot steam pipe—a torturous, elaborate, symbolic, and paraphilic gesture. No obvious sexual assault, both shoes taken by her killer.

It later turned out that one supplemental key detail never made its way to the microfiche records in Dallas-Fort Worth that might have been useful to know before Linda set out on her journey; in the end, the trip was a dead end. It turned out that local cops had actually made an arrest three weeks after the murder of Cynthia Hellman, picking up a local schizophrenic living near the Randolph-Macon campus who had gone on to attack another student. After receiving two hundred words as a blotter item squeezed between the obits and the open houses in the Fredericksburg *Free Lance-Star* on April 28, 1973, the story disappeared. Linda couldn't find a cop, reporter, or anyone on campus by the winter of '79 who remembered anything more—who knew anything of it for that matter. Like Christine, young Cynthia Hellman was from out of state, a transplant whose death didn't set off any alarm bells or make any lasting impression. Another case of yesterday's news. Undaunted by yet another dead end, Linda took a belt of coffee at a diner in Fairfax, flipped open a Rand McNally road atlas, and focused on her next stop—the dump sites of the Ypsilanti Ripper.

In the summer of '69, a Canadian-born sexual sadist named John Norman Collins had been arrested for a series of murders in and around Ypsilanti and Ann Arbor—most of the victims were young coeds at Eastern Michigan and University of Michigan. Although he had only been charged with one of the seven murders, the other six being "cleared" to him, Linda knew "cleared" was police code for the cops thinking that Collins was probably responsible for them despite never being indicted—a time-honored trick that allowed police departments to artificially ratchet up their statistical "solved" rate. The "probably responsible" caveat allowed cops to link the crimes on paper and then close the books—to "clear" rather than indict Collins and thus close the cases in the more traditional sense. It's a seldom-discussed consolation prize that remains the lifeblood of many homicide divisions across the country, allowing open/unsolved files to be cleared off and a public left tenuously satisfied without the need for trials. But Linda didn't buy it.

A couple of years after Linda's dark odyssey took her to Michigan as the latest stopover, the Atlanta Child Murders, perhaps the most egregious example of questionable clearances—with all twenty-eight-plus slayings being linked en masse to a local pirate-radio disc jockey named Wayne Williams—once again raised issue with this same practice. Williams was a malignant narcissist and sexual deviant who unquestionably killed at least two young boys; however, as recently as 2015, various individuals and groups ranging from famed FBI profiler John Douglas to the US Department of Justice have been jackhammering the concrete around what was once taken for granted as rock-solid fact—that Williams had not only killed two boys but all of the thirty cases cleared to him.

But the Atlanta Child Murders weren't yet a news item in the winter of '79 when Linda banked on the Ypsilanti Ripper task force being eager to pin all of the open/unsolved Michigan sex killings on Collins, much the same way that Wisconsin lawmen would soon be looking for someone's neck to hang the Capital City Killer sign on. With Jorgensen in the wind, they'd need to find a local patsy they could publicly and bombastically attach to every murder after Christine's. In its zeal, the Michigan task force had even linked an eighth coed victim in California to their man Collins. But Linda would soon discover that the MO and victimology also matched both the Rothschild and Williamson slayings to a tee.

The one murder for which Collins had been charged and convicted of in August of '70, the final one of the Michigan set, had been the July 23, 1969, murder of eighteen-year-old Eastern Michigan University student Karen Sue Beineman. Last seen on her way to a nearby wig shop, her ravaged body was found three days later dumped in a gulley near the Huron River. First sexually assaulted and stripped naked, a piece of clothing inserted inside her vagina, she had been tortured after being forced to drink an unknown corrosive chemical and then both strangled and bludgeoned to death. Curiously, the wanton and reckless brutality in this final murder seemed to differ from the specificity of the previous six slayings that had been cleared to Collins. In the other six, specifically the two slayings from the summers of '67 and '68—the victims spaced nearly a year apart—both young women had been stabbed in excess of twenty times in the torso while the murderer used improvised ligatures fastened from either their own clothing or electrical cords. The ligatures were then fastened around their throats with additional items inserted into the mouth—just like Christine. Linda was curious to know how and why these linkages to Collins had been made by police; both of the notable earlier cases also had been moved from storage locations, presumably at or near the primary crime scenes, to their final dump sites outdoors. After their deaths, these two victims, in classic necrophilic fashion, had also been kept partially preserved through refrigeration, either as lifeless sexual surrogates or for Polaroid snapping purposes—or both. Linda already knew from his erstwhile roommate that Jorgensen had come to Madison from New Jersey and Michigan in his convertible Benz, the reason for the convoluted routing never explained. It left a question mark seared into Linda's mind. Irony abounded.

For Linda, the road from Fairfax to Ypsilanti that February to follow this lead was death on a stick—a snow-and-ice-laden gauntlet with not a plow to be seen. Factor in that Linda was also way out of practice with her winter driving since becoming an unlikely Texan. A jackknifed rig—an Exxon tanker—sideways across I-76W, plus a second truck deadheading bobtail, and a state trooper sedan, all in the ditch. The slalom of winter road spinouts soon forced her on to US Route 24, through Defiance, Ohio—at dusk. Desolate and perilous, what they call iceblink superimposed against an empty horizon quickly fading to black, the snow blowing lengthwise through the barn lights in the distance looking like stardust. Eyes heavy, a weary Malibu with even wearier, threadbare wipers—traction control and ABS both still science fiction—Linda's car hit a patch of something unforgiving beneath some virgin snow and spun counterclockwise into a four-foot drift that was partially burying a Burger King signpost. Upon bouncing the rear fender off the signpost and getting the car back on to the road—the snout now facing westbound in the eastbound lane—it was then that Linda had something of an epiphany. It was the most significant moment of pause and introspection since that day at Picnic Point when she first made her promise to Christine, long since dead and buried in a grave she'd still been thwarted from visiting back in Chicago by virtue of her hunt—her promise. It occurred to her that her journey to find the elusive Dr. Jorgensen might be just a big one-way spindrift in its own right. It occurred to her that one of these times she might just end up running out of road and out of time—that she too might end up like Christine. Between the man she was chasing and the law of averages, she was playing with fire—and she knew it. But, there she sat, in an idle car in the black of night, like a painted ship on a painted ocean as the wind howled at over sixty miles per hour and the snow swirled. At the same time, back in Madison, an 8 mm film hissed and sprocket holes framed shaky newsreels as a ragtag assemblage of cops in the dark—both literally and figuratively—watched archived Mad City murder flicks. Those films included CinemaScope surveillance footage of the Debbie Bennett and Julie Ann Hall funerals as detectives scanned for exemplary oddballs lurking around, or anyone worthy of a roust as the cases went further into permafrost. They were grasping at straws, looking for a fall guy. Meanwhile, Linda was looking for trouble. She was prepared to take the risks the cops weren't.

Linda hit the Ypsilanti main drag at just after 10:00 p.m., the drive that should have taken ninety minutes from her last stop clocking in at just under five hours. Overnight she made a flashlight tour of the Eastern Michigan U campus, all of the locations she'd verified as places where victims were last seen or where remains or evidence were discovered relating to the murders of '67—the first two of the set for which Collins, though deemed responsible, had never been charged. The next day, she made the drive in comparatively civilized weather conditions to the only place left to go, the forbidding Romanesque monolith known as the Marquette Branch Prison, perched high on the north shore of Lake Superior—another six hours away. Two years earlier the building had been federally listed on the National Register of Historic Places. Twenty-five years before that, the Detroit Red Wings played—and predictably throttled—the prisoner's hockey team in an outdoor exhibition game as the guards slung 30-30 carbines, and cheered and jeered from the towers. But today it was all business. Linda had to see Collins face-to-face—she *had* to ask him herself about the first two girls killed between the summers of '67 and '68, ask him the questions the police never did about what he knew, what the ligatures and insertions in the throat in lieu of conventional rape might have meant—what they *still* meant in his mind.

Even if Collins, and Collins alone, was good for these killings as the police suspected, she theorized that he and Jorgensen might have crossed paths, might have co-developed the MO and signature seen again elsewhere, such as in the Mad City. Otherwise, an audience with Collins in its own right—like Clarice Starling's tutorials gleaned from Hannibal Lecter's cryptic repartee in *The Silence of the Lambs*, a consultation said to be inspired by Washington State Detective Robert D. Keppel's real-life consultation with Ted Bundy during the Green River Killer investigation—might provide her with better insight into what exactly made Dr. J. tick. It might also be another dead end.

When Linda got to the prison just prior to closing, she'd learn before even breaching the main gates to sign in that Collins had been moved to full lockdown—watertight segregation, zero privileges. It was a necessary measure imposed by the warden following a foiled escape plot hatched by Collins just three weeks earlier, an internal investigation into an incipient tunneling scheme still underway. The new policy mandated no visitors. No exceptions. Linda regrouped, rummaged for change, and dropped a quarter in a pay phone to call Bill Share back in Milwaukee. Before she could fill him in on the details of yet another failure to launch, he did her one better. A contact on the inside with Uncle Sam—a "journalistic source" if there ever was one—had done him a solid. The source had found matching SSN and known-alias data previously used by Jorgensen—used as early as back in New York in the summer of '68—as part of a credit check for a rental application in Flagstaff, Arizona. And Share *had* the address. It was fresh. It was vetted. A message appeared with flashbulb instantaneity in Linda's mind's eye, one Etch-a-Sketched with monochrome clarity: **The Lead Is Solid. This Is the End of the Line. Seize. This. Moment.**

Taken

As Linda crawled her way out of Michigan to begin the nearly two-thousand-mile drive to Flagstaff, twenty-year-old Julie Speerschneider clocked off work to make her way to a local Madison fixture on University Avenue. The date was March 27, 1979; the time was 6:00 p.m. The place was the 602 Club, a charming dive bar carved out of the ground floor of a multipurpose tenement located, as the name implied, at 602 University Avenue—a straight shot south of the UW campus and situated near the student ghetto. More Main King Tap than Cardinal Hotel, it was a place whose local history was about to get a makeover as another unremarkable Madison watering hole soon to be soldered to the legend of the Capital City Killer.

In the spring of '79, the 602 Club was a Mad City enigma. Having defied the encroachment of disco music and its trappings into nearly every element of the local nightlife, the 602 "club" didn't even have a jukebox. As other taverns of comparable size relied on old ceiling-mount television sets showing Packers, Bucks, and Brewers games to draw sports crowds, or rows of pool tables and other table games to keep patrons entertained

The interior of the 602 Club as it appeared in 1979, located at 602 University Avenue in Madison, a hole in-the-wall tavern with a cult following of both UW students and local regulars.

and instinctively guzzling booze, the barkeeps at the 602 kept the one and only set behind the bar powered off. The result was that human conversation was the only racket patrons would hear upon darkening the door of the tiny hole-in-the-wall perched at the corner of University Avenue and Frances Street. The lone electronic devices that existed in the 602 were actually an odd set of intercoms installed in the various booths, allowing drinkers to simply buzz the bar for refills and relay orders through a loudspeaker mounted in the wall—pure genius, pure kitsch. Having once been known as the House of Sparking Glasses, by 1951 the aged building had been renamed to reflect its address before later morphing into the city's first gay bar. In due course, the antique, flowered ceiling would rust and yellow to a rancid copper-tone brown after absorbing the smoke of countless cigarettes sucked to the filter by the eclectic assortment of regulars who came to call the place home. To this day, no one is sure how or why Julie Speerschneider ended up there in March of '79 or whom she came to see. The even bigger question is what happened after she left.

As with Debbie Bennett, the circumstances surrounding the final hours of Julie Speerschneider's life were destined to remain shrouded in mystery. After leaving the 602 Club mid evening—just after 8:30 p.m.—no one is certain what happened to her. Before leaving, she had first phoned a friend from the pay phone inside the bar and indicated she was on her way over. As usual, Julie's intended method of travel was to be hitchhiking. The path would have taken her up Johnson Street from University Avenue, a short distance of under two miles. The difference is that, unlike Debbie Bennett and even Julie Ann Hall, she had a known, intended destination and someone waiting for her. When she didn't turn up as expected, there was concern that something might be wrong. Within twenty-four hours, Julie's friends and family had reported her missing to police. Within another twenty-four hours, both the *Capital Times* and *Wisconsin State Journal* ran features on the case, complete with a reward of five hundred dollars for information leading to her whereabouts. On April 1, 1979—April Fool's Day—a dark headline of "Missing Woman, 20, Sought," along with a recent photograph of Julie, spelled out what the carefully veiled blotter item wouldn't: that she was less missing as much as she was taken.

The offer of the reward—albeit a modest one—coupled with the publicity, confirmed that Julie had been quickly shunted by the police into a high-risk category of missing person known as *endangered missing*. It meant that, in effect, someone had made her go missing, had made her disappear—that she was in life-threatening danger if not already dead. With no history of running away and with a pending destination she never arrived at, there was no other inference to be drawn. But there are countless cases of endangered missing women that never get reported as such, women like Debbie Bennett who, despite being in danger or already dead, nobody ever stops to worry about, much less goes looking for. Julie Speerschneider as *endangered missing* subsequently ensured that she was the first of the recent set of Madison victims not to fall into the dreaded category known as the *missing missing*—a person who is so socioeconomically alienated and devoid of personal support that their disappearance and even their murder goes unnoticed. Often, the person is not known to be missing or in jeopardy until it is too late, such as when a body is recovered and their final days, weeks, and even months and years are unaccounted for. While the fact was that Julie Ann Hall was an anomaly in this respect, as she was gainfully employed and had family and friends in Madison, Debbie Bennett would of course not be given a second thought until such time as her charred and ravaged corpse turned up in a ditch outside Cross Plains. Today, across countless cities in America, things remain largely unchanged.

From Debbie Bennett as an example of the *missing missing* to Julie Ann Hall as a less flagrant version of the same—her disappearance more ignored than simply unknown—to now Julie Speerschneider as *endangered missing* complete with above-the-fold publicity, all indicators were that by 1969, Madisonians were beginning to realize that forces were now at work in the city that would change everything. Going back to the Rothschild job in '68, a fuse had been lit that it seemed no one could put out. Indeed, things began to look even grimmer when the newspaper publicity and solicitation for information brought forth a man who claimed to have recognized Julie as the hitchhiker he picked up on the night she was last seen alive—when she walked out of the 602 Club by herself. The problem was that she wasn't really by herself.

Despite being alone when she set out for her friend's address, the man claimed that Julie was hitchhiking in the company of another man who appeared to be squiring her through the three-way junction where State, Johnson, and Henry Streets converge—about half a mile from the 602 Club. Speaking to Julie and the mystery man through an open driver's window, he was told that they were looking for a lift to the corner of Brearly and Johnson, a quick jaunt just over two miles up the road to the east. The motorist had told them to hop in, he said, before soon after dropping them off—a silent car ride the whole way—at their specified location less than one block from Julie's friend's home. When asked to provide a description of the mystery man squiring Julie that night, the driver drew a blank. There was nothing about him, whether good or bad, that managed to stand out. Good Samaritans aren't, after all, particularly known for their observation skills. But there was one thing about the brief interaction that did stand out for the motorist, something he'd found unsettling. After checking the rearview mirror while he drove up Johnson Street only seconds after pulling away, the two hitchhikers had vanished.

As weeks became months and months became years, the modest five-hundred-dollar reward for information on Julie's whereabouts went unclaimed. In time, her classification as endangered missing unofficially changed to presumed dead. Although there had been no confirmatory evidence, behind closed doors Madison cops had effectively shelved the file. All the while, her parents Joan and David Speerschneider became increasingly reclusive in their small Lomax Drive home while still holding out hope. But while they stayed clear of the public eye, Julie's friends pounded the pavement and doled out leaflets emblazoned with her photo. They diligently documented and passed on to police the details of countless false sightings offered by well-intentioned but mistaken Madisonians;

they heard countless false "visions" and dealt with the bunk offered by fraudster clairvoyants. During this later period, little to nothing was done by police in terms of public appeals for the mystery man—the vanishing hitchhiker seen in the company of Julie when she was last alive—to come forward and present himself for questioning. Unlike the multijurisdictional task force working the Bennett murder and subsequent torching, which used intermittent media blitzes in an attempt to ferret out whoever had mailed her room key back to the Cardinal, no one in the Speerschneider investigation apparently ever followed up in an attempt to locate the unknown male seen at Julie's side the night she disappeared. He was at the very least a key witness, even more likely her killer. The investigation was further hampered by the fact that, all speculation aside, there was no proof to confirm that Julie was in fact dead. There was also no crime scene, no body, no evidence of an actual crime. It was the missing link between Julie's sudden disappearance and the series of other murders plaguing Madison—and the murders yet to come—that within the next two years would become tragically resolved.

Familiar Figure

Back in the vicinity of the Main King Tap, the sketchy watering hole east of the Capitol Square where Julie Ann Hall was last seen alive in June of '78, there was, by the end of 1979, a new hangaround whom the police would later describe euphemistically as a "familiar figure." By December of that same year, as Christmas shoppers shuffled along West Main and Pinkney and their children peered into store windows, twenty-four-year-old Susan LeMahieu had become a Main and King Street habitué. She could be frequently found loitering near that same intersection while popping in and out of the various bars and coffee shops that by then were known haunts for some of the prostitutes who had migrated from the Cardinal Hotel after the Debbie Bennett murder.

Young Susan was not, however, a street worker or even a drug user. She was simply one of the forgotten, a cognitively delayed woman whose amalgam of mental and physical disabilities had left her partially paralyzed on her left side. She had largely been forsaken even by her own family as a result of her disability and later would be described insensitively—perhaps a sign of the times—as "retarded" in newspapers during the coming months. She was for all intents and purposes relegated to being the village idiot and a soon-to-be inconvenient victim for police amid the deluge of more photogenic missing and murdered coeds. Sent off to live in a state-funded chicken coop of a group home by her family, Susan resided at Allen Hall on nearby State Street where she was given room and board, but had taken to roaming the Mad City streets during the Christmas shopping season in hopes of finding some kind of human connection with somebody—anybody.

By the time she was reported missing to Madison PD by the group home staff the night of December 19, a Wednesday, after she failed to turn up for the home's imposed curfew on the previous *Saturday*, a belated and begrudgingly written report was filed but no media release was made and no real investigation undertaken. A "retarded" and physically disabled woman wandering the streets in subthermal conditions—with the Capital City Killer on the loose no less—was apparently little cause for concern. It's also unclear whether the group home or police notified Susan LeMahieu's family, parents separated, with her mother still residing in their East Madison home—not far from Allen Hall—where the rest of the family was apparently preparing to celebrate Christmas, apparently without Susan. If her mother Ruth—or even her father Gary who was by then living in the town of Mauston some eighty miles away in Juneau County—was notified, it would likely have been too much to bear. They might have thought, and would later know for certain, that history was repeating itself. Indeed, both Susan's status as a burden and her parents' marriage were casualties of family tragedies past.

In 1966, when Susan was only ten years old, her two youngest brothers, Bill and Doug, age four and six respectively, suffocated to death after being trapped inside an abandoned old refrigerator left to rust in the basement of the family home. With four other siblings left alive, Susan—from a huge family like Julie Ann Hall and similarly being overlooked time and again—was sent to East Madison High before being apparently sentenced to life in an overcrowded group home. After successfully completing high school in 1974 but deemed unable to provide for herself or live alone, the supported living she was supposed to receive at Allen Hall, a long-term convalescent-care facility, amounted to three hots and a cot. The rest of the time she was left to wander the streets unsupervised. In fact, she was only admitted into the facility at all, given her age, following a fatal fire at the multistory sardine can a year prior, a five-alarm blaze that led the administrators to reexamine the risk of having too many enfeebled seniors on-site.

Originally built in 1962 to serve as a women's dorm for UW students, by the end of '69 the Frances Street building was repurposed into a facility for the disabled. Less than four years later, on January 8, 1973, a sixty-year-old resident burned to death and a twenty-two-year-old part-time care worker—a UW–Madison student to boot—died of smoke inhalation. The student had been trying to use a simple fire extinguisher to battle an accidental fire that, after mysteriously starting in a resident's room, quickly consumed the entire structure. Scores more were seriously injured, including three firefighters, as wheelchairs became entangled in the lobby amid unleashed mayhem. With the student employee left for dead by the other staff and the residents left scrambling, the Red Cross quickly arrived to stabilize the situation and assist emergency personnel. Several days later, after a second resident died of injuries, questions started to get asked. Amid the scrutiny, the ensuing room vacancies led to Susan being short-listed.

After six years of a proverbial life sentence at the recently renovated Allen Hall, a despondent Susan had taken to wandering the streets rather than remaining in solitary confinement in her meager room. No one can blame her. Although the home's policy required that police be notified after Susan failed to return on the night of December 15, they failed to do so. Ditto for December 16, 17, and 18. Only on the night of December 19, a full four days after last being seen alive, was Susan reported missing. By then, there was also no confirmed last sighting of her for police to go on. While perhaps a "familiar figure" in the area of the now-infamous Main King Tap, no one knew her name or thought much of seeing her or not seeing her. No one, it seems, was paying attention. For whoever's attention she did get that night, she was the ideal victim. In Madison, she was the invisible woman, another one of the missing missing.

As December 1979 dissolved into January 1980, reporters at the *Capital Times* and even the *Wisconsin State Journal* surprisingly had no tough questions for local, county, and state police about the mounting number of open investigations and apparent lack of progress: Julie Speerschneider and Susan LeMahieu, both missing without a trace; Julie Ann Hall and Debbie Bennett also missing and later found dead, both girls having met with horrific endings to their brief lives. Christine Rothschild all but forgotten—yesteryear's bad news. Questions for investigators, if any, at news briefings, if any, were lobbed in—underhand, no spin—and typically prefaced by some apologetic qualifier. The usual police platitudes about "ongoing investigations" and "every avenue" being vigorously explored were then lobbed back at the press and taken at face value. Madison was riding the jet stream at a comfortable cruising altitude. No one, it seemed, was as worried as they should have been. With the truth of what really happened to Susan LeMahieu waiting to be discovered, 1980 picked up speed—someone turned on the faucet.

That year started with a shot. The new decade started with a leap year, one that this time would signal the start of a new era. It was a decade whose unrivaled blend of innovation and hedonism would trigger the highest violent crime rate across the United States in the history of the republic, with events in Madison being ahead of the national curve. Linda had missed Jorgensen by a matter of hours in Flagstaff the previous March; he'd left town at the same time Three Mile Island was melting down and when there were distractions galore. He had previously been known to fly by night but now, by the close of the 1970s—over a decade after Christine's death—and age wearing on him, he was prepared to move in the light of day hiding in the long shadows of the American Southwest. Even with favors called in by Bill Share and the earnest tips of other nomads running from their own past lives—meaning those who met Jorgensen passing in the night—Linda had, by the spring of '80, resigned herself to the fact that Jorgensen would always stay one step ahead of her. Her own private all-points want on his whereabouts would need to evolve; it would need to move from hunt and peck to something more nuanced, more insidious. In time, she would learn to use his own tactics against him. He was adept at running. He had been running in some fashion his whole life, ever since sending his own brother to a watery grave. That's why, as she believed, *The Love Pirate* was penned as one part catharsis and one part treasure map.

The book was mother Heidi's profile of her own malevolent creation—an itinerary of Jorgensen's life that came before and that would come later. Wherever he went and whatever he did—whatever identity he assumed and whomever he killed—he would always be the obsessive Dr. Francis Corcoran. To know Corcoran was to know Jorgensen. Linda wanted to get inside his head and torment him as he had tormented Christine and the other lives she believed he had laid to waste. If she couldn't get to Jorgensen in the conventional sense, she would have to bring him to her—draw him out, provoke his compulsions. And so a new era of psychological warfare would begin.

On January 2, 1980, just after 9:00 p.m., a warmer-than-average winter Wednesday in the Mad City, seventeen-year-old Shirley Stewart left her part-time job as a night maid at the Dean Clinic, a franchised family wellness center still in operation across Southern Wisconsin. But that 9:00 p.m. in the dead of winter in the Mad City might as well have been the small hours, the city streets largely devoid of traffic and potential witnesses as it sat eerily still and poised on the brink of what would be its most unsettling year to date. As young Shirley—a native of Nebraska, devout member of St. Bernard's Catholic Church in nearby Middleton, single mother to an infant daughter named Christina—ventured out into the streets of East Madison to walk home, she made a fateful foray into a mostly deserted streetscape—a barren and frozen landscape apparently devoid of witnesses. There was, however, one person watching—and waiting. As to precisely what happened next, no one can be sure. What is certain is that in the following days, Shirley was reported missing to police and the tragically predictable waiting game began once again. As in the case of Julie Speerschneider, the speed with which Shirley was reported missing immediately raised the otherwise flaccid antenna of local authorities. Like Speerschneider—the very real vanishing hitchhiker—the Stewart girl's case was quickly updated to endangered missing. By the time the first news release hit the papers and local Mad City airwaves, all evidence pointed to the fact that she was already dead.

The Lost City

As the Madison city cops tossed around ideas about a search area when the start of the Wisconsin spring thaw would surely, or so they thought, reveal the body of Shirley Stewart, the Intra County Investigative Squad that had been assembled in the wake of the Debbie Bennett murder was about to have an improvised and unexpected reunion. The Madison PD, state police, Dane County Sheriff and, for the first time since the Rothschild murder—deus ex machina—the UWPD, were all to join forces after a group of morning joggers happened upon a discovery that would stir up ghosts of the past. It was a discovery that would confirm that, assuming the Capital City Killer or killers did in fact exist, he or they were still fixated on the UW campus proper. The killings would soon return to where they began with Christine Rothschild's death twelve years earlier. Although Julie Ann Hall had worked on campus, and both Debbie Bennett and Julie Speerschneider had last been seen near campus, locations nibbling at the edges, the university proper would soon go from being a common denominator in the string of recent city slayings to ground zero for a recurring MO.

In the spring of '80, there existed—and still exists—an expanse of UW property officially constituting the university's arboretum. An assortment of prairies, woodlands, and wetlands, the arboretum was developed principally as a place to protect the ecology of the "original Wisconsin"—a snapshot of a time and place untouched by humans where students and faculty scientists could study the countless number of trees covering the expansive 1,200-acre nature preserve south of University Avenue. But it wasn't always so.

In the 1920s, in a swampy and isolated portion of the preserve known as Gardner Marsh, a specific section of land was cleared to make way for a subdivision known as Lake Forest, a tony suburb thirty years ahead of its time, when the postwar boom led to flight from American urban centers and toward the perceived utopia of suburbia. The development, however, being too isolated—too radical in its concept—for its time in a then conservative Wisconsin capital, quickly floundered. In due course, bankrupt investors and builders abandoned the model homes that had dotted the site, the wood-frame structures reclaimed by nature—consumed by the same land cleared to accommodate the buildings years earlier. By the 1970s, the homes were rotted shanties mostly reduced to foundations hidden among the trees and other vegetation that had come to erase the past. The grim mosaic of homes sinking into the Wisconsin marshland was an elegiac panoramic of a place that soon came to be known as the Lost City Forest. It was the real-life Madison version of the legendary lost city of Atlantis that, like all isolated curiosities locked away in the woods, would inevitably attract the curiosity of enterprising youths and, not surprisingly, explorers of another kind.

The doomed Gardner Marsh development had been known for much of the 1960s and '70s among Madison and Dane County locals as a good place to "go park" as they say. The Lost City, with only two access points for visitors arriving by car, was just isolated enough to double as a lovers' lane and was an ideal place for Mad City teens to bring their dates away from prying eyes. The problem is that, as we now know, once an isolated location is earmarked as a known make-out spot, it's not only starry-eyed lovers who show up to use it. In criminal investigative analysis, these lovers' lanes are today referred to as "known vice areas," having been identified by the FBI and others as key locations for predators to develop their fantasies while spying on others. Peepers, prowlers, and other offenders with deep-seated imagistic regimes and twisted fantasies—what are known as *scopophiliacs* in the related forensic literature—often cut their teeth in these locations before moving on to more serious crimes. They voyeurize those people using these locations engaged in everything from teenaged over-the-jeans heavy petting to reefer madness and more illicit acts by sex-trade workers and even trysts between secret lovers. They also learn how to best conceal themselves in such places and to pick up on social cues from those subjected to their bizarre surveillance activities.

Because these same places, by virtue of being so-called "vice" areas, also attract johns with prostitutes on board, offenders may often try to experiment with bringing prostitutes to these locations for more nefarious purposes. They may engage in exhibitionist activities and other preparatory or rehearsal activities at these same sites before then returning with a targeted victim following complete psychological and emotional decomposition—after succumbing to their need and desire to indulge a related "attack" paraphilia, including sexual murder. As a staple of 1970s' driving culture, killers like the Zodiac in California and David Berkowitz in New York—the self-proclaimed Son of Sam—would frequent these locations and attack victims, ambushing after first voyeuristically stalking them. It was also an MO used by the Texarkana Phantom of the 1940s and the Monster of Florence over a seventeen-year period from 1968 to 1985. Offenders who use lovers' lanes to develop their fantasies and return there with their victims to act them out—or who simply attack victims they happen to find there—know full well that anyone else there, absent another voyeur, will be minding his or her own business. They know that anyone parked there will not be overly curious about who else is parked there, and that there's usually not a cop to be seen. It's for this reason that known vice areas are considered to be among the most telltale signs of the makeup of an offender's background when a murder victim is found discarded at one of these places. To know of the existence of such a place and to be confident enough to travel there with a body on board—alive or dead—suggests that the killer in all likelihood will have been there before. However, as seen in most cases, he lacked the proper socialization to be there with a consenting partner. Typically, he will have been a regular, there as a deranged voyeur—a scopophiliac in the technical sense—in order to stoke existing and aberrant fantasies while watching others from afar. Simply put, the killer knows these same places only as either a hunting or dumping ground, but seldom, if ever, as a proverbial Don Juan with a willing participant.

Lovers' lanes in the light of day are often *not*, however, known vice areas, and can double as lawful spaces with lawful users. On the morning of April 17, 1980, a group of joggers, parking their cars in the same lot that doubled as something else under the cover of darkness, set out for a springtime group run around the perimeter of the Lost City. It was shortly after embarking on their usual fun run, just a hundred feet into those same dark woods that had swallowed up the model homes in what had once been planned as the Lake Forest community, that the group found the body of Susan LeMahieu. No one is quite sure when someone first noticed the body, or what led them that far into the forest and off the path to investigate. One thing for certain is that the group was so traumatized by what they found, as were some nearby bird-watchers who they alerted to the discovery, that it wasn't until later that afternoon that someone summoned the courage to call police and escort officers back to the spot. Police noted that the civilians were simply "too frightened" and too taken off guard to mentally process the gravity of what they'd found, so the lost hours didn't end up making much of a difference. Susan had been there, it was later estimated, before she had even been reported missing. With a delay of four days back in December of '79 and a delay of nearly a full day in April of '80, it seemed no one felt compelled to act as an advocate for Susan either in life or in death. No one in town, quite simply, could be bothered getting involved—again.

Like Julie Ann Hall, Susan LeMahieu's body had been stripped naked. Like Julie Ann, Susan had also been placed in a surface burial position, concealed from immediate view by decaying leaves, branches, and debris from the canopy of trees above. It was a manner of disposal, or what criminal profilers call a disposal "pathway," that relied partly on the killer himself piling material pulled from the forest floor and partly on additional material that the changing seasons would cast loose from the trees of the living forest as the barely buried body began to decay. It was less a shallow grave than it was what's known as a surface burial—the body secreted in a pile of readily available organic material and left exposed to the elements and the wildlife of the surrounding area.

There are a number of reasons an offender might use this disposal method. The killer might lack the tools or strength to dig a proper grave that might prolong the time before discovery; he also might not want to. He may wish to conceal the body from immediate view of passers-by but still be able to find it when he returns back to check on it—to gaze upon it, snap exposures of it, and do whatever else he wants. There are, as horrific as it seems, several documented cases of this occurring among organized offenders operating within the necrophilic spectrum. But the concealment technique—whether instrumental and part of the MO or expressive and part of the signature—wasn't the only item in common between the remains of Susan LeMahieu and those of Julie Ann Hall, who had been seen leaving the same bar where Susan was a "familiar figure."

Given the state of Susan's body—much of the torso eviscerated by scavengers and her bones found scattered in a large perimeter surrounding where her skull was found—no precise cause of death could be established. An autopsy was, for this reason, deemed moot and was altogether avoided. Instead, what remained of Susan was expeditiously laid to rest in a private, quick-rigged service at the Schroeder Funeral Home on E. Washington Avenue—no visitation, no donations. The obituary in the *Capital Times* listed Cherry Street—with her mother—as her last address and not the home on Frances Street, where they should have been watching out for her welfare, though her disappearance was ignored for a total of four days and nights. As for UW, this new victim to end up on the campus was a problem cleaned up in record time. Like Christine Rothschild, Susan LeMahieu was an outsider; unlike Christine, there was no Linda to keep the memory of young Susan alive, the momentum going, and her killer looking over his shoulder. The four-agency task force, with the UW campus police at the center and declared to be "partially activated" on the morning of April 19—half measures once again being the order of the day—was little more than window dressing. In reality, the investigation fizzled by the summer solstice two months later. The predictable lack of progress in finding a solution to now several Madison murders was becoming a recurring theme. By the summer of '80, people were scared as hell. If they weren't already, they'd soon have reason to be.

The Sweetheart Murders

As plainclothesmen from Madison, Dane County, the UWPD, and both the Wisconsin State Police and Department of Justice (DOJ) scoured old tip sheets and carbons of original crime scene summaries looking for clues that would never materialize, history was about to get turned on its ear. Along with those few investigators looking for genuine clues, there were of course also those, subscribing in whole or part to the Capital City Killer theory, looking for someone on whom they could pin the tail on the donkey and be done with it all. While the official police decree was that none of the cases were connected, the public was bewildered by the spate of murders—not to mention the seemingly accelerating pace of the slayings. By the end of the summer of '80, the police would get their first of two chances to try to assign a name to the Capital City Killer and make it all go away. That name was Edward Wayne Edwards.

The straight life never really squared with Edwards, a small-time punk hailing from Akron, Ohio. Orphaned by his mother upon her unforeseen suicide, he bounced around various youth homes, boarding houses, and juvie lockups before enlisting with the marines and being dishonorably discharged in near-record time. He later wandered Ohio and Kentucky as a nomad, working briefly as a traveling vacuum cleaner salesman in Louisville before ending up back in the slammer in his hometown for an assortment of petty crimes.

Then, in 1955 at the age of twenty-two, he hit the big time. After escaping custody by pushing past an inept jail guard in the city of Akron, Edwards roamed the US, robbing gas stations in part for the money and in part for the fame. It worked. By 1961 Edwards, like the Sterling Hall bombers to follow, landed on the FBI's Ten Most Wanted Fugitives List and eventually got scooped in Atlanta in January '62. From there he was sent to the infamous United States Penitentiary, Leavenworth, in Kansas where—as a model prisoner—he was paroled in 1967, going on to marry a local rube and become a motivational speaker. But it was all a ruse—a brief layover before he chose to reveal his true nature.

By the mid-seventies, Edwards's bizarre sexual fixations, sadistic impulses, and lust for fame had boiled over. Following two unremarkable game show appearances that he unsuccessfully tried to leverage into TV stardom, Edwards—much like "Dating Game Killer" Rodney Alcala later did in between slayings—was soon consumed with a brand of sexual anger and malignant narcissism that caused him to place great erotic value on destructive and violent behaviors. Starting first as an orphaned petty burglar and later graduating to setting false fire alarms and committing check fraud—the type of criminal versatility common to both criminal psychopaths and serial killers alike—by 1977, and just five years after an appearance on the CBS panel show *To Tell the Truth*, Edwards would claim his first two murder victims back in Akron. By the summer of '80, those crimes still unsolved, he had made his way northwest to the Badger State.

On the night of August 9, 1980—a pristine Midwestern summer Saturday—high-school sweethearts Tim Hack and Kelly Drew, both nineteen, left a wedding reception at the Concord House. The joint in question was at the time a dance hall located in Sullivan, a rural water-tower town about forty-five minutes east of the Mad City. Tim, a hard-working farmer who drove an old tractor he nicknamed "The Lonesome Loser," and Kelly, a recent graduate of a local beauty school, were last seen walking hand in hand toward Tim's car in the parking lot. The next morning, Tim's car remained the only vehicle still parked in the Concord House lot; his wallet lay untouched inside. The couple had made it to the car, if only for a moment. What happened next would remain a mystery until five days later. Less than a week after the murder, Kelly's clothing and undergarments, slashed to ribbons, were found three miles down the road from the parking lot. With no bodies or other evidence to go on, local cops started by questioning the guests at the reception and the hall's staff. But that was just the start.

That staff included the facility's new handyman, Ed Edwards, who had dried blood—his own—caked around his nose from a recent impact injury when investigators showed up. He explained the bloody nose away as an accident sustained while deer hunting in the nearby woods. It was an obvious deception and a glaring clue that should have been picked up on but wasn't. Within two weeks, Edwards had quit the job and fled back to Louisville. Two months later, now October, the bodies of Tim and Kelly were found in the woods about five miles from the clothing pile and a total of eight miles from the hall—one straight line.

The scene of the murder, puzzling given the distance covered from the hall, suggested that the two teen lovebirds, initially unharmed, might have gone willingly—or under duress—into a deathtrap in the woods. Once there, it appeared that Tim was quickly stabbed to death while Kelly was tied up, raped, and then strangled. Given the use of restraints and control of the scene by the killer, the cuts to the clothing were likely carried out postmortem—expressive violence not committed against the body itself but to the temporary keepsakes to be taken from it and gazed upon later. The finding of some clothing remnants discarded on the way back to the abduction site, the Concord House, and not on the way to the kill site, meant the killer was retracing his steps. The presence of DNA on various bits of Kelly's clothing—matched to Edwards almost thirty years later—verified this horrific but somewhat predictable order of events.

Even without the DNA match at the time of the initial investigation, the apparent itinerary quickly puzzled investigators. He *had* to go back to the scene, they thought, but why? He had to be back at the party, maybe back working *at* the party, the cops thought. They thought right, and they soon followed Edwards to Louisville to question him a second time about his movements that night. He played them. In his twisted mind, he was a Midwestern sex creep Hall of Famer, the paragon of a smooth criminal and the consummate serial killer; they were small-town, small-time cops out of their jurisdiction and out of time—with scattershot hunches and a one-night's hotel budget.

What the cops certainly didn't know is that Edwards's first double murder, another young couple snatched right out of the man's car in a parking lot back in Akron, was near identical in MO and victimology. They also didn't know that while they waited him out—and waited some more—that same MO would change. Once the heat was off, Edwards would bring his next victim to him, adopting a young orphan boy who he'd later murder in 1996 for the insurance money. Confessing and pleading guilty in Ohio to both the Sullivan double murder and the earlier Akron double murder, he was sentenced to life in prison. His confession and guilty plea to his adopted son's murder would land him on death row. Unlike many craven killers who, once caught, hide behind the bureaucracy of the system, Edwards said he would not appeal the decision and wanted to die by lethal injection. Only one month later, he was granted his wish but not as he had hoped. Before having to take the needle, he died of natural causes.

With Wisconsin media's attention diverted from the summer happenings in big, bad Madison to what they were now calling the "Sweetheart Murders" in sedate, leave-your-doors-unlocked Sullivan, a small scrum of detectives with the multiagency Mad City task force had a light-bulb moment. Edwards was already by then a known person of interest in the Hack-Drew double murder in state police circles. There were also some elements of that case that were close enough to a number of the Madison murders to make the short list of potential connections.

The forest—check; access to a car—check; notable distance traveled—check; removal of all female clothing—check; the use of a knife and strangulation matching two of the Madison victims—check. What no one bothered to determine was that Edwards hadn't even arrived in Wisconsin until approximately the fall of '79 at the earliest, well after the first barrage of murders in the Mad City. Besides the erroneous timeline, the flimsy connections—over 48 percent of serial murders committed in the United States since 1800 and almost 90 percent of sexual murders on record involve at least some degree of strangulation—and at the same time the abduction-murder of couples being among the rarest of MOs, the crime scene behaviors were in the ballpark purely by default based on the odds. As police in Sullivan pondered their next move, back in Madison, with a quick stroke of the pen the Capital City Killer at least had a placeholder name to be pocketed for a rainy day: Ed Edwards. But before long, he'd be bumped from the list for a better contender as the police spent the next few years shuffling the deck chairs and reverse engineering a plausible narrative—rigging the evidence to serve the existing myth of a local boogeyman. It was a new strategy and one that would allow history to be more favorable to them and replace Edwards with a more believable stand-in. As the next wave of murders was set to hit, they'd soon have their replacement killer.

Chapter 7

Deadfall

I detest all men; some because they are wicked and do evil, others because they tolerate the wicked.

—Molière, *The Misanthrope*

Tutelage

By the winter of '81, no one is sure exactly when, Jorgensen had joined an outfit known as the Sierra Singles, a ragtag and mixed-age California social group that used hiking in the Sierra Nevada Mountains—about an hour from where Donna Ann Lass's car was found abandoned at the California-Nevada border—as an icebreaker for mingling and hookups. That same organization, not unlike many singles services of the day, ended up being little more than awkward humdrum, a deflator of expectations. Jorgensen used the yawning chasm that was the distance between those lofty expectations of the members and the more banal realities of real life to assert himself as their de facto leader in no time flat. In an age defined by self-styled pseudocelebrities and avaricious larger-than-life psychopaths who seized the public eye—televangelists, stock swindlers, corporate raiders, bombastic hoteliers—Jorgensen was finally in his element. A man for all seasons. Like any intuitive cult leader and faith healer of the era, Jorgensen talked in clichés and oozed grandiosity as he sought to dominate—as he looked for his next unsuspecting target either within the group or as part of its many excursions. It was the Memorial Library in the spring of '68 all over again, but with even easier targets. Easier, it seems, than Christine turned out to be.

Donning his army-issue jacket, perhaps for the first time since that fateful Sunday at UW, Jorgensen sought to make it clear to the members of the Sierra Singles that he *knew* the terrain; he was their leader and that was that. It wasn't difficult for him to assert himself with what amounted to a remarkably pedestrian group of people who took to nature hikes and other wholesome activities while their colleagues surfed, played the stock market, and immersed themselves in the yuppie consumer culture of early-1980s Southern California. The Sierra Singles were also a captive audience to Jorgensen's twisted stream of consciousness—his largest audience yet. Sometimes his stories made sense, sometimes they didn't. Sometimes they were pure fiction and sometimes—as Linda later pieced together—they amounted once again to cryptic confessions of one type or another. Confessions about what he had done and would do again. With his outlandish claims about World War II and his intuitively braggart nature, Jorgensen attracted less the attention of the women in the group as much as one young man named Ezra Jameson. Like Jorgensen, Jameson had a different axial tilt than most Californians of the day—a type of synchronous yet retrograde orbit with the world—that made Jorgensen the ideal mentor. Quid pro quo, Jorgensen, like all malignant narcissists, of course wanted—and needed—a young protégé. Before long they were hand in glove—the minion and the master alike. Jameson was unwittingly to become a real-life manifestation of Quong Sha in *The Love Pirate*, an irrationally devoted and brainwashed servant who is a "sane and sober influence" on Dr. Corcoran's actions, and who serves as a foil for the police once the fictive Inspector Dowling and Sergeant Mentzer, the fictional equivalents of men who would later become Detectives Josephson and Lulling, track the missing Annabel to Paradise Valley. But what neither Jorgensen nor Ezra Jameson knew in the summer of '81 was that their unlikely friendship would also trigger the indirect involvement of a neutral third party in nearby LA. Their partnership put Jorgensen two degrees of separation away from a woman who, unbeknownst to either of them, had been cultivated as a confidential source by Linda after decrypting the turgid middle chapters of *The Love Pirate* beginning on page 103:

"A woman was hanging up a few clothes to dry in the yard [and] seemed surprised at the sight of the girl. 'This is Annabel. Miss Jane Brown,' he presented them. 'Annabel's just—er—my niece.' Jane Brown put a little tousled jet black toy into Annabel's hand."

Jane Brown, Dr. Corcoran's neighbor in Paradise Valley, aware of the captivity but believing the cover story, unsuspiciously believes that Dr. Corcoran is a "missionary" and can do no wrong when she first appears in *The Love Pirate*. She even makes Annabel's confinement more tolerable, unknowingly and unintentionally assisting the doctor in his scheme. Linda believed that Jane Brown's real name outside the diegesis of the novel was Rita Baron, a name Linda had found in Jorgensen's high school yearbook at North Hollywood High. She'd been a family friend from day one. As expansive as the continental trek of America had been—as far and wide as the game of cat and mouse she and Jorgensen had been playing for over a decade—by April of '81, when Linda let off the gas and gave Jorgensen some breathing room, he proved to be as predictable as his ghastly crimes and brought Linda right to him. Linda actually had no idea that Jorgensen had joined the Sierra Singles until she reached out to Rita as part of an ingeniously deceptive ploy to coax details from her on what Jorgensen's activities had been—what his future plans might hold.

Posing as an NBC researcher doing preliminary background checks on potential candidates for a rebooting of the Ralph Edwards bio program *This Is Your Life*—arguably America's first genuine foray into reality television—Linda contacted Rita by telephone. It was under the pretense that Jorgensen's name had been put forward as an ordinary yet extraordinary American whose story would be told in the pilot episode of a thirtieth-anniversary network reboot studio execs were considering in development meetings. As with every episode in the show's original run from 1952 to 1961, the research would need to be conducted in absolute secrecy to surprise the guest on the air in front of a studio audience to elicit genuine emotion that his life was about to be profiled. In other words, Rita could not tell Jorgensen of their conversation—nor the conversations to come. Linda even made the call from a pay phone in

Burbank just in case Rita got hinky and rang the operator for the outgoing exchange. It was clockwork cloak-and-dagger.

Sure enough, Rita bought into the ruse and gave up Ezra Jameson's name, told her that she hadn't seen Jorgensen in person since '67 when he left for summer "hunting" in Michigan before heading to Madison to finish his residency. Said she'd been to his father's funeral in '74 and was shocked to find Jorgensen pulled a no-show—that he'd been told by his mother Heidi not to come. Rita also went on a bit about "poor Søren" and a family splintered, how it was good that Jorgensen recently put his practice on hold in either Arizona or Nevada to come back and look after his mother. "She isn't well, you know . . ." Rita stressed with an odd and curious inflection. She told Linda about Ezra Jameson, described as a "loner" who looked up to Jorgensen. It wasn't immediately clear how Rita knew Ezra but it was a lucky connection that Linda played out for all it was worth—near real-time intelligence for the first time in over a decade. While Rita hadn't seen Jorgensen since the summer of '67, it seemed Rita saw Ezra weekly, and he reported back to her about their mutual friend. Good ol' Dr. Jorgensen, Sierra Singles pedagogue—what a guy.

Even in her first phony phone interview, the details gleaned from a clueless Rita were jarring and struck like a cleaver. Ezra, it seemed, was especially impressed how Jorgensen could trap and skin a rabbit with a penknife while the rabbit was still alive. Linda's blood curdled; he'd not aged out of his sadism. He wasn't through with his depraved proclivities—and they weren't through with him. Over thirty years before the FBI finally started tracking and cross-referencing cruelty-to-animal cases against unsolved murder sites—with *zoosadism*, or sexual excitement through animal torture and mutilation being a known precursor to attacks on humans—Linda instinctively felt that Jorgensen was rehearsing his next crime under the auspices of being a small-game hunter. Ezra didn't know the difference; he seemed to believe whatever Jorgensen would tell him—did whatever he told him. The next part was predictable save one additional detail. As Rita gushed about Jorgensen's "heroism at the Bulge," she also divulged one item that even Ezra had found odd, notably the state of the army jacket that served as the sole material evidence of Jorgensen's fabricated exploits. Despite allegedly being to the Western

Front and back, narrowly escaping with his life and injured leg intact, it seems that Ezra questioned the appearance of recent tattering and fading on what should have been a well-preserved memento of his time in battle—a reminder of fallen friends who never made it home. Knowing full well the whole story was a con, Jorgensen being one of countless frauds to later lay claim to military service, Linda pulled an old trick taught to her by Bill Share back at the *Sentinel* and feigned genuine ignorance—as though she were hearing of the jacket for the first time—and pined for further details. She empowered Rita as narrator. "Well, you see he had to wash a lot of blood off of it," Rita volleyed back.

"Whose blood," Linda countered. Rita didn't know because Ezra hadn't asked; all he knew was that it was blood spilled *after* the war.

"I didn't think rabbits would shed that much blood," Rita quipped. Linda considered a response she kept to herself. They don't.

The Julie Murders

Back in Madison that same April, the history of things past would also reveal itself with an early spring thaw. Just over two years to the day after she was last seen walking along Johnson Street in East Madison, the question of where Julie Speerschneider went after vanishing into the black of that cold March night was answered by a teenaged boy named Charles Byrd. While hiking through the brush along the banks of the Yahara River in the nearby township of Dunn, a river that forms part of the majestic Mississippi's expansive watershed, Byrd happened upon a skeleton concealed beneath some decaying leaves and brush. It was becoming a tragically familiar tale in rural Wisconsin going back to the Debbie Bennett case. Someone minding his own business soon found himself hurled headlong into the inner workings of yet-another murder mystery, the unwitting discoverer and unlikely witness to a ghastly and enduring scene. By sundown on April 18, 1981, as Dane County Sheriff's deputies arrived to tape off and guard the scene until first light the following morning, the question of what had happened to Julie Speerschneider was finally answered, and the lore of the Capital City Killer took on a new dimension. Within hours, the existing narrative was already being supplemented by a new sound bite—what the cops themselves were already calling the "Julie Murders."

The murders were conjoined by a common name and victimology, as well as a number of similarities with respect to MO, including being driven and dumped just under thirty minutes from Madison but both still in Dane County—Hall to the north in Vienna Township, Speerschneider to the south in Dunn Township. The deaths of the two Julies, as the latest succession of Mad City sex slayings, made it clear that, whether or not a single serial killer dating back to the spring of '68 was fact or fiction, the city was in the throes of a gathering storm. Most drew the conclusion that the latest victim at the very least suggested that the last two cases, the Julie Murders, were the work of a single culprit—a mobile and motivated killer relying on a very specific body disposal pathway. Found by Byrd positioned in a prone, or facedown, position the body was devoid of clothing, jewelry, or any other belongings save an elastic band found entangled in what remained of the hair that was still intact on the skull. Presumed to have been dead for the full two years since her disappearance, the timeline was in part established through the presence of adipocere on the skeleton. A grayish and gruesome waxlike coating, adipocere can be used to help forensically determine the season in which the decaying process began, with cool and damp conditions at the time of disposal typically leading to the presence of adipocere and some living tissue remaining intact—including scalp hair. Beyond this one item overlooked by the killer, the postmortem movement of the body not only mirrored the circumstances of Julie Ann Hall's murder, but more specifically a specific breed of organized offender.

An *organized offender*—versus a *disorganized offender*—is one who puts tremendous planning into his crimes and has access to resources that often elude the disorganized offender. Both of the Julie murders reflected sexual motivations and, despite the absence of a cause of death or a confirmed sexual assault, disposal of a naked corpse is by definition a sexual homicide, especially since the kidnapping, murder, and concealment of a young female stranger or acquaintance in such circumstances has no other cogent motive. Another one of the principal differences between organized and disorganized killers is that the former owns or has access to a vehicle, a fundamental game changer that opens a realm of possibilities in terms of crime-scene behavior and transportation of a victim, whether dead or alive. No place to where a body is moved is therefore ever random, as traveling with a victim onboard a vehicle, dead or alive, is a rare and risky enough behavior in its own right.

An organized offender, before doing this, will typically know precisely where he is going before the journey begins, the killer having visited the dump site location on more than a few occasions. He will know it and know it *well*. That includes knowledge that the likelihood of being interrupted in the middle of the night while carrying, dragging, posing, and otherwise concealing a body there is remote. The killer will also have an excuse at the ready for being at the site on the off chance someone may be a witness prior to disposing of the body, or being stopped and questioned by police en route. That ready excuse will come easily because of some prior lawful use of the property, and it will provide a feigned purpose for returning there once again. It's but one of countless well-rehearsed cover stories organized sexual murderers are accustomed to telling. The place ultimately chosen to dispose of the victim inevitably is somewhere previously visited while wearing the mask of normalcy between crimes.

Organized sexual murderers who go to the trouble of stripping a body of clothing, jewelry, and all personal effects are also not doing so strictly to interfere with the identification of the body. If that were the sole intention, then it should follow that these offenders would also remove the teeth to prevent dental identification or the hands to prevent fingerprint identification in the event the body was found before fully decomposing. Instead, rendering the body naked, whether during or after the murder, is more expressive than it is instrumental; it is an expression of the same abhorrent and violent sexual fantasies—attack paraphilias—that fueled the offender's actions in the first place. The removal of earrings and other discrete personal items is similarly paraphilic. It is a reflection of a bizarre and often violent erotic attachment to unusual objects or scenarios that prompts an offender to keep souvenirs of his crimes.

The collection of homicidal keepsakes, for instance, just like the sexually degrading disposal of the body itself, satisfies the offender's disordered visual compulsions, the disposal site itself often having some fantasy-driven purpose in a larger narrative the killer may have envisioned. In fact, an emerging area of study that sits at the crossroads of criminology and forensic psychology is what's known as the *narrative theory* of offending. Based on a long-term analysis of the transcripts and hand-drawn maps or other sketches created by violent offenders as they mentally re-create and then retell their crimes suggests that all violent criminals—including sexual murderers—are actually reducible to four distinct storytelling and artistic typologies.

These same typologies reflect the very specific ways these offenders see their victims as characters in an ongoing life story—their crimes the action of that story. This narrative impulse among criminals includes the "revenger" type, an offender who sees his or her crimes as striking back at an unjust society; the "professional" type, an offender who sees his or her crimes as part of a larger vocation and a calling; and, the "tragedian" type, a self-aware antihero—like Othello or Hamlet in Shakespeare's tragedies—who sees future events, including his eventual downfall, as preordained, and who in the meantime is compelled to make the world burn. By contrast, the fourth type, the "hero," sees his crimes, however brutal, as an adventure and rationalizes their actions as part of a righteous journey—a cowboy's ride into indulgence. For the hero in particular, locations aren't therefore just spots on a map. They are stages for action and mechanisms for theatricality, for self-aggrandizement—pure show business. And like all such locations, they are first scouted.

These locations also often have some other intrinsic—and often historical or symbolic—value for the killer. Sometimes it's a mix of both. As an example, Gary Ridgway, the so-called Green River Killer already mentioned, chose disposal sites for the naked corpses of his victims, both secluded and also accessible to him. These sites would be near landmarks that, on foot and with a flashlight, his car parked nearby, he could return to in order to gaze upon the decaying remains of his innocent victims. At times, retracing his steps and returning to these same spots to admire his work led to such intense excitement and arousal he would actually fornicate with and further sexually defile the corpses where they lay in the woods. On at least one occasion, this occurred while Ridgway's children waited back in the family car idling on a county road. Just as organized offenders have a believable story when either driving to or stopped at the disposal site—a story that, among serial killers in particular, itself forms part of the larger "hero" narrative—Ridgway had a similar believable cover story to explain to his children why he was stopping, why he was venturing into the woods by himself.

Synchronicity

The Julie Speerschneider dump site matched the Julie Ann Hall murder in more than a few ways. The subsequent homicide investigation that finally lurched to a start also had many of the same cast of characters, including Dane County Coroner Clyde Chamberlain, now known as "Bud" Chamberlain in the press as his media profile continued to grow. It also featured some newcomers and other bit players to add to the ballooning cast of police detectives who, in the ever-expanding rotation of city, county, and state investigators being yo-yoed ad hoc in and out of the investigations, came to symbolize what psychologists call the *diffusion of responsibility*. At its simplest, the diffusion of responsibility describes how too many cooks in the kitchen not only translate into predictable redundancy, but also a natural unwillingness to take personal responsibility for actions and their consequences when there are others present to hide behind—others to whom blame can be deflected.

Sometimes taking the form of what's known as the *bystander effect*, the phenomenon of diffused responsibility remains most infamously illustrated with the case of Kitty Genovese, a New York City woman attacked and murdered outside her Queens apartment by a sexual sadist and necrophile named Winston Moseley in March of '64. While being chased down in the street like an animal and stabbed to death at random, Genovese cried out for help in a densely packed neighborhood where it's estimated that thirty-seven of the thirty-eight witnesses sat and watched without intervening or calling police—each one of them expecting, and wrongfully assuming, that someone else would. In the meantime, her attacker returned and finished her off while neighbors are reported to have simply stood and watched like an assembly of slack-jawed gawkers.

While today some researchers, contesting the actual number of bystanders who failed to act, have suggested that newspapers of the day may have overestimated—or outright exaggerated—the total number of witnesses, Genovese's murder endures as a criminological parable that strength in numbers, rather than producing responsible action, often results in the opposite—inaction characterized by an assumption that someone else will take care of it. The consortium of the Madison area police agencies once again drawn into an inconvenient alliance by virtue of the multijurisdictional nature of this latest murder opted to take a different approach. Inaction was replaced by blaming the victim.

Speerschneider had been holding down two jobs, paid her apartment rent on time, and was generally described as a "really nice person" according to the newspapers of the day. But the police spin on the Speerschneider killing was one that framed it as a one-off slaying in spite of the specificity of the offender's behavior and disposal pathway matching the murder of Julie Ann Hall. The official version was that it was personally rather than sexually motivated, not random as the previous Julie murder had been. Although there was no evidence to support the hypothesis, and Speerschneider had no criminal record—she was, after all, cleared to work as a day-care attendant—the police reverse engineered a drug-world narrative to contextualize the whole affair. In an interview later granted to reporter George Hesselberg with the *Wisconsin State Journal*, the latest "lead investigator" and public face of the most recent Madison murder, Dane County Sheriff's Investigator Steve Urso, would only describe the case as the antithesis of black and white. It was a cipher intended to suggest that Speerschneider somehow had a role to play in her own death, the operating theory being that drugs were somehow involved. Contrary to outward appearances, because Julie Speerschneider, it was hinted, was somehow embedded in the Madison criminal subculture, there was "a lot of gray" coming up in the investigation. Carrying on, he clarified that when "you get into the drug area, it turns into double-gray." Urso never properly explained these tortured metaphors, including why the case was shaded in "double-gray," whatever that meant.

The "double-gray" declaration in the press was, however, used to bend the narrative, used to militate against any further talk of the Speerschneider murder being another slaying attributable to the Capital City Killer.

Regular Madisonians need not worry, so it was inferred, because the case, rather than being random, was the inevitable result of what happens when one gets into bed—either literally or figuratively—with the wrong people. With the police grasping at straws, the statement was little more than propaganda, what's known as the propaganda of integration—versus agitation—and where the objective is to restore social harmony and blind faith in the status quo. The Julie Speerschneider case was used as a Mad City moral lesson about not only the dangers of hitchhiking but also a "this is your brain on drugs" allegory years before the same antinarcotic PSA became what was arguably America's original meme. Since one cannot libel a dead person, Dane County cops effectively had carte blanche in terms of proffering theories and pontificating at length, of dispensing guesses about the hows and whys of Julie meeting her killer—how she may have somehow even invited it. This was, sadly enough, a strategy for shifting blame in a number of stalled sex crime and homicide investigations involving female victims of the day. But, just in case readers didn't buy the unfounded and accusatory explanation as to why the police were awash in a field of gray, the investigation cold before it started, there was backup Plan B locked and loaded—maybe the Speerschneider girl wasn't murdered at all.

In the same interview with the *Journal*, Urso—despite having lamented about investigators being mired in "double-gray"—also saw fit to challenge the official findings of the senior and widely respected pathologist who oversaw the autopsy, a Dr. Billy Bauman, who officially reported that Speerschneider's death evinced "high suspicions of homicide." Despite the fact that he was unable to say with certainty how exactly she died—manual strangulation being a *contributing* cause of death in over 90 percent of sexual homicides typically not leaving obvious evidence on skeletal remains—Dr. Bauman's findings were based as much on common sense as forensic medicine.

Julie's body had been found naked, stripped of all personal effects, and buried beneath dead foliage along a riverbank some fourteen miles from the Madison city limits. Julie, who didn't own a car, had for all intents and purposes never been to the site as best anyone who knew her could estimate. Since she had last been seen with a still-unidentified male only a hundred paces from her intended destination, other than homicide, there was simply no other logical inference to draw. As the newspaper reported, Urso, so incensed by this expert conclusion that managed to pull on the threads of the tattered story the police were spinning, smashed his fist into a pile of typewritten statements and carbons relating to the case while exclaiming "they can't say that" to the bemused newspaper reporter running the interview. The "they" in this case was, of course, the senior pathologist at the state crime lab whom the police relied on every day. While some were pairing the Hall-Speerschneider slayings and calling them the Julie Murders, others, it seemed, were prepared to pretend at least one of them never happened. In short order, it already seemed to be "*Julie who?*" within the ranks of the city and state homicide units.

Sadly, Julie Speerschneider, her slaying little more than a pawn for police politicos and her death manipulated to suit a certain city agenda and contain a burgeoning multiple murder panic, was neither the first nor the last time a victim—usually a woman—has been inferentially held to account for her own murder. Known as *victim facilitation*, it's a concept attributed to Yale victimologist Hans von Hentig and his foundational 1948 treatise *The Criminal and His Victim*. The book built upon Hentig's research in Weimar, Germany, where, prior to the rise of the Nazi party, collaboration between police agencies and the intelligentsia—academic experts specializing in the evolving field of criminal psychology—was in its heyday. In his monograph, Hentig devised a comprehensive taxonomy of thirteen common victim types that he felt reflected biological, socioeconomic, and psychological circumstances contributing to victim facilitation, and the degree to which a victim's own actions might contribute to his or her victimization being measured as either low, medium, or high in nature. A few of these categories, such as "The Wanton" (someone often involved in criminal activity and an inveterate stimulation seeker and risk taker) and "The Tormentor" (someone who seeks out conflict and ends up going from would-be victimizer to victim) fit within what we might consider as being the realm of high facilitation.

Hentig's purpose in designing this table was not to indulge in victim blaming but to instead account for offender motivations in targeting specific typologies of victims. Over the years, however, a trend has emerged—one spearheaded and perpetuated largely by people who have never heard of, much less read, Hentig's work—to equate certain victims or categories of victims with high facilitation as a matter of course. In certain communities in America, simply suggesting that a victim might have dabbled in recreational drugs is enough to move them from one category (such as Hentig's "Woman" category) to a typology such as "The Wanton," often triggering a reduced inclination to work the case. The tacit implication that the victim is somehow less worthy of an all-out effort compared to other more conventionally "innocent" victims soon seeps into collective thinking and takes on a level of official acceptance. Even today, depending on which zip code a genuine, low-facilitation murder victim finds himself or herself in, this trend remains disturbingly prevalent.

The X-Factor

By the time Julie Speerschneider's skeletal remains were discovered along the banks of the Yahara River—coated in adipocere, an impromptu surface burial—Wisconsin police were fresh out of options. The decision to throw the young day-care worker's memory under the bus and brand her as a druggie and down-and-outer whose luck with shady men and hitchhiking had predictably run out was nothing if not shortsighted. It may also be a reflection of just how desperate the cops had become. Intuitively knowing there would be more victims to follow, it seems that police had launched a spring counteroffensive with casualties unfortunately needing to be the victims themselves—those victims followed in short order by the truth as yet another casualty. It's an understudied variable in homicide investigations that might be called the X Factor—that human factor that can override the best intentions, investigative techniques, and forensic technologies. Not so much human error, in fact, as much as human meddling and malevolence—self-serving sabotage.

The last few years had seen a spate of disappearances later determined to be homicides after remains were located. Following the discovery of Julie Speerschneider's remains in 1981, there were still more abduction murders to come as Madison continued to face a tidal wave of violence.

Worse still, the consortium of police agencies loosely joined together had nothing in the way of leads. The Debbie Bennett Intra County Investigative Squad was played out and the Julie Ann Hall investigation, if one could call it that, had ground to a halt. Then of course there was the subtext of a Mad City ripper making a mockery of local law enforcement by snatching girls in the city and dumping them out in the counties to buy time and space. Incredibly, at least by today's standards, the police got off easy in terms of public pressure until the Speerschneider discovery—the initial revelation of the so-called Julie murders.

What no one bothered to examine amid the rewriting of Speerschneider's biography, and then later branding her as a drug player, was the number of salient linkages in terms of MO and even signature between the Julie murders. The contrast between the slaying and disposal of Debbie Bennett, quite clearly immersed in the Madison drug culture, managing to garner a full-blown task force, and the Julie Speerschneider murder, relegated to a listless and perfunctory investigation, spoke to a certain fatigue that consumed the same triad of agencies which, since Christine Rothschild, had inherited Madison's unsolved homicides whether in whole or in part. It also spoke to the arbitrariness with which murders are investigated, including by whom and for how long, based on variables ranging from internal promotions and transfer needs within a police agency to factors as academic as to when a murder occurs within a department's fiscal cycle.

The truth is that if the general public knew just how many murders are solved due to luck or silly mistakes and oversights made by offenders with respect to leaving physical evidence or not keeping their mouths shut—versus crackerjack sleuthing the way it's done on TV—people generally would be horrified and never leave their homes. Here's a hint: in some of the largest US cities, the homicide clearance rate hovers under 40 percent—even lower in the case of random murders, closer to 20 percent, or one in five. Some notable outliers, as confirmed by the Murder Accountability Project, are even lower than 10 percent. In fact, there have been more Americans killed in still-unsolved murders in the last thirty years than the combined total of all US military personnel killed in all global armed conflicts since World War II.

Curiously there are also fewer murders solved per capita in America today than there were in 1965, an era before DNA, before sophisticated ballistics and blood-spatter testing, before sex-offender registries, monitoring bracelets, and watch lists, before other investigative advantages that detectives have today. Equally, although there are fewer murders across America today than in previous generations, fewer of these fewer cases are being solved, thus leaving more killers than ever to remain at large. The question is why. One theory is that the conveniences enjoyed by police today have dulled investigative intuition and old-school instincts upon which cops once relied. It has been suggested that, when a case yields no DNA evidence or other offender clues to be plugged into databases or submitted for standardized testing, modern police are often quickly out of their depth.

The second theory is more frightening. It suggests that, while the number of domestic and intimate partner murders has been decreasing in recent generations through improved social services and intervention techniques—in fact, the US murder rate as a whole has been decreasing steadily over the last thirty years—the number of stranger-on-stranger murders has actually been increasing. Historically speaking, domestic murders pointed to clear and obvious suspects and motives, suspects frequently being collared by uniformed first responders at the scene. On the other hand, murders with no obvious suspects and no apparent motive—whether random, personal, or sexual in nature—are essentially impossible to solve absent some lucky break such as a tip from the public or a deathbed confession. A single random-stranger crime is essentially a needle in a haystack. In the case of a serial killer, new individuating details are often revealed with each new case until linkages can be made after a comfortable and emboldened killer eventually cuts corners and makes a sloppy mistake that puts the police on to him or her.

But there is also a third and more controversial theory that tries to explain why America's unsolved murder rate is climbing while violent crime and the total number of murders are actually going down—the X-Factor. It describes the unforeseen human variable that is less about a lack of investigative smarts as it is the deactivation or otherwise purposeful derailment of investigations to suit the objectives of those occupying middle and senior management positions. These are, for the most part, the decision makers and pencil pushers who often have little involvement in day-to-day investigative work and who essentially occupy bureaucratic roles—the puppet masters. In the business world, this myopic and often toxic management style has little regard for what effect these decisions have on the morale and lives of subordinates and other stakeholders. Such decision makers have even been called corporate psychopaths—people whose insatiable need for admiration and penchant for grandiosity is a veiled form of the same sadistic behavior exhibited by criminal offenders in the outside world. In fact, some variations of the corporate psychopath have been found to score on par with convicted sexual murderers in the standardized forty-point Psychopath Checklist Revised (PCL-R) test that has for the last several decades, despite some controversy, been the gold standard for evaluating offenders in both clinical and forensic environments.

Recognizing the damage done by psychopaths who manage to infiltrate the workplace (positions such as CEO, lawyer, surgeon, television personality, and police officer being among the most overrepresented of jobs), many progressive organizations have implemented their own test to screen for psychopathic indicators during the hiring process. Because no such testing yet exists in law enforcement beyond some rudimentary—and easily defeated—psychometric true-false evaluations completed at the time of initial hire, there is by comparison no way to measure or account for such psychopathic tendencies in the police workplace that might eventually be exhibited by senior managers. As the proverbial elephant in the room, the role of psychopathic behavior in police case-management practices—an investigative X-Factor that no one seems prepared to confront or address—remains the most plausible explanation for how and why such egregiously outrageous decisions are often made regarding unsolved homicides. It might also explain the reluctance or outright refusal to revisit what appear to be wrongful convictions. This sometimes means willfully ignoring new developments and exculpatory evidence, the infamous cases of the "Central Park Five" and "West Memphis Three" being but two examples that still resonate widely with the American public. Leaders in law enforcement in such cases are effectively prepared, it seems time and again, to ignore or betray their oaths in name of empire building—tin-pot tyrants.

In the case of the Julie murders, apart from the mishandling of the other Mad City sex slayings that came before and after and the influx of tips provided by Linda as she pursued Jorgensen, the X-Factor looms large as the most plausible explanation for how the dual investigation went so wrong. It remains, in fact, the only explanation for linkages between the Julie cases being so summarily denied, the pathologist's ruling of suspected homicide in the Speerschneider case being questioned, and the maligning of the victim in the local and state press by police. It's also the only explanation for the apparent refusal or failure to recognize the identical surface burials, transportation distance and vector, the specificity and limited access to disposal sites, the stripping of the bodies and collection of souvenirs, and the indeterminate cause of death—manual strangulation or suffocation implied in both cases.

After factoring in the similarities in victimology—age, appearance, last seen at or leaving a bar near UW—there is simply nothing in law, current criminal investigative analysis methodologies, or old-fashioned detective work to justify the way the Julie murders were handled, particularly the Speerschneider case. Someone, for reasons we may never know, perhaps pride, perhaps a "my way or the highway" management style, stood in the way of these cases being properly linked or investigated. Although the discovery of Speerschneider's body should have been an appropriate time to raise the alarm, the opportunity was missed given the way the Julie murders were characterized as being unrelated. Even if the Capital City Killer legend of years past was fiction, these last two cases at least had some striking similarities. It was not inappropriate to at least consider that a serial killer may have been at work. The Madison powers that be pulled the oxygen out of any such talk by taking the stance they did, effectively failing the Julies—and the whole of Madison.

Just over ten years after the recovery of Julie Speerschneider's body, all documents relating to her investigation were also destroyed. On whose orders, no one ever could determine, and we will also likely never know. What is clear is that, by then, whoever was behind the curtain, pulling the strings on the Julie murders, certainly would have had reason to worry, to cover his tracks. As early as that summer—July of '81—the cavalier manner in which the Julie murders had been dismissed by area police would reveal itself as a mistake with another grisly find in the offing.

Ghost Camp

Out in the hinterland of Dane County, in a densely wooded area near the town of Westport, four archeology students from UW made their way into the woods on the muggy afternoon of July 16, 1981, a Thursday, in order to map new territory for a proposed nature preserve in the tradition of the university arboretum. Lake-effect humidity moving in from the majestic nearby Mendota made the trip through the region, plunked squarely within the Madison census metropolitan area, more arduous than expected as the foursome lugging cumbersome surveying equipment and paper maps made their way to Camp Indianola just south of what locals knew to be the old Reynolds farm. The farm, owned by local Westport resident Henry Reynolds, had become the de facto landmark in the area since the summer of '67 when Camp Indianola was leveled by a late-season tornado that killed two women living nearby. The camp had just let out for the summer, saving hundreds of potential child victims who had vacated the grounds the day prior, but the owners never recovered. The camp, first run by a UW psychology professor named Frederick Mueller, never reopened. By the summer of '71 it was a veritable ghost town peppered with the remains of summer memories—the detritus of the wooden lodgings and outbuildings that had once stood there. It was a lost summer camp in much the same way that Lake Forest had become Madison's forsaken city.

The private boys' summer camp, first opened in 1910, had seen some notable Wisconsin and other Midwestern residents pass through the gates over its fifty-seven-year history, particularly after the operators started placing an increased focus on theatrical productions and dramatics ahead of athletics. These included famed Hollywood actor, director, and venerable luminary Orson Welles, later followed by National Public Radio fixture Scott Simon, and others. That's not to say that all time at Indianola was devoted strictly to the arts. In fact, another one of the camp's defining features was its "Gypsy Trip," a five-mile expedition that required campers to obtain detailed cartographic knowledge of every hidden nook and cranny, every isolated county road and waterway in the area—a combination of bird's-eye reconnaissance and Boy Scout grit. Campers were also required to swim five miles across Lake Mendota and understand its current, and learn how to follow and respect the force of the Yahara River. Whoever abducted and killed Julie Ann Hall, Susan LeMahieu, and Julie Speerschneider also had an encyclopedic knowledge of the greater Madison countryside and most of its wooded areas. He knew and respected the Yahara—he was following its path. He also knew the Lost City, maybe as a lovers' lane voyeur, maybe as an adventurer who'd scouted it more than once. As the hapless survey team dispatched by UW would soon discover, he also knew Camp Indianola.

The decaying old boathouse at the abandoned Camp Indianola borders the spot on the map where, in July of 1981, the body of Shirley Stewart was discovered by UW archeology students in the nearby woods. Courtesy: Wisconsin Historical Society.

Just prior to 4:00 p.m. on the sixteenth, the archeology majors happened upon what appeared to be an addendum to the Julie murders—the decomposed remains of missing seventeen-year-old Shirley Stewart. The native of Middleton, a Madison suburb, had been placed by her killer in an identical fashion to that of other recent victims. Covered in deadfall only a little over fifty feet into the woods and off the trail, Stewart's skeletonized remains were still relatively well intact considering the wildlife and scavengers that roamed freely in the area. The maid uniform she was last seen wearing at the Dean Clinic the night she vanished was, however, found nowhere near the body. As with the others before her, all of Shirley's clothing, jewelry, and personal items had been plucked from the corpse at some point prior to the killer leaving her naked and supine on the forest floor near a set of old summer camp storage buildings. As with the other deaths, Phil Little, the coroner replacing "Bud" Chamberlain, revealed that no cause of death could be firmly established. Again, as with the last three deaths, the state of the skeleton seemed to rule out severe trauma, such as a gunshot or bludgeoning. The inference then, as it is now, was that the murder amounted to another choke job on a random stranger—a sexual homicide.

Given that all estimates pointed to Shirley being at the site since the night she vanished or shortly thereafter, the arithmetic was simple. Her death brought the total number of victims to four, found in similar ways, in Madison between May 1, 1978, and January 2, 1980—less than two years. Four women ranging in age from seventeen to twenty-four had been snatched off the street, murdered, and dumped naked in remote locations no further than thirty minutes from the city center and in locations strategically selected for their isolation—not to mention their apparent expressive value. All victims had been stripped of all clothing and all jewelry save the lone ring left on LeMahieu, the elastic hair band seemingly overlooked in the Speerschneider murder, and a Timex watch—later ordered destroyed—discovered near Stewart's body. All the women had been covered in deadfall in carefully executed surface burials, and all had been strangled or suffocated in some capacity based on the available evidence. Whether sexually assaulted or not, the motive in every case had been explicitly sexual, and the offender's signature remained constant with all four victims. Although the Capital City Killer might have started as a concoction of the lunatic fringe, this latest volley of murders—every murder after Debbie Bennett—seems to have made it a reality.

As Linda followed the trail of Jorgensen—the city's first serial killer of the era—on one side of the country, it appeared that another one had made his way to the Mad City just as Jorgensen had once done. Maybe it was the legend itself that had drawn him. Or maybe, unlike Jorgensen, he was an existing local who had been created by the city itself—the harvest of what the previous two decades had sown. Maybe he was once a small boy with incipient perversions and violent predications who had been sent to summer camp at Indianola to get straightened out. Maybe that's exactly where he ended up cutting his teeth.

Repudiated

The reality is that the center block of murders to plague the Mad City during its thirty-year reign in sexual violence—the Julie murders plus the LeMahieu and Stewart slayings—overwhelmingly point to the work of a single offender. It's the legacy of a serial killer, one born from a legend the police sought to hide from rather than repudiate, one who disappeared as quickly as he materialized. By the time he'd come and was gone again, like Jorgensen before him, other lone wolves would follow in his wake and target Madison's young, most vulnerable, and most easily forgotten. It's a story of a serial killer whose crimes filled the middle innings of one city's sordid but suppressed criminal past and, as a consequence, it's a story without an ending. The killer—the heir apparent to a local legend that started soon after Camp Indianola was shuttered—will in turn most likely never be caught. Assuming he's still alive, absent a corroborative confession, there is simply nothing left from these cases to test using modern scientific techniques save one—what's known as *geographic profiling*.

Owing its origin largely to the pioneering work of senior Canadian police detective D. Kim Rossmo's PhD dissertation, geographic profiling employs a series of calculations based on what's known as the "buffer distance" between known crime scenes, including body disposal sites, attack locations, areas where evidence is recovered, or simply an estimated location where offender-victim contact was first initiated. Based on the calculated buffer distance, a pattern in an offender's movements can be inferred by relying on the assumption that, especially in the case of murder, the killer comes and goes from a regular home base, usually his primary residence. The more of these confirmed locations the police have to work with, the more accurate the ensuing calculations and the more precise the estimated "hot zone"—the most probable area where the offender's home base is located—with the operant theory being that serial offenders in particular will tend to follow repetitive patterns in their behavior. While the MO and disposal sites may change between crimes, the primary and secondary crime scenes will, when examined in aggregate, eventually begin to paint a picture of how the killer navigates his space and exploits his physical environment in selecting attack and disposal locations. The proprietary program designed by Rossmo for this purpose, known as RIGEL, has been employed successfully in a number of high-profile serial crimes, as have variations of RIGEL relying on the same mathematical principles. These cases include, most notably, when geographic profiling was used to zero in on the home base of a serial rapist named Randy Comeaux in Lafayette, Louisiana.

By 1995, Comeaux had snuck into the homes of at least seven women in a middle-class Lafayette neighborhood after beginning his spate of home invasions in 1982. Using a flashlight to blind his victims, he ambushed them while they were asleep. Comeaux would then sexually assault and torment the women before forcing them to shower and later giving them a bizarre fatherly lecture on the security oversights of their homes that had been their Achilles' heel—how they had essentially allowed him to break in and brutalize them through their own negligence. Once the attacks were definitively confirmed as connected to a common serial rapist, the task force investigating the crimes was nonetheless disbanded in 1998 after coming up dry.

Then, an article on Rossmo's innovative and—unlike conventional behavioral profiling—scientifically rigorous geoprofiling method was seen by a senior detective in the pages of *The Police Chief* magazine. In a last-ditch effort, the Louisiana cops contacted Rossmo and a profile using his formula was developed and indicated that the hot zone was in fact immediately next to the neighborhood where the attacks had clustered over the thirteen-year period in question. Later, Randy Comeaux—actually a police officer with the Lafayette PD who previously had inside information on the task force's activities—was revealed to be the elusive serial rapist. It was also revealed that he lived in the mean center of the hot zone. It was the first of several big wins and validations for geoprofiling and the RIGEL program, one that has been used in cases of serial murder, serial rape, and serial arson—all compulsively sexual crimes that will bear out common denominators in attack-retreat patterns.

The method has, since Comeaux's arrest in January of '99, seen generous fictionalized treatments in some prime-time cop shows, most accurately in the FX series *The Shield*, but is otherwise strangely still very much in a beta stage. It's a system that has been woefully underutilized by law enforcement, and for no justifiable reason. Somewhere between being confused by the applied mathematics and computer schematics, and being irrationally suspicious of outsourcing serial investigations to the handful of experts around the world who know how to apply the formula—Dr. Rossmo having rightfully since left policing for academia—geoprofiling remains curiously arcane in spite of its successes. Many police managers also, in fairness, simply don't know it exists and that it's a logical next step in cold cases when looking to narrow the size of the haystack. They should.

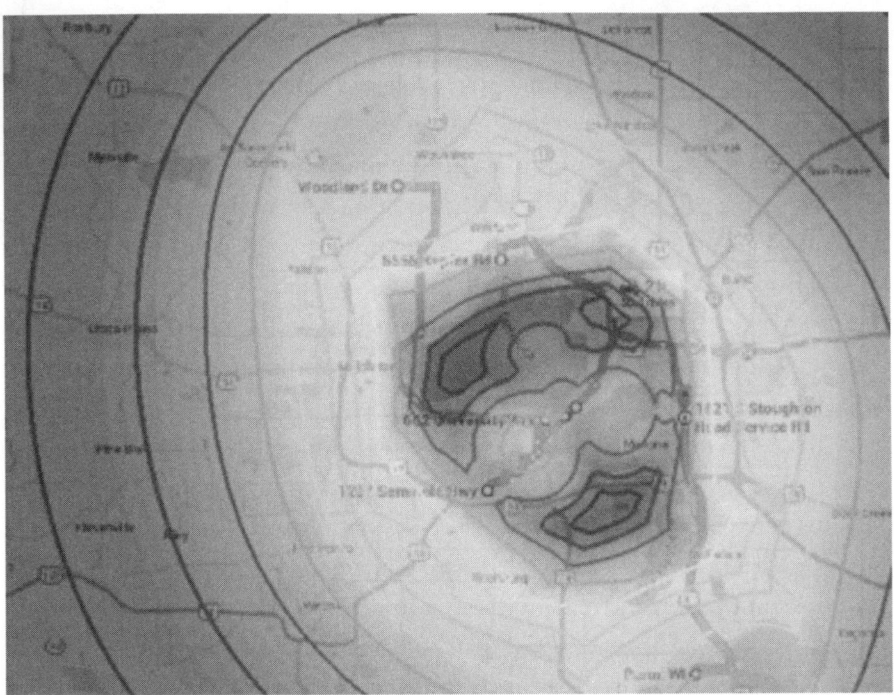

A geographic profile, applying Dr. Rossmo's formula and using a variation on RIGEL, indicates that the four connected Madison sex slayings were all committed by a killer living within this darkest region at the city's center and circumscribing both Lake Mendota and the UW campus. It's a narrow circular band that simultaneously points most strongly to the nearby community of Five Points and also to the village of Windsor, both exurbs of Madison. One or both areas reflect the most probable "home base" of a single killer over the course of the murders, factoring in both the abduction sites and disposal sites as the data points. The combined male populations between both locations would, in 1981, have numbered fewer than three thousand. Courtesy: Western University Cold Case Society & Peter Leimbigler at the University of Toronto.

In the case of the Julie murders plus LeMahieu and Stewart as part of an apparent set of four linked sexual murders in the Mad City, applying Rossmo's geoprofiling formula to the total of eight confirmed locations reflecting known or suspected contact points and disposal sites, a clear picture of the killer's probable home base—the so-called "hot zone"—comes into focus for the first time in decades.

Beyond the retroactive use of geographic profiling, however, the reality is that the way these crime scenes can today be digitally plotted on a map—antiseptically clean, precise, conscientious—doesn't reflect the reality of how they were found or processed. Between the mishandling of evidence and the fact that the killer took all of these girls' immediate possessions before dumping them in the wilderness—items that today might hold valuable and perishable DNA evidence—there is little else to work with. Years ahead of the Human Genome Project that ultimately led to the establishment of databases such as the Combined DNA Index System (CODIS) and allowed for offender-crime scene cross-referencing, the killer who operated in Madison between the spring of '78 and early winter of '80 had dotted his *I*s and crossed his *T*s. He put enough time and distance between himself and his victims to ensure, by the time they revealed themselves to shocked passers-by, that there would no trace of him or what he had done to his victims. In the unlikely event that he might have missed something, the Dane County Sheriff's Office or UWPD might have helped him out.

Eventually, the key exhibits from these cases: the umbrella and handkerchief in Christine Rothschild's murder, the hair elastic in the Speerschneider murder, the ring mysteriously left on LeMahieu's body, the watch at the Stewart scene at Camp Indianola—any and all related documents and photographs—were either lost or, more likely, destroyed. Although the sheriff and the campus cops blamed each other, it was all just a grand punctuation mark in a game of duck and run. Indeed, by the time Shirley Stewart's skeleton turned up in the summer camp forest near Westport and a fourth victim now matched the victimology, MO, disposal pathway, *and* the specific signature of the last three women—the full disrobing of the corpse and collecting of jewelry, watches, and other items as souvenirs—the police had a new slant. An unnamed police source sought to distinguish the Stewart case from the others because she had no association with downtown Madison. Seemingly no longer speaking directly to the media for attribution purposes, a colossal failure of leadership in its own right, the four police agencies involved instead deferred to the Dane County deputy coroner, a man who, unlike Bud Chamberlain, Phil Little, or other senior medical experts they couldn't control, seemed prepared to read lines. The spin, it turns out, was no spin. And so entered Don Scullion, a knuckleballer pulled up from the minors and used as a closer for the county, state, and both city and university police departments. He'd been tested with the earlier discovery of Susan LeMahieu when he pussyfooted around the whole find, coyly stating that they would "rule out" its possibly being a murder. They would rule out a delayed twenty-four-year-old who'd never left the city by herself to have ended up naked in the dense underbrush of an abandoned forest subdivision half an hour from town, in the dead of winter, as being suspicious. True to form, amid an ongoing police blackout, the press kowtowed for the scraps they were tossed—wartime rations.

In light of recent events, including Urso's official take on Speerschneider's case, the discovery of Shirley Stewart's remains under similar circumstances indeed meant that the whole "double-gray" nonsense failed the smell test once and for all. No police investigator was at that point prepared to stand in front of a bank of news mics or even meet with a reporter on the QT to float theories until the task force had some better idea of who or what they were dealing with. Scullion, with no specific police or investigative qualifications, seemed to be providing his own guesswork, suggesting a lack of linkage because Shirley Stewart was neither kidnapped from, nor known to hang out near, either downtown Madison or the UW campus. With that, the state of Wisconsin officially stepped back in time almost fifty years in terms of understanding victimology. As Hans von Hentig spun in his grave like a lathe, once that same theory made it above the fold in the July 18, 1981, edition of the *Journal*, the killer of those four young girls officially got away with it—with *all* of it.

By the end of 1981, the Madison PD and their consorts with county, state, and UW campus, having been variously involved in all of the murders going back to Rothschild, had a conflicted relationship with the idea of a serial killer being good for all of the Mad City's mayhem—being single-handedly responsible for now six unsolved sex murders in just thirteen years. The fear and loathing in the city, in Dane County, and outward across the expanses of the whole state of Wisconsin posed both a problem and solution. Police leaders, normally gluttons for face time on the evening news, were indefinitely avoiding the press like the plague. To admit that the cases were connected would likely have left an already-concerned public outraged. Such a tacit admission of colossal failure, even by the amateur standards of the early '80s, would help sow the seeds for internal investigations, public inquiries, and possibly firings—lawsuits galore.

At the same time, to acknowledge that in at least the last four cases, the lore of the Capital City Killer might actually have some merit also meant, whether fact or fiction, that someone might one day be caught and all those cases solved in one fell swoop. It was a long shot that would first require backtracking on previous conjecture—the need to come to terms with the fact that police quite simply didn't understand victim patterns in the manner we do today. Although it wasn't necessarily their fault, while they were too busy not looking for clues, the killer of Hall, Speerschneider, LeMahieu, and Stewart seems to have moved on. But he wouldn't just stop. Like Jorgensen, he simply couldn't. What he more likely did was to pack up and move on. One possibility was that he was in prison on other unrelated charges. The more likely possibility was that he was in another city and county where he picked up where he had left off—perhaps even with a change of MO just subtle enough to ensure that the cases never became linked. Ahead of what the FBI, in later petitioning Congress in 1984, would describe as an "epidemic" of serial murder in the United States born of the larger rise in violent crime, whoever briefly and anonymously took ownership of the Capital City Killer title in Madison knew what police didn't about murder victims and MO.

Unlike signatures, which remain stable across crime scenes and reflect deranged visual schemes generally understood as originating with a certain form of childhood trauma known as the "vandalized love map," MOs can change as often as the weather. Every criminal offender has an MO, and it simply means that they have a customary or preferred method of carrying out their crimes. The difference between MOs and signatures was actually first noted in a serial robbery investigation—all bank jobs—back in the 1970s. Once the FBI finally took over the cases, it found that the bandit's MO changed with every crime. In some cases, he'd hit the vault at opening, other times the registers at closing. Sometimes he'd vault the counter; other times he'd also rob the other customers of their valuables. In one case, he'd produce a weapon, and in the other, a note. The differences were salient enough to ensure "linkage blindness" among the different police agencies that failed to recognize a common signature until the feds got involved and looked at the big picture nationally. In every case, regardless of MO, there was a common signature: the female tellers had to undress before he left the bank. The truth is that the robberies were never about the money. They were part of an elaborate and violent sexual fixation.

These same findings with respect to distinguishing MOs from signatures were later supported through interviews with Edmund Kemper, also known as the "Co-Ed Killer," a wannabe cop who picked up, murdered, and frequently decapitated hitchhiking college girls in northern California between 1972 and 1973. These crimes supplemented the murder of his mother and both grandparents in separate incidents, beginning as far back as 1964. He had managed to get away with his crimes for so long in part because his MO varied so widely, thus ensuring the same linkage blindness later seen in the Mad City. A *process-focused* (sadistic) killer at heart, Kemper preferred to strangle his victims if possible and prolong the rush of the kill while maximizing their pain and terror. If, however, things didn't go as planned and spiraled out of control when victims resisted, Kemper would then stab them as a matter of convenience, taking on a more *act-focused* (efficiency-based) method of operation. All the while, his necrophilic signature common to all of the murders—including taking body parts up to and including victims' heads he would later adorn with makeup—consistently went overlooked.

But in Madison, it seems that no one got that memo and no one thought to ask for the FBI's help. While Debbie Bennett's risk factors and violent fiery disposal pathway strongly suggest it was indeed a standalone event, the quick succession of events that included the bludgeoning of Julie Ann Hall, the strangulation of Julie Speerschneider, the suspected stabbing of Susan LeMahieu, and the apparent second strangulation of Shirley Stewart all showed minor changes in MO while having a common signature—the naked surface disposal at select or symbolic wooded locations and the accompanying collection of souvenirs. As these are among the rarest of accompanying actions seen in sexual murders in America, the evidence at the time should have screamed "serial" even to the untrained eye. The additional fluctuations in victim type—three victims from the downtown, one from the east side—that led the cops to kibosh the idea of a serial murder is in fact less of a distinction than is the fact that the girls had a relatively varied age range and drastic differences in appearance and lifestyle.

Despite that, just like a changing MO, subtle changes in victim type are equally par for the course. As Kemper and plenty of other serial offenders have demonstrated, every sexually motivated killer—especially an organized killer with a car with a near-endless number of spots to troll and later dispose of victims—has a preferred victim, or an archetype who fits an existing or developing fantasy image that has been festering for weeks, months, or even years. When, however, that same archetype—blonde or brunette, child or adult, male or female—can't be found or accessed, the need-motivated killer will move on to the next closest match. In Jorgensen's case, Annabel was the literary template for his preferred victim—a type of woman, Christine Rothschild included, who, it seemed, turned up dead or vanished any time Jorgensen passed through town during his dark wanders of America. However, a rare minority of particularly sadistic serial sex killers fit the bill of being what's known as *polymorphistic* in their victim selection, meaning that any gender, age, or body type will do in a pinch—typically for domination and torture. Like any person seeking a partner, they are quite simply prepared to settle on the closest reasonable facsimile to their "type." Everyone's settled at some point—or will. One would be a fool to think that sexual murderers aren't equally as flexible.

Looking back at the Mad City between 1977 and the start of 1980, it's still unclear which of the four girls most closely fit the killer's template as the preferred victim and which ones were deemed sufficient replacements. Replacements who, on a cold winter's night, were deemed "good enough" once his options were limited and the ability to control his impulses exhausted—the compensatory cooling-off period at a breaking point. The fact that three of the four victims were taken or first targeted in Madison's core and Shirley Stewart, unlike the others, was well outside the downtown area is purely academic. That's also maybe why no cop ever put his name to the theory that Shirley Stewart's murder and disposal at the ghost camp of Indianola was unrelated. The idea that her murder didn't fit with the others was a stretch—even then. It was ulterior motivated; it defied common sense; it stunk to high heaven. But as it turned out, nobody ever really questioned it. Policing in Madison and Dane County at the time was the new Flat Earth Society—the dark age of reason. Before long, that darkness would call to others. To the imitators.

Chapter 8

Gate 4

History, with her volumes vast, hath but one page.

—Lord George Gordon Byron, *Childe Harold's Pilgrimage*

Valentine Sally

It was February of '82 when Linda made her eighth full read of *The Love Pirate* from start to finish. It was onerous, the prose was tedious and boringly repetitive, but each new reading offered new and revelatory insights as she simultaneously cross-referenced events of the past against Jorgensen's suspected movements. The original manuscript—copy one of two—had been left abandoned on the fly back in Jorgensen's Madison apartment and recovered thanks to George Johnston in what already felt like a lifetime ago. In so doing, a number of entries returned Linda to the case of Donna Ann Lass, the Tahoe casino nurse whose body was never found. It seemed as if the tenuous connections made by Linda might actually have been intended by the story's author, Heidi Jorgensen. They amounted to low-hanging fruit that anyone who knew the details of Jorgensen's life and crimes could easily pluck from the vine. When Dr. Corcoran warns young Annabel that "any kind of intimacy with people arouses me in a nearly nauseated aversion," Heidi, it seems, was speaking to those who, like her as Jorgensen's mother, knew of the driving force behind her son's psychopathic disposition—his malignant narcissism and his apparent preference for the company of the dead. Like Dr. Corcoran, it was evident to the two women who knew Jorgensen and lived to tell about it—Linda and his mother Heidi—that only intimacy with the living led to this aversion. Jorgensen's bizarre fantasies were better met in the company of the dead and the collection of their modest belongings.

As Jorgensen regaled the Sierra Singles with his knowledge of the California-Nevada countryside nearby and impressed his friend and doting admirer Ezra Jameson with the adept swiftness and cruelty with which he killed small game not for food but for mischievous fun, Linda paused to ponder new themes. She ran scenarios; she had new questions; intrusive thoughts intruded; she had even more questions—she drove herself nearly mad. Why wasn't the body of the Lass girl ever found? How far could it have been driven before being buried or burned, maybe both? Who would actually try to bury a body in the desert by themselves? Could it be that Donna Ann Lass was actually left in plain sight still waiting to be discovered, having perhaps been seen but dismissed as a mannequin by anyone driving by and only half paying attention, just as Christine had been? If Jorgensen was good for the Lass murder, as Linda believed, why did both the MO and signature vary so greatly from Christine's murder and what she thought was also the connected slaying of Judith Williamson, herself abducted, murdered, and stripped of belongings at Jorgensen's alma matter after homecoming '63? Soon enough, Linda was back to the library microfiche and immersed in a periscope view of the murder and mayhem being wrought during the 1980s across the United States. All the while, she scanned for common denominators no one else considered. She scanned for clues plain and simple—clues and connections everyone else, it seemed, was too busy *not* looking for.

Scanning the fiche for open/unsolved cases—missing and murdered women and teens in particular—Linda expanded her search across the whole of California and the American Southwest dating from the time she knew Jorgensen had returned to California to live with his aging and frightened mother. Idle hands—the Devil's workshop—and his knowledge of the area made him especially dangerous, she believed, even more so than in his younger years. She considered him even more dangerous in light of what she had learned regarding Jorgensen's recent activities within the singles' club and the new protégé he was grooming. Grooming for what, Linda wasn't sure yet, although she believed that there would be other victims if she didn't stop him. She, by then, also knew that there already might have been other victims despite her best past efforts—the years immediately after New York when he became the one that got away for Wisconsin police, with an insurmountable head start. Beginning in reverse chronological order, it took Linda under an hour to find what she thought might be yet another linkage missed—an errant piece pulled off of the floor but still fitting into an expanding puzzle that she alone was assembling. At first blush, the possible linkage seemed too close a fit and the timing too opportune not to at least merit a second look. Moreover, it was recent—well within the window of Jorgensen's Sierra Singles interests and within reach of his recent desert and mountain expeditions. They called her Valentine Sally.

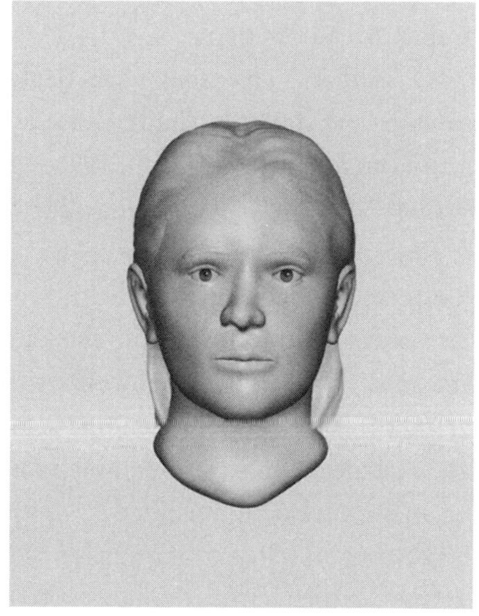

Left: An artist's rendering, created in 1982, of how the Jane Doe murder victim known as Valentine Sally is likely to have appeared while alive. Right: An improved twenty-first-century digital rendering of Valentine Sally based on 3D imaging of her skull, released over thirty years later in hopes of finally identifying the young woman—and by extension her killer.

A Jane Doe, an unidentified female with no known name or next of kin, had been found by pure fluke only a month earlier by a highway patrolman prowling a desolate stretch of I-40, about eleven miles west of the town of Williams, Arizona. Discovered lying beneath a cedar tree on the afternoon of February 14, 1982—Valentine's Day—the body, affectionately named "Sally" by cops and morgue staff, had been positioned just twenty-five feet off the highway where it had sat undiscovered for at least ten days, certainly long enough to mummify in the desert heat and be otherwise decomposed beyond immediate recognition. Estimated to be between sixteen and twenty-one years of age, Valentine Sally appeared to have been either strangled or suffocated, likely sometime on February 4 when a girl of similar description had been seen at the Monte Carlo Truck Stop in nearby Ashfork. Although no precise cause or date of death could be verified given the state of the body, all indications were that she was not sexually assaulted and that her clothes were left untouched by her attacker. Linda knew that the choice not to take trophy souvenirs would set the murder apart from Christine's case and others. One other piece of startling evidence, however, did not. A high-end handkerchief had been found with the corpse.

Flashback—fourteen years back—to the drizzly morning of Christine's murder and the men's hanky left beneath her ravaged head as she lay in the grass outside Sterling Hall. Jorgensen had used it to send a message—his signature. Now, Linda thought, the same signature was reappearing with a body posed in plain view in the desert—once again accompanied by a white men's handkerchief. Although a slightly varied MO as part of this latest decompensation and the ensuing compulsion to kill—in essence the end of a serial killer's refractory, or cooling-off, period between his crimes—it fit the same general visual scheme. It fit the same narrative.

Valentine Sally, someone who unlike the others wouldn't immediately be missed, also represented a subtle shift in victimology as compared to Christine and any other earlier victims, including Lass and Williamson, with even the victim's dental record checks having come back with negative results. One possible dental lead, however, was that the victim had recently been prepped for root canal work, a procedure that never ended up happening. Even with this detail made public, no one came forward to ID the body—no family, no dentist, no friends or coworkers. Valentine Sally was the quintessence of the *missing* missing and now the unknown dead. If her murder out on the desert was indeed once again the work of Jorgensen, Linda sensed he was getting more brazen, now going after perfect strangers rather than targeted strangers, acquaintances, or family. He was settling on whomever he could find. So long as no one found the bodies or knew the victims, he'd remain untouchable. The clock was ticking, and there was now no waiting for the police. Linda, to know for sure, would have to take a risk, to poke around in an attempt to get inside his head. She would have to stick her neck out to draw him from the shadows, provoke him out from under his rock. Valentine Sally became the excuse Linda needed to begin a new tradition, one she'd start belatedly in the winter of '82. When she got home that same afternoon in late February, she mailed Jorgensen a cryptic and belated Valentine card to his Washington Boulevard address in Marina del Rey. She dug up the past. She made a jab. She chose to reveal herself and her mission at once. She upped the ante.

> *Greetings from Texas,*
> *Remember when you worked at UW–Madison in 1968? I'm sure you recall that Chief Hanson sent two detectives to speak with you after you fled Madison.*
>
> *If you ever want to chat about the good ol' Badger days, please call collect at 817-294-XXXX.*
>
> *Would be interesting to reminisce since we have a friend in common.*
>
> *Happy Valentine's Day,*
> *Linda*

Knowing the danger she might be placing herself in but also knowing the time for half measures was long since gone—that it never really existed—she even included her full name and return address on the envelope. Then the waiting game began. It was a wait, taking decades, that would begin a new chapter in her hunt, one more subtle and telegraphic than before but no less tactical. As they both advanced in age and Christine stayed forever frozen at eighteen, Linda's tactics, now taking on a more nuanced dimension, would also leave her open to a possible counterattack for the first time. What ensued was a chess match that Linda now controlled, at least in the early days. It was a match played over a fifteen-hundred-mile distance but one with life-and-death stakes. It was a match in which she'd chosen to make a dangerously aggressive opening move—what chess players call the Halloween Gambit—an early sacrifice for a tactical upper hand and a psychologically elevated position. Valentine Sally, the Halloween Gambit—both references to secular observances; however, the next ominous event of consequence back in Madison would be linked to yet another and, for the moment, deadly observance: Independence Day. But in the meantime, a bizarre development that brought forth the first plausible suspect—or more accurately a patsy—for a good chunk of the unsolved Mad City murders to date. Maybe even *all* of them.

On the afternoon of March 1, 1982, Lincoln Elementary in Madison let out early to allow teachers to prepare for a PTA meeting and parent-faculty interviews. A third grader named Paula McCormick attended the school and set out to walk home alone when she was approached by a sex offender on probation living near the school and offered one dollar to babysit for him for a mere five minutes. The trusting girl followed a twenty-seven-year-old pedophile, petty shoplifter, and daytime B&E loser named Roger Lange into his apartment on Cypress Way where she was quickly overpowered, bound, gagged, sexually assaulted, and murdered—the precise order of the rape and murder not being clear. The girl's body was then placed in a garbage bag and again into an empty television box before being taken to a mini-storage warehouse on Copps Avenue across the lake in the town of Monona, where Lange had rented a drive-in unit to hide the girl's corpse. After the girl was reported missing, Madison PD didn't know where to start and it might have stayed that way if Lange, citing news reports of the girl's disappearance, hadn't offered them his services as a "psychic."

Claiming he was a psychic and was having "visions" that could help lead authorities to the missing child's whereabouts, on the evening of March 3, Lange quite incredibly brought the police to his own storage unit where the lead detective would claim that it became clear Lange had a personal connection to the disappearance—that his clairvoyant routine was disingenuous at best. In the unit, the police of course found the body of young Paula McCormick stuffed in a garbage bag, and Lange was immediately placed under arrest, much to his protest that he was only following his visions. Not surprisingly, he would later plead insanity while his lawyers argued with gusto that the pedo-necro sex creep should go to the state forensic mental health hospital—the same "puzzle factory" where grave robber Ed Gein was still locked up—rather than to the big house. But the jury didn't buy it. It was one of Madison's worst sex murders amid a torrent of killings blamed on some specter known as the Capital City Killer. Now, at last, the public had a name and a face they could assign to at least one of the murders, and they'd take it. Lange was convicted of first-degree murder, kidnapping, and a host of other felonies—convictions later upheld on appeal in 1989.

In the meantime, by the spring of '82, the police were publicly naming Lange as the replacement for William Zamastil as a possible suspect in other unsolved Mad City sex murders—in fact, in *all* of them. The city's newspapers of record—the *Capital Times* and the *Wisconsin State Journal*—were even citing police sources that Lange was now the prime—and only—suspect. This, in spite of remarkable differences in MO, signature, victimology, organization, disposal pathway, paraphilia, and weapon focus, in the murders of Debbie Bennett, Julie Ann Hall, Julie Speerschneider, and Susan LeMahieu. All the cops needed was for the deluge of random stranger-on-stranger murders in the Mad City to stop—at least for the short term—in order to keep Lange in play as "their man" for nearly every unsolved murder after Christine Rothschild. But then someone threw a wrench in their plan.

The Long Walk

July 2, 1982, fell on a Friday. It was also the last working day before the Fourth of July weekend—one of those rare occasions when it's actually *on* a weekend. With the usual Madison Independence Day parade in the offing, a mile-long asphalt flotilla lay waiting to set sail: marching bands, pom-poms, and pickups laden with festooned amplifiers all locked and loaded. It had been just before midnight on July 1 when twenty-three-year-old Donna Mraz finished her shift at a restaurant known as Bittersweet. Located just beyond the Capitol Square at 117 State Street—near the historical society in the 800 block of that same street where Julie Ann Hall once briefly worked—Donna had been waitressing there for nearly three years while balancing her studies at UW. It was her nature to keep active and lead a purpose-driven, hardworking life, a routine that earned her the nickname "buzzy"—as in a busy bee—among her family and closest friends. While preparing to embark on her senior year, Donna had even become a regular name on the Dean's Honor list. It was a mild early summer night when, directly in front of the restaurant, she managed to catch the last bus and set out for her campus-area rental home on Van Hise Avenue. It would be her *last* last bus.

While she had some distance to travel that night compared to the brief routes taken by other young Mad City women and teens before they had previously vanished, it was one that young Donna, with her board-straight brown hair and mile-high cheekbones, had been accustomed to taking since the spring of '79 when she first started working at Bittersweet. The route would have taken her, in a roundabout way, as it always did, through UW and past the general vicinity of Sterling Hall. It would also have taken her directly past Camp Randall Stadium where the university's NCAA Division I Badgers still play and where she was to be let off, a mere two blocks from her home where she lived with her two roommates. The unanswered question that endures is why whoever was waiting outside the stadium when she arrived was also on the UW campus that night. Why was he drawn back to the same vicinity that had been the epicenter for Madison's nearly fifteen-year reign in blood?

It was a bygone age before smartphones allowed people to remove themselves from the reality of their surroundings and instead actually look ahead to what lay in front of them—who was behind them. It was a time when journeys on foot or by bus, like the one Donna undertook that fateful night, were single-task undertakings that required engagement with the real world and not opiating oneself with scrollable social media pages or Pokémon GO. The result was that people actually paid attention—to be vigilant about who might be shadowing them—and were generally expected to have their wits about them. Thus, the fact that Donna made it three-quarters of the way through her journey without incident suggests that she hadn't been followed. That is not, however, to rule out that she wasn't specifically targeted; yet, as her friends, family, and coworkers back at the restaurant would later tell police, Donna was also smart enough to always vary her route. Over a decade before, people—especially young women like Donna—were urged to regularly change up their routines and paths to and from their usual haunts, and she practiced that good habit. Without necessarily knowing what it was called, Donna understood what criminologists just a few years earlier had begun to refer to as the *routine activities theory* of crime and victimization.

The truth is that, man or woman, young or old, we all follow routines. The structure of modern society is such that we also seldom deviate from them. Suburban family homes are targeted for daytime break-ins because thieves know that the weekday routines of people who own those homes is one that puts the occupants at work, at school, or out running errands during that same time. The result is a predictive soft target that can be identified based solely on the routine of the owners. But the routine activities theory of crime suggests that this same model can be applied to nearly all types of offenses, not just burglaries. The nuts and bolts of the theory states that where a motivated offender and a vulnerable victim meet at a particular time and place in the absence of a "suitable guardian"—police, eyewitnesses, video surveillance, and so on—a crime is more likely than not to occur.

In the crime-plagued New York City of that same year, 1982, unforgiving places like Battery Park and the 191st Street Station—the reputed "Tunnel of Doom"—were living laboratories that quickly proved the soundness of the theory. Jogging paths frequented by young women and concealed by hedgerows, staircases to the subway, they were all easy targets for the various forms of societal flotsam that laid claim to the city once the sun set. They knew who would likely be in those places and when. Much like taking down a stagecoach at the pass, all they had to do was wait. Within twenty-four months, the city reached a breaking point after crack hit the streets and changed all the rules. Later, Bernie Goetz went *Death Wish* on four black kids on a subway car in Manhattan with an unregistered .38, and by the end of '84, America suddenly awoke to the dimensions of the new decade—the realities of what was yet to come. One didn't need to live in New York City to know it. Back in the Mad City, Donna already knew it. She knew where the world had gone and was going and always played it safe. She paid attention—always. That's why what happened when she got to Camp Randall Stadium that night, just after midnight on July 3, is all the more puzzling. What was even more puzzling is where it happened.

As her boss and longtime owner of the Bittersweet, Gene Konitzer, would later tell reporters with the *Capital Times*, Donna was "unafraid," which is not to say she was fearless. She was too smart to be fearless. Even in her placid west-end suburb with its coach lights and welcome mats, she knew the world was a dangerous place. She also knew how to protect herself from the evil that men do. In fact, until the small hours of July 3, she also seemed to have done everything right. Donna was an accomplished varsity basketball athlete, National Honor Society member, and state scholarship winner. She wasn't helpless or clueless; in fact, she was as physically agile as she was smart. There could and would never be any "double-gray" area with respect to Donna's brief, bright life in the way that Julie Speerschneider's existence had been so readily dismissed. Tragically, it was still no assurance that Donna too wouldn't fall between the cracks—wouldn't be yet another byproduct of a local and regional system that, with industrialized efficiency, churned out unsolved murders in assembly-line fashion. By the time the national crime rate tore through the stratosphere, Madison had already become something of a cold-case foundry—a place whose chief products were little more than human tragedy and misery.

Shortly after midnight on July 2, after Donna disembarked from the Madison Metro Transit bus that picked her up outside the Bittersweet, residents of the nearby Breese Terrace Apartments, a network of walk-up multidwelling units within view and earshot of Camp Randall Stadium, heard a blood-curdling scream. Most of the occupants who were still awake dismissed the noise as an early start to Fourth of July revelry, part of the usual weekend benders that descended on the neighborhood once the summertime subtenants moved in.

But there was at least one tenant, a twenty-two-year-old UW male student from nearby Milwaukee, still holed up in his student apartment well into the summer, who thought differently. He was sufficiently jarred by the unsettling pitch of the scream that he looked out his second-story window to see a woman running from the vicinity of the stadium's gate 4 before collapsing on the concrete walkway leading from the stadium to a series of small apartment structures, the Bresse Terrace buildings included. Momentarily darting his eyes away from the woman on the ground to the dim amber glow thrown onto the stadium's student entrance, labeled as gate 4 (what is today gate 5) by the metal-halide street lamps nearby, the same witness saw an amorphous silhouette—some kind of shape in the night—running in the opposite direction to the east. Although he was the closest thing to an independent eyewitness to a Madison murder in nearly two decades, in the end, the details of what he saw wouldn't end up mattering. What the student in the window didn't yet know was that the woman lying prone on the walkway was Donna Mraz and the shape in the night was her killer. What he also didn't know—and Donna couldn't have known—is how long that same mysterious figure had lain in wait in the shadows of Camp Randall Stadium for this very moment. What no one will ever know is whether Donna was a previously targeted victim or someone in the wrong place at the wrong time. Like so many of Madison's other girls.

Hypnosis

Upon seeing that Donna—he wouldn't know her name until after it was all over—was no longer moving, the student, now a key witness, ran down to the walkway to find her unconscious, her arm slashed, and her chest spritzing blood in sync with her elevated pulse as she went into shock. All the while, Donna's purse remained untouched, her clothing unmolested.

In the dark of night and concealed by the long shadows of the stadium, her attacker had emerged from the black and plunged the knife with surgical precision through Donna's heart. The slash to the arm, running shoulder to elbow and cutting down to the bone, revealed an initial plunge of the knife that Donna deflected by trying to shield her face, and which in process managed to inflict a deep glancing slash. Even to the untrained eye of the Good Samaritan, the evidence spelled an attack from close quarters—from ambush—with the blade having been directed down from overhead. It had been plunged from above with tremendous force and purpose, the intent from the outset to deliver a horrific and inevitably fatal blow. Panicked, the witness managed to maintain the presence of mind to run back inside and call an ambulance from his apartment before then grabbing a blanket off his own bed to bring down to Donna. By the time he got back to her—maybe a minute, maybe two—there was a second man present tending to her as well. No one knew where he came from. No one ever even got his name.

Within three minutes of the initial 911 call, fire department EMTs converged on the scene, followed soon after by both UW and Madison PD uniform officers who strung up yellow tape and built perimeters. Paramedics worked on Donna at the scene for a total of twenty minutes—too long—before transporting her to the campus hospital, wheeling the ambulance into the same ER receiving bay across from Sterling Hall used for Christine Rothschild, effectively retracing the steps of May of '68. Different faces and names, the same dark history on autorepeat. In the meantime, police scanners went berserk at all the local affiliates—NBC, CBS, ABC—with news crews scrambling to the scene to roll electronic news gathering, or ENG, videotape. Within two hours, Donna Mraz was pronounced dead. She'd made it thirty feet from where her attacker emerged from the blind spot by Camp Randall Stadium's gate 4 before collapsing from shock and blood loss. She never regained consciousness. She never got to ask, *Why?*

Page 2, Section 1 Wisconsin State Journal, Saturday, July 3, 1982

UW Officer Rexann Lemke guards scene where Donna Mraz was stabbed (circle).

— State-Journal photo by Carolyn Pflasterer

A circle delineates the area outside Randall Stadium's infamous gate 4 (today gate 5) where Donna Mraz's body was found in a pool of her own blood. UWPD officer Rexann Lemke stands guard at the outer cordon of the crime scene, one surrounded by student houses left abandoned for the Independence Day holiday weekend. Courtesy: Wisconsin State Journal.

Donna's murder came at the tail end of a week that, even for Madison and 1980s Middle America, saw a remarkable torrent of violence. The previous Sunday, June 27, a young woman walking along Regent Street near Monroe Street, just south of the campus and less than half a mile from Camp Randall Stadium, had been slashed across the back of the leg in an apparent random attack. A basic description was obtained in what was thought to be a mugging gone bad, the case written off with no composite drawing and no public plea for tips. There was also no canvass run of the street made famous for its slanting homes—the leaning houses of Regent.

On the night of Donna Mraz's murder, there had also been two stranger-on-stranger sex attacks across the city. The first incident occurred immediately *before* the attack on Donna—a mere matter of minutes before—at the rear of a dive bar called the Shuffle Inn on West Beltline and just five miles from the UW campus. In that incident, a woman walking through the bar's small parking lot was attacked when a man jumped out from in between two parked cars, dragged her to a nearby embankment, and severely beat her face while raping her. No usable description of the attacker was obtained. In a strange twist of fate, the Shuffle Inn would burn to the ground six years later when Mad City serial arsonist Fred Long—a depraved pyrophiliac with a penchant for setting nightclub fires—landed a job there as the night janitor and later set the place ablaze. It was the last of his three intentionally set Madison nightclub fires, one claiming a life, that had reduced three buildings to rubble. At the time of Mraz's murder and the contemporaneous attack at the Shuffle Inn, Long would have been seventeen years old. Although perhaps a long shot, as a serial pyrophiliac with abnormal sexual desires, he probably should have also been considered—or the very least cleared—as a "possible" for the three knife attacks in the summer of '82. He wasn't.

The second of the two stranger-on-stranger sex attacks to occur during the Devil's hours on July 3, this one occurring immediately *after* Donna was stabbed to death, was even more notable. A little over an hour after Donna was pronounced dead at UW hospital, a single thirty-one-year-old woman was asleep in the bed of her apartment on Fiedler Lane, located just south of the UW arboretum. About 4:00 a.m., rolling around in the midst of a deep sleep, something jarred her awake. It was then that she too would take note of an indiscernible figure—one in this case standing immediately above her bed. The nocturnal intruder, apparently having cut electrical service to the apartment to prevent lights from being turned on, had some time earlier managed with some deftness to enter the apartment in what can only be surmised to be a targeted stranger attack. When the ambient light outside came through her bedroom window to reveal the brief glint of a blade surface, the victim attempted to instinctively shield her face, as Donna did, while the intruder slashed her and severed the tendons of her right hand. The attacker then held the knife to her throat and proceeded to sexually assault her before slipping out into the predawn twilight and leaving her bleeding in bed. Somehow, she survived.

Although no description or DNA profile of the bedroom intruder was ever obtained, Madison PD later assured the public they were "closely examining" whether the attack on Fiedler Lane was related to the murder of Mraz, as well as the knife attack on Regent Street the week prior. For the cases not to have been related would mean that *three* knife-wielding suspects were walking the streets contemporaneously, attacking female strangers independently of one another over the course of the same week—and all in the same general area of Madison. Not surprisingly, this was somewhat consistent with the approach taken with the previous four murders and the reluctance to *seriously* entertain the possibility of any linkage in those cases, particularly the last two murders of Susan LeMahieu and Shirley Stewart. Another area of consistency with the Mraz murder was to reunite the custom-built Intra County Investigative Squad of days gone by, once again cobbling together an assortment of city, county, state, and campus cops but with one key difference—this time the campus police were in charge. Just as they had been responsible for the Christine Rothschild investigation back in May of '68, so too would a member of the UW Five-O be tasked with heading up the investigation into Donna Mraz's murder. The new boss there was a Lieutenant Gary Moore, a man who, before long, realized that being a campus cop in charge of a major case task force was a real gas. It was regular detective work à la mode—a little more sweet, a little more self-indulgent—in that investigative decision-making was all his, even if it involved an unorthodox method or two. In fact, the sky was the limit in terms of harebrained ideas. He was, after all, a man playing with house money.

It would be tough to beat the mishandling of the earlier Mad City murders, especially given that Donna was a homegrown all-star with wall-to-wall friends and family. Somehow the task force would manage to outdo itself. Within only hours of the girl's death, Lieutenant Moore didn't assign his detectives to focus on the potential linkages to the other stabbings, or even re-interview the other potentially related victims. Nor did he apparently have them corralling other possible—and previously unidentified—witnesses by doing a thorough canvass run of all nearby residences, maybe even a proper grid search or, more appropriately, what's known as a fingertip search of the stadium and surrounding area for trace evidence. Rather than ordering all hands on deck to search for blood droplets, cigarette discards, footwear impressions, or other trace evidence, the investigation was taken in another direction—and into a black hole. Instead, within the first forty-eight hours—that critical first two-day window following the murder—the task force under Moore's leadership quite incredibly, and incredulously, put its faith in the power of hypnosis. It soon became the first major step taken in the investigation.

It was tragicomic; it was pure lunacy; it should have led to the disbandment of the Intra County Investigative Squad and intervention of the US Justice Department for egregious violations of basic investigative adequacy standards. The Justice Department has certainly intervened and solicited consent decrees from other police departments for less. But no one in the Mad City, it seemed, knew any better. Amid some questions of optics and subtle shoulder shrugging by the local press—the *Capital Times*, the *Wisconsin State Journal*, and even the *Sentinel* from where Linda's confidante and man on the inside, Bill Share, had just retired—the papers reported that arrangements were made to have the unnamed eyewitness who first called 911 meet with a hypnotist. It was being brokered on the quick in a bid to have any missing details extracted about what he saw that night—the *previous* night. Ostensibly, it was to be used to help retrieve forgotten details of the mysterious shadowy figure seen near gate 4 brought to the surface, but it more explicitly served as a portent of things to come: hocus-pocus, mumbo jumbo, a fire sale on common sense. It was the Independence Day weekend of 1982. It might as well have been 1892—back when H. H. Holmes was building his Murder Castle and the Pinkertons collared killers.

Notwithstanding that hypnosis is now and was then regarded by the courts as junk science, it has been occasionally used in a last-ditch effort to recover the "repressed" memories of victims—not witnesses—about events long since passed. This controversial technique has also been linked to instances where it has managed to fundamentally twist and override existing accurate memories. The subject under hypnosis also needs to be willing to undergo the often-awkward ordeal, or at least to play along with the game. The student witness from the window was having none of it. After hearing what was planned, he skipped town and headed home to Milwaukee. His roommates later told the papers as much, saying that he was "spooked" by the whole affair and how it was being handled. The cops never got a forwarding address or alternate number. In fact, they didn't get anyone's information—possible witnesses, persons of interest, even viable suspects—or where they might be spending that holiday weekend. Police, when later embarking upon a delayed canvass, complained that most of the names on mailboxes of surrounding houses or on the buzz boards—building intercom systems—of nearby apartments, such as those on Breese Terrace, had six or seven entries apiece. Markers on masking tape over other masking tape contained the names of student tenants and their sublets—couch surfers and summer flings all staying off lease. It was an absolute mess. The investigation seemed to be over before it started—again.

As Lieutenant Moore later lamented to police, the holiday was "hampering" police ability to flush out either witnesses or the "hard clues" they so desperately needed. He tried to lighten the mood by later suggesting to *State Journal* reporter Marvin Balousek that he and his team were using the down time, as the case went cold before their eyes, to "catch up on [their] reading," an offhand reference to the file itself. That "reading," of course, was the Mraz murder book, including coroner's reports on the brutality that had been wrought upon the body of an innocent girl just trying to make her way home that night, the witness statements of the Good Samaritan, the EMTs who had tended to her, and the handful of local residents who confirmed hearing the screams—Donna's final horrific moments. All bumbling and ill-timed jocularity aside, the newsman responded by asking what leads the crackerjack task force had mined with respect to potential suspects, and the lieutenant was more candid. "Absolutely nothing," he admitted. That was just thirty-six hours in. With the half-baked hypnotist idea kiboshed, the task force was already bleeding out on the mat and Moore had thrown in the towel and was publicly prepared to announce as much. Unlike his circumspect predecessors during the Major Case Unit's earlier iterations, it seems he was at least prepared to fall on the sword—on the front page of three newspapers, no less.

Publish or Perish

After the fireworks had all burned out and the miniature star-spangled banners were tucked away under Madison staircases alongside Christmas ornaments for yet another year, it was back to business on Tuesday, July 6. It was also the day Donna Mraz was laid to rest during a private service at Roselawn Memory Gardens in the nearby town of Monona. Two days prior, the actual Fourth of July, a visitation had been held at the Betzer Funeral Home in Delevan, about an hour's drive from the Mad City. Despite the distance and the competing holiday festivities, a sea of mourners—friends, family, UW classmates and professors, coworkers and customers from the Bittersweet, first responders to the crime scene—arrived in a continuous stream for upward of five hours to pay their respects to Donna, her parents, and her brother Mickey. Most of the Major Case Unit sleuths were no-shows.

Back in Dallas, Linda knew of the latest Madison murder, knew that UWPD was at the helm, and knew they would likely muddy the waters until no one could see the bottom. She also knew of the plan to hypnotize the lone eyewitness who had been scared away by the fact that other potential witnesses had never been identified or short-listed for proper follow-up. But she'd been to this dance before. She also knew of the holiday visitation and Tuesday morning burial, and that the Mraz girl wouldn't rest in peace. As the coming months would prove, she was right in the most literal sense. But Donna's murder had also brought back a wave of saturnine feelings that even the latest torrent of killings hadn't. She couldn't shake the similarities between Donna and Christine as victims—she wasn't sure why. The murder rekindled nightmares that she had otherwise put up on the shelf while trying to keep her eye on the ball, her focus trained on Jorgensen and her attempt to stop him from killing again. She feared she'd already failed at least twice after Christine while Jorgensen was off the grid and out of reach—Donna Ann Lass was a good bet and Valentine Sally a solid maybe—and there would no doubt be more to follow. As the Major Case Unit would soon begin to create the Capital City Killer in effigy and turn it over to the feds to get themselves out of the corner, Linda was chasing the only verifiable serial killer—name, address, Social Security number all confirmed—to have lived and killed in Madison. By the summer of '82, she had stopped calling the cops with updates.

That same week, Linda did, however, make a call that would chart a new course—the next move on the chessboard that spanned the distance from Dallas to Marina del Rey. Again assuming the role of a studio executive doing research for the now-imminent anniversary reprise of *This Is Your Life*, she called Rita Baron asking for any updates on Jorgensen's life—anything that might help ensure he was chosen as the feature persona of the show's supposed network return. Indeed there was an update.

"Well, you heard that as his mother's dying wish, he finally helped her get her book published? Niels would do *anything* for his mother, you know."

Linda tried to compute these latest details, facts much more quantitative—and ominous—than her contact's earlier nondescript and sycophantic riffs from the last phone call. *Dying? Published?* Linda zeroed in on these two tidbits, now legitimately curious beyond the purview of the research cover story. "Poor Heidi hasn't got much longer they say. She never leaves the house. Niels got her old manuscript published as a book as a final gift; Ezra is selling them on consignment in LA for him."

Linda bristled. "*What* book?"

With a slight pause, Baron came back with the title as though Linda should already have known, as though it was common sense. "Well, *The Love Pirate* of course. It was the children's book she wrote over ten years ago. Such a wonderful story."

Linda was flummoxed but quickly put it all together—her cryptic Valentine card with its tacit reference to Valentine Sally and its jab about Jorgensen's running from the Mad City back in '68. She had expected to provoke him and had also anticipated a knee-jerk response. She had even considered it possible that he might have concluded that the woman who sent the taunting Valentine card might have read and decrypted the abandoned Madison copy of *The Love Pirate*. In this new level of psychological warfare and proverbial chess game that Linda was orchestrating, Jorgensen had made his own unanticipated strategic move. He had met Linda's Halloween Gambit with an opening "sacrifice" of his own in the form of full disclosure, a move Linda hadn't been expecting. He had chosen in a way to reveal himself by tauntingly putting the coded book into the hands of American readers—indirectly revealing his proclivities in black and white for unknowing readers. He'd gone public.

A single, meager print run with now-defunct Vantage Press—a New York–based vanity publisher—spit out a total of fifty prepaid hardcover editions of the book, all destined for Southern California where Jorgensen would have Ezra Jameson—a true-life version of Quong Sha from *The Love Pirate*—sell them out of the trunk of his car or even give them away to members of the Sierra Singles. Although publishing the book with its veiled references had in theory left Jorgensen exposed, he knew that no one would make the connections that Linda had. Moreover, now that the book was in print, Jorgensen knew that any linkages that Linda might now try to draw from it—or at least speak publicly about to the police or others—would only make her appear obsessed. He no doubt thought that Linda's valid connections, referencing what was once a memoir, private cipher, and roman à clef but now a public document, would likely have her written off by cops and reporters who'd recently seen such linkages—incidents still very much in the news in 1982.

Like Mark David Chapman, John Hinckley Jr., and the countless others drawn to J. D. Salinger's *The Catcher in the Rye*—Chapman's 1980 murder of John Lennon revealed his possession of the novel when arrested; the book was also recovered from Hinckley's hotel room in March '81 following his attempted assassination of President Reagan—publishing the book was principally a strategic move. He no doubt banked that the police and whoever else might listen would summarily paint her as a woman who never got over May of '68, a woman tilting at windmills and mistakenly interpreting the book for something it was not. As Heidi waited out death in the condo she shared under the domineering control of her son, the book, now published, was her mea culpa about the monster she had unwittingly created. Jorgensen had, however, turned it into an insurance policy against Linda. Beyond that, he also would relish in the double entendre and hidden meaning of every page—that he was in fact the devious Dr. Corcoran. As a malignant narcissist in the psychopathic spectrum, he may have thought that people might come to understand and even admire him.

Linda, still on the phone, in processing these short- and long-term implications and realizing what her incendiary Valentine card had touched off, asked Rita how she might go about getting a copy. "The network studio would love a copy to review ahead of final selections," she qualified. Although she wasn't certain the industry jargon she was throwing around made sense—that the nomenclature rang true—it was enough to pull a final one over on the naïve Rita.

"I'll get two from Ez when I see him this week. I'll tell him the second one is for the beauty salon. Will they show the book on TV?"

Linda replied with a confident "no question about it" before then providing the KVTV address. "Come to think of it, send it COD to my professional PO box." Knowing not only that she could never in a million years manage a parcel intercept at the CBS affiliate office, she also knew she didn't have a PO box. As another ruse, she provided Rita with her actual home address and prefaced it with a bogus PO number. It was an address that by then she knew Jorgensen already had by virtue of the earlier Valentine card, so if he found out, she would be in no greater danger than she was already. Linda could hear Rita was distracted, jotting down digits and not caring one way or another about where the book was headed or why. For a brief moment Linda even felt badly about falsely lifting the kind woman's spirits and suggesting that a book written by Jorgensen's mother might in some way help in his selection for a television show. Rita, she realized, having fallen under Jorgensen's psychopathic spell, had believed his stories and believed he was special. Although Linda's playacting with this trusting and pleasant woman had been nothing personal, Baron unfortunately had to be used as a pawn in the ongoing chess game. This conversation would mark the last time they ever spoke. Linda officially retired her ruse exactly eight business days later when the package from California arrived.

The dust jacket cover of The Love Pirate *following its lone print run after being self-published by Jorgensen through Vantage Books, the now-defunct vanity press.*

In peeling open the red, white, and blue box with the USPS logo, Linda dumped out the lone item onto her kitchen table where it spun slightly clockwise, the dust jacket facedown to reveal a blank rear side. Linda turned it over to see the front cover. The dust jacket design, a weird cottage country motif created by some anonymous hack, didn't square with the images conjured in Linda's mind by the original unvarnished manuscript she'd pored over so many times, the passages she'd decrypted and digested. She had envisaged something more literal and in keeping with the title—the taking of Jorgensen's twisted definition of love by violence, by ruthless piracy—as opposed to the infantile and benign image ultimately chosen. On the front of the matte dust jacket, a pontoon plane vectors left toward a small lake circumscribed by pine trees and low-rise mountains—an interpretation of the volcanic lake from the story where he hides his captive—as a full moon and starry night illuminate a makeshift runway along with a glass-like surface of the still water. In the bottom foreground, the silhouette of a crudely sketched timber-frame cabin, its first- and second-story windows illuminated from inside, its dock extending well out into the lake. And there it was, *The Love Pirate* in published form, Jorgensen mocking Linda, Judith, Christine, and his other victims past and future—mocking his own mother as its author—all at once. The specs: a 6" x 9" hardback, 239 pages, ISBN 533-04835-4. Suggested retail price: $10.95 USD, copyright Heidi B. Jorgensen. Inside the dust jacket, the front flap, the book's description for a commercial market, a two-hundred-word summary written on the quick by a marketer back in New York who never knew the *real* meaning of the book, who had no idea that he or she was drafting a précis of Jorgensen's murderous career. Nonetheless, the "hook" for potential future readers—whoever they might be—as composed by an impartial third party boiled down with disturbing accuracy to a semifictionalized psychological assessment of the real Dr. Corcoran, the novel's bizarre antihero—real name: Niels Bjorn Jorgensen.

> *Dr. Francis Corcoran [. . .] gets what he wants [. . .] then he meets Annabel in San Francisco [. . .] he must have her! She resists, he lures her into his car [. . .] he assures her that, after a time, he will return her to society unharmed [. . .] does he sacrifice all and become persecuted as a kidnapper? Read* The Love Pirate *and see!*

Linda fixated on a single word in the cover description that hadn't appeared in the original unedited manuscript: *persecuted*. In Heidi's outré narrative, Corcoran is a sexual psychopath, inveterate predator, and kidnapper whose actions are sanded down to the puerile and purely silly to conceal their truly aberrant nature. The term "persecuted" thus never appeared, it couldn't have—the story was an R-rated horror drive-in movie transformed into a G-rated after-school special for those who bothered to notice the veiled warnings embedded in the text. The moral couldn't be spoon-fed; the vernacular couldn't be proscriptive; the antihero's actions could never be mitigated. Heidi knew it like Walt Disney knew it; she simply followed suit. Old Walt had by then already sanitized countless folktales borne out of medieval sexual depravity, and done so with great success. His 1950 film *Cinderella* and every version that's followed is little more than a family-friendly reinterpretation of a darker folktale that appears across multiple languages in the Middle Ages known as both "The Persecuted Heroine" and "Cruel Relatives in Law." Similarly, the 1937 classic *Snow White* is distilled from numerous folktales collected over the years by anthropologists and consolidated in the Grimm Brothers' macabre story "The Glass Coffin," first published in the nineteenth century and derived from the German folktale "The Sleeping Beauty" (also the basis for the 1959 Disney film, *Sleeping Beauty*) and the Italian legend known as "The Young Slave," both of which have much less happy endings—ones that annual visitors to the Magic Kingdom are likely unaware of. To therefore suggest that Dr. Corcoran as the metaphorical Dr. Niels Jorgensen would not be rightfully *prosecuted*, but would instead be *persecuted*—most readers not distinguishing, much less appreciating, the difference between the two—was a bottom-of-the-ninth edit by Jorgensen himself. He had made himself the hero, all those who opposed him the villains. He was rewriting history on a single print-on-demand run.

But the shrewd substitution was also an editorial decision made and an Easter egg inserted on Jorgensen's orders to the publisher, no question about it. In his mind, he was and always had been taking what he was owed in life; to deny him was merely to provoke him. It was not his fault that, in his twisted mind, his superiority was his curse. To hold him accountable for what nature made him was to wrongfully and hypocritically condemn him. Like those persecuted before him, he saw himself as the real victim, a righteous man whose punishment and ill-treatment was more political than it was moral or legal. Niels knew that Linda would eventually find her way to the book and this one word—his sole editorial contribution to the book based on his deeds, his book of secrets—and it was his countermove to Linda's opener in their expanding match. Rook takes knight pawn.

Machinations

As Linda thought carefully about her next move, the Major Case Unit in the Mad City was contemplating one of its own. It was a new strategy, a latter-day whisper campaign to introduce a reinvented iteration of the Capital City Killer as the prime suspect, not just for Donna Mraz's murder, but for *every* murder. It was a theory developed in a darkroom—the *camera obscura*—that held that a single killer, should a suitable one be found, might indeed be deemed responsible for everything that had ever happened in recent memory. There were and are still conflicting reports about who was by this time actually pulling the strings—who the master puppeteer controlling the money and the narrative of the investigation actually was. Come the fall of '82, things were set to change. In a big way.

Although there had previously been a denial by police in front of cameras that the Mad City murders were connected, the Mraz murder was the proverbial fly in the ointment. Not since Christine Rothschild had a victim so galvanized the city and its single largest employer, the UW campus. Not since Christine had a victim been killed and left directly on the campus as a single homicidal event. The thought of one killer terrorizing the state capital and claiming its young at random was terrifying enough given the size of the city at the time. The idea that one, two, as many as five or six killers were walking the streets at any given time in Madison—and were equally fixated on either the campus or any girl even loosely affiliated with it or in its vicinity—was a poison pill no right-minded Madisonian would swallow.

Avoidance and incompetence gave way to denial and eventually to deceit. Madison wasn't the first city to go through such a crisis, nor will it be the last. Yet, eventually, after a few years—though it varies by city—that same scheme comes to work against every lawman who, whether officially on camera before the state and now national media, or behind home plate at little league games, needed to come up with a way to placate those who actually lived the reality of the era. A year earlier—only a month earlier for that matter—none of the killings on the books were related. That was the official credo. But after Donna Mraz, things changed. Those same books could be cooked. No one would ever know. The machinations of a Middle America scheme no one ever knew existed soon took shape. All the Mad City needed was a name.

The stark reality is that there is never any shortage of people ready and willing to confess to crimes they didn't commit, especially if it comes with the cachet of being a serial killer. The motives for this run the gamut; however, disturbed people whose precise whereabouts can't be verified—or won't be verified by authorities for fear of letting the truth get in the way of a good story—have often inherited serial killer titles as part of some mutually beneficial agreement even when not already facing a murder charge. Their confessions aren't part of some plea bargain or defense strategy, but for some other intrinsic reason most of us will never understand. The looser the linkages between cases, the more difficult it is. Like in the case of Whitechapel murders attributed in whole to Jack the Ripper, they are more difficult to assign to a named person; however, sometimes the connections are just close enough, the suspect just believable enough in his pathetic need for attention, that the public buys it.

To try and stem the flow of nutcases who come out of the woodwork during multiple murder panics claiming to be responsible, and to allow themselves to focus on finding the real killer, most police departments limit key information relating to MO, signature, victimology, disposal pathway, and other sensitive details to a handful of lead investigators within the inner circle of an investigation. This inner circle is intended to function as something of a containment field, a way to keep what's known as "holdback evidence" out of the public eye. That same privileged information can later be used to test the stories of those coming forward, claiming responsibility. False confessors can be weeded out if, when questioned on certain details, they can't recite what was held back from press reports and seem to just be aping what they read, saw, or heard in the news.

The value of having a holdback evidence policy was first suggested in Edgar Allan Poe's 1842 short story *The Mystery of Marie Rogêt*, a fictional treatment of the actual 1841 murder of a young New York tobacconist named Mary Rogers, and arguably the first piece of true crime ever written. Holdback evidence, as first recommended by Poe though not by using this precise terminology, is a list of facts about an open or unsolved case that are concealed from both the public and even rank-and-file officers who inevitably talk too much. Aside from being a good practice to identify false confessions, it was also proposed by Poe, in a roundabout way, to deter copycats. In reality, the two phenomena are closely connected. Albert DeSalvo, who had confessed to being the "Phantom Fiend"—the Boston Strangler's alternate nickname—back in 1964, is confirmed by DNA to have murdered the thirteenth victim attributed to the Strangler, Mary Sullivan, but questions remain as to whether DeSalvo actually killed the other twelve women. Some ponder whether he was simply a copycat seeking attention and also educated in how to offend based on the leaks about the Strangler's MO and signature in the local press. Others have suggested that there may be as many five Boston Stranglers—plural—and that the failure of the Boston police to maintain a holdback evidence policy when the first linkages were made in 1962 actually opened the door for a wave of other paraphilic psychopaths to begin escalating to murder by mimicking the Strangler's successful methods and forensic countermeasures. Lucky for them, DeSalvo admitted to them all.

But in Madison the linkages were even looser, the murders more spread out over space and time. To have someone willing to admit to them all would require a number of things to occur simultaneously. An offender would need to be in custody for a similar or related crime, preferably a sexual homicide. That crime would need to be substantively similar to at least one of the Capital City Killer's crimes, much like DeSalvo's murder was close enough to the other twelve credited to the Strangler. Lastly, ideally the offender, if old enough, would need to be willing to confess to all of the crimes dating back to the Rothschild murder and allow the cops to close the books, or alternatively there would need to be some other connection that would allow public opinion to make that linkage. Although it wouldn't be a frame-up, it would, if such a person confessed, be a convenient solution for so many unsolved attacks. With Ed Edwards already well off the table as a potential Capital City Killer at the time of the Mraz murder, by the fall of '82 the cops had a new name. While his age didn't necessarily make him a match for most of Madison's previous outrages, he could take the heat off the stalled Donna Mraz investigation and some of the more recent attacks. His name was Lonnie Taylor.

Exhumed

On November 3, 1982, the UW Police Department, a Captain Robert Hartwig now doing the talking, confirmed that they had obtained a judge's order to exhume the body of Donna Mraz, her remains having been interred just four months earlier—nearly to the day. While exhumations would in later years become increasingly common for the purposes of procuring DNA samples and performing other more contemporary forensic tests, they dug Donna out of the ground for a more rudimentary procedure—to check her teeth. All things considered, it was actually a good hunch.

A week earlier, Madison city cops arrested eighteen-year-old Lonnie Taylor, a local creepo who'd been seen slowly following a young woman down Regent Street as he stealthily rode a ten-speed bicycle in the wake of her heel clacks—along the same block no less where a series of random slashings had occurred in the weeks leading up to Donna's murder. The student witness in the window of the Breese apartments outside Randall Stadium of course hadn't seen the killer on a bicycle but rather a silhouette fleeing on foot into the night. That posed a problem given that there was nothing to suggest any possible linkage to Donna's murder or the other previous slayings that the police now seemed increasingly—and officially—prepared to chalk up to the work of a single serial killer. The witness who had reported the suspicious cyclist on Regent Street made, however, an additional revelation that police glommed onto. Taylor, the witness insisted, was also the same man he'd seen trying to break in to a home on North Randall Avenue, immediately to the east of the stadium where Donna was attacked. Once confronted in that incident, the burglar pulled out a blade—a stiletto knife, in fact—and threatened the witness before fleeing the scene. In that case, the same perp fled not on a bicycle but on foot.

Young Taylor's presence near the leaning houses of Regent, cycling behind an oblivious female while inferentially preparing to pounce, might well have been a coincidence. He might have also been part of the next wave of Mad City paraphiliacs, someone inspired by the generous reportage of the earlier incidents that were all still unsolved. If so, he would have learned of the previous attacks in the same Regent Street corridor that offered a plethora of young women walking alone and, in keeping with the routine activities theory of crime, available as soft targets. Whatever the reason, it paled in comparison to the significance of the attempted B&E and subsequent knife threat. Not only did the MO and weapon mesh with the home invasion that immediately followed the Mraz stabbing, the *style* of knife—a thin stiletto edge consistent with a switchblade—was also believed to approximate the weapon used on both Donna and the later rape victim attacked on Fiedler Lane.

The daytime break-in on Randall Street, whether sexually motivated or not, is also in keeping with the activities of habitual or serialized offenders as they experiment with new crimes. Contrary to popular opinion—and misconception—serial offenders, whether serial killers, serial rapists, serial arsonists, or other, don't continuously and unidirectionally escalate their offenses. Since all serial offending is defined by fluctuating intervals of compensation and decompensation, some offenders abstain for a time from committing crimes entirely while others may revert to the same default behaviors that often preceded their current fixations. More often than one might think, that means breaking and entering.

One example is Timothy Wilson Spencer, dubbed the "Southside Strangler," who graduated from financially motivated burglaries to being a nighttime intruder and sexual murderer in Arlington, Virginia, between 1984 and 1987. Murdering at least five women in the area, Spencer continued his financially motivated breaking-and-entering exploits simultaneous with his murderous home invasions, each MO complementing the other. Spencer is, however, a notable but lesser-known case of the correlation between residential break-ins motivated by theft and what are known as "hot prowl" burglaries, motivated by sexual assault and, often, homicide.

The better-known example is, once again, Richard Ramirez, the LA "Night Stalker" mentioned earlier. A self-avowed Satanist, he terrorized residential areas between Los Angeles and San Francisco through a series of home-invasion rapes and murders, which a California judge would later describe as displaying "viciousness beyond any human understanding." Claiming a total of fourteen victims, both male and female and ranging in age from nine to eighty-three between 1984 and 1985, Ramirez first began by burglarizing guest rooms with a master key while working as a Holiday Inn night clerk. Eventually, as his twisted and sadistic perversions began to overtake any remaining ability to function normally, Ramirez's intrusion skills were used to facilitate nighttime rapes and murders as he continued to still commit daytime B&Es with theft of property. The crimes, though seemingly poles apart in terms of motive and MO, weren't always mutually exclusive, one crime often complementing the other in terms of technique or knowledge gained. On at least one occasion, he first targeted a home for property, then used his newly gained knowledge of how to defeat the locks to return months later to rape and murder the female occupant and whoever else was there. Ultimately receiving thirteen death sentences, Ramirez was supposed to have been gassed in the green room at San Quentin State Prison—the infamous "Big Q"—where in 1996 he married his equally deranged long-term pen pal Doreen Lioy. He ended up cheating the hangman—or by then the needle man—and died of B-cell lymphoma in 2013 shortly after the couple divorced.

But before Ramirez was even on the radar, before he had even started simultaneously burglarizing and killing in California, cops in Madison had, to their credit, realized that the break-in on Randall Street was likely just the tip of the iceberg and the key to other unsolved crimes. Once in custody, Taylor was found to have a dated injury to his arm, right or left was never clarified, which still hadn't healed. Upon closer inspection, investigators were able to discern a pattern to the wound, one consistent with human teeth marks. Someone in recent weeks had clearly bitten the young man, but the question remained who, since Taylor wasn't talking. The woman attacked in her apartment within hours of Donna Mraz's murder hadn't bitten her intruder; Donna, on the other hand, was the type of girl who might have. Headstrong and assertive, an accomplished athlete and leader, she wouldn't have gone down without a fight—as best she could have. The problem was that the two sexual assaults that bookended Donna's murder aside, there were eight other stranger attacks followed by rapes in Madison that same week alone. It also might not have been a female bite mark, perhaps the result of another unreported scuffle that Taylor had gotten into during his various criminal exploits. No one is sure who made the final snap judgment—who swore out the affidavit for exhumation—but the Major Case Unit would go for a Hail Mary win and bank on the bite mark matching with Donna's teeth. If they lined up, it would put Taylor at the scene. He would be confirmed as Donna's killer and could even inherit the Capital City Killer title as an addendum if he was willing to cop to it. Explaining how the previous victims were taken so far by bicycle before being dumped and posed might be a problem, as would trying to convince the public that the serial killer terrorizing the city started when he was just twelve years old and burned the remains of Debbie Bennett, but they'd cross that bridge if and when it came. It didn't.

After the body of young Donna Mraz was pulled from the earth—her family having no say in the matter and never even being told why, or what the police were looking for—a forensic odontologist at the state crime lab compared her plaster teeth impressions to the pattern on Taylor's arm. Rather than simply trying to rely on a dental X-ray, the extraordinary step of exhuming the girl's body was no doubt in part due to recent well-publicized success in this fledgling area of forensic science. As a comparison examination technique used only sporadically in the past, it had generally been considered a controversial methodology since bite wounds are continuously changing in their form. The technique came of age, however, three years prior during the 1979 trial of Ted Bundy for the Chi Omega sorority house massacre in 1978 when four women were viciously attacked, two of them murdered. Bundy had bitten one of his victims deeply in one of her buttocks during the attack, and two leading forensic dentists, Richard Souviron and Lowell Levine, were able to conclusively match castings of Bundy's teeth to the wound. It turned out to be key evidence in the case and looking for bite-mark evidence became an increasingly acceptable investigative technique into the 1980s. In most cases, however, the technique was and still is used, almost without exception, to match a killer's teeth to wounds on a victim's skin, not the reverse. That meant that, in the end, the exhumation of Donna's body turned out to be a long shot that missed the mark since experts were unable to confirm that the bite marks on Taylor matched Donna's teeth. That is not to say that they weren't from her, only that four months later a conclusive match that would hold up in a Wisconsin court couldn't be made.

As Donna was reinterred at the Roselawn cemetery, Lonnie Taylor was free to go. He was never convicted of the B&E on Randall Street but, as if by odd coincidence, the end of November saw the string of slashings, sex assaults, and break-ins in Madison subside as quickly as they began. The university, however, was another story.

Chapter 9

Rural Route

Those who make the worst use of their time are the first to complain of its brevity.

—Jean de La Bruyère, *The Characters*

As Seen on TV

There's a widely known saying, unknown in origin, that simply states: "May you live in interesting times." It's intended not as a blessing, wishing well for the future, but rather as an ironic curse, generally wishing one times of turmoil, uncertainty, and disorder—in essence a foreboding wish for troubled times to come. Once known as the "Chinese curse," no confirmed origin of the statement can, however, be found in Dynastic Chinese writings, with its earliest known English reference dating only to the twentieth century. In fact, despite the negative connotation given to it today, the saying seems more apropos of something one might find in a Chinese fortune cookie—itself an American invention first popularized in California—than anything with its dubious and disputed roots of Eastern origin. What is clear is that the statement and the corresponding idea are generally associated with bad luck. Bobby Kennedy even referenced the saying in a famous speech before a group of university students in Cape

Town with a more positive spin, suggesting that interesting times can also be creative times. That June '66 speech in South Africa was not long after Jorgensen claimed to have completed his final mission there. Two years later nearly to the day, as Jorgensen fled to NYC, Bobby was assassinated in downtown LA by a stable worker named Sirhan Sirhan, the latest casualty of violence associated with the so-called Kennedy curse.

The year 1984 certainly signaled the start of interesting times, both in Madison and across the whole of America. It was the same year that the FBI petitioned the US Congress for the money needed to fight the new scourge of the serial killer and when, as some criminologists have suggested, coverage of the FBI's clarion call to Congress in the *New York Times* served to create the first social panic about serial murder in America. Two years earlier, President Ronald Reagan had declared the War on Drugs but now the bureau, citing an estimated ten thousand victims of serial murder a year in America alone, had a new offensive to mount. Names like Ted Bundy, John Wayne Gacy, Richard Chase, and Angelo Buono and Kenneth Bianchi—the Hillside Stranglers—all still resonated with the American public. In truth, they scared the hell out of them, and the feds knew it. A sea change was underway in relation to how many murders were committed and the way in which they needed to be investigated. Until it knew exactly what they were dealing with, the FBI needed a proverbial blank check to bankroll new initiatives. These initiatives included its new Behavioral Sciences Unit, now the Behavioral Analysis Units—actually five in total—all attached to the National Center for the Analysis of Violent Crime. By 1983, the "Mind Hunter" program, as it was colloquially known, was still putting the finishing touches on what would ultimately become the genesis of offender profiling as we know it today.

Profiling, or criminal investigative analysis as it's more commonly cited, is never conducted as seen on TV. Contrary to what is portrayed on nonsensical series such as *Criminal Minds*, profiling is only used during the third wave of an investigation *after* all conventional methods have been all but exhausted. Unlike serialized television, those conducting the analysis also don't fly between cities on private charters to take over investigations from local law enforcement or make arrests and indulge in shootouts. The fictional investigative fantasia depicted in network prime time simply doesn't exist. The truth is that there are actually a large number of accredited experts—including clinical and forensic psychologists, psychiatrists, and noted criminologists—who are the real-world analysts properly trained in this area. Some of these same authorities on the subject have delved into this issue and suggest that, with the actuarial method having a success rate of roughly 5 percent, about the same as any random outcome involving pure luck, law enforcement should get out of the profiling business altogether and leave investigative applications of psychology to the properly lettered, published, and peer-reviewed authorities on the subject.

The first case to receive the benefit of an outside, expert perspective—specifically in the field of forensic psychiatry—was the lesser-known "Babes of Inglewood Murders" of 1937. The profile drew on the perceived success of Dr. Thomas Bond's Whitechapel suspect mock-up and sought to narrow a field of persons potentially responsible for the murders of three little girls aged six to nine. It eventually identified a local school-crossing guard named Albert Dyer who had used the position to lure unsuspecting grade-schoolers to their deaths. Later, in the mid-1950s, public pressure led to an outside expert being similarly recruited by the NYPD to prepare a psychiatric profile of the then unidentified "Mad Bomber" of New York City. As a lone-wolf domestic terrorist, he targeted, seemingly at random, public buildings by hiding explosives indiscriminately while trying to kill civilians and to generally wreak havoc, all the while sending bizarre Ripper-like ramblings to the local press.

Between 1940 and 1956, a total of thirty-three of his homemade explosives were planted in crowded public places, usually hidden from view—in a locker at Penn Station, underneath a seat cushion at Radio City Music Hall—collectively resulting in twenty-two explosions that injured a total of fifteen people. Miraculously, despite injuries, no one was ever killed. In an era before the post-9/11 omnipresent security of today, it had not been a challenge for the brazen bomber to smuggle in and secrete explosives in these places. Recognizing that the bomber wouldn't stop until he was caught, and that fatalities were both likely inevitable and imminent given the frequency of incidents, detectives enlisted the assistance of prominent Manhattan forensic psychiatrist Dr. James Brussel. Like all psychiatrists, unlike psychologists, Brussel was first and foremost a medical doctor. In addition to being a physician by training, he also had a significant personal and professional interest in the criminal mind and specialized in the pharmacological treatment of criminal offenders. By the time the NYPD asked him to develop an offender profile on the bomber, Brussel already had a significant number of patients he could use in what is now called a *typological approach* to assist him in developing a list of probable personality traits—to help him pin down the psychological characteristics of the suspect.

In examining all of the elements of each crime scene as well as the post-offense behavior—in essence suspectology—which included the taunting letters sent to the newspapers, Brussel theorized that the bomber likely had a background in mechanical work (given the complexity of the bombs), that he likely lived alone and was unmarried (given that his activities in bomb making would be noticed), and, that he was likely a middle-aged man with a specific grudge against Consolidated Edison, New York City's main power company at the time (given that the company was named in at least one letter). Brussel also theorized that the bomber had no specific political objectives and that the attacks were likely carried out as a result of some misplaced anger or desire for revenge.

While these conclusions seemed overly specific to many at the time, and while Brussel also made a number of other recommendations that proved to be inaccurate, many of the key details proved to be accurate once a former Consolidated Edison employee named George Metesky was arrested in 1957 and admitted to being the elusive Mad Bomber. Police were tipped off to Metesky by a human resource administrator at Consolidated Edison who knew him to be a problematic former employee, injured on the job, and displeased with the compensation he'd received. He had been sending the company threatening letters for several years, including some that were found to contain a number of the same terms used in the anonymous letters sent to the media. Just as Brussel theorized, Metesky had been a mechanical worker with the company, was middle-aged and unmarried, and was angry at the world about his predicament.

He was also legally insane, and was subsequently sent to a mental-health facility rather than doing his time at Sing Sing.

Just over fifteen years later and over two thousand miles away during the early morning hours of June 25, 1973, seven-year-old Suzie Jaeger—innocent, helpless, fast asleep—was snatched from her sealed tent while camping with her family at a campsite in Montana. The girl had been overpowered and subdued in her sleep before she could scream and alert her parents and siblings asleep in their own tents just a few feet away on the small site near other populated sites. No ransom note had been left or was ever received. After the Jaeger case had been subsequently referred to the FBI by local law enforcement, agent Howard Teten—inquisitive, innovative, a UC Berkeley psych grad—became involved and quickly knew the evidence at the campsite spelled abduction by an experienced peeper-prowler. He theorized that the offender would almost certainly be acting out on a number of paraphilias, including Peeping Tom and sleep-watching activities, precursors to more serious crimes and behaviors ignored five years earlier in the days leading to the murder of Christine Rothschild.

Using simple deductive reasoning, the hallmark of Sherlock Holmes with whom the term is generally associated, Teten was able to draw specific conclusions based on certain generalities. Relying on a combination of experience and common sense, what Holmes would call "elementary" observation, Teten knew that someone unaccustomed to stealthily prowling on private property at night would not likely be so brazen as to enter a tent with several witnesses within immediate earshot. Theorizing that the offender had likely killed Suzie Jaeger and would kill again—that the motive was sexual and that the offender would be sure to never allow the child to identify him or testify—he additionally postulated that the perpetrator would also likely have kept clothing items as souvenirs to visually re-create the crime as part of an elaborate fantasy related to his paraphilias. Because peepers and prowlers are highly visual offenders, he concluded that this visual regime was necessary to prolong the fantasy well beyond the completion of the act of murder. Teten also theorized that the severity of the offender's paraphilic impulses were such that they had likely previously landed him in trouble with the law and that he was already in the system—on file or in police records somewhere.

The very next year, in September 1974, a twenty-three-year-old drifter named David Meirhofer was arrested in the nearby town of Manhattan, Montana, where he had, it was later determined, hidden souvenirs from his various crimes in the walls of his apartment as Teten had suspected. Although he only had a minor criminal record, in an interview with the police, in addition to confessing to the abduction and murder of Suzie Jaeger, he admitted that he had also killed three other people in Montana between 1967 and 1974; he'd also kidnapped one of those victims while she was sleeping. After his arrest and subsequent confession, Meirhofer later hanged himself in his jail cell. Glad tidings. Good riddance.

Orange Socks

By mid-1983, with the profiling methods professionalized and standardized by Howard Teten—a system now generally referred to as the "Teten technique"—at the core of its fledgling offender profiling system, the FBI was mobilizing agents all over the country to combat the new national scourge of the serial sexual murderer. Yet, despite apparently having resurrected the idea of the existence of a single Capital City Killer—a Ripper by any other name—responsible for some or most of the Mad City campus-related murders, no one in Madison or elsewhere in Dane County saw fit to ask for the bureau's help. This, despite a previous working relationship with the feds and their many agents who were on the ground in the aftermath of the Sterling Hall bombing in the fall of '70. Then, in the summer of '83, it seemed that a break finally came. Wisconsin police eyes soon turned to an Okie drifter who'd been collared in June of that year in Texas for felony possession of an unregistered firearm. The Texas Ranger who made the bust, a cop named Phil Ryan, later went on to television fame after cruising on the notoriety of that same arrest, becoming the technical consultant for the camp '90s CBS action-drama *Walker, Texas Ranger*, starring Chuck Norris. The itinerant man he busted, however, went on to even bigger things himself, demonstrating his even more fervent flair for the love of drama.

Henry Lee Lucas, the man stopped by Ranger Ryan that day, was a scraggly and soulless drifter who'd done horrific things he couldn't wait to boast about. Lucas's past was a story of veritable mistreatment and depravity, both as victim and victimizer. A shiv job from his own brother at the age of ten took his left eye and left him with a shoddy glass replacement. His prostitute mother forced him to wear women's clothes and watch her fornicate with violent johns in their squalid Blacksburg, Virginia, home, wanton abuse that later turned him into a sadistic paraphiliac beyond rehabilitation. His mother was thought to be his first victim; that is until, as has been recently revealed, he killed a girl when he was fourteen in order to conceal having committed sex crimes against the victim, also age fourteen. After being in and out of juvie facilities and state care, a twenty-three-year-old Henry Lee beat his mother Viola Lucas to within an inch of her life in January '60, leaving her in a pool of blood where she eventually died of a heart attack triggered by the trauma of the assault. The cops later picked him up in Ohio while on the run but, by 1970, he was already kicked loose from the big house while serving a twenty-year bit, ostensibly due to prison overcrowding and the assessment that he was at low risk for committing additional offenses. He was back in custody within the year after trying to lure three schoolgirls into his car. He was out again by 1975, and within the year had settled in Jacksonville, Florida, where he met Ottis Toole, a panhandler, pyrophiliac, and inveterate fire starter in a local soup kitchen. Then things took a turn for the worse.

A native Floridian, Toole had an IQ somewhere near room temperature and, like Lucas, had been tormented by his alcoholic mother to no end. He too, by strange coincidence, had been forced to wear girls' dresses and acquiesce to horrific emotional and physical abuse, including incestuous sexual assaults by relatives, both male and female. His chance meeting with Lucas was, like the beginning of all team killer partnerships, something that would confound cops and criminologists alike for decades. It still does. It would leave them to wonder what the odds were that two forces of such depravity—like Ian Brady and Myra Hindley in England

and their heinous "Murders on the Moor," Leonard Lake and Charles Ng in California and their want-ad murders of young couples along with video-recorded torture rituals, Paul Bernardo and Karla Homolka and their "Schoolgirl Murders" in Canada—ever finding each other could have been, and how history might have been different if they hadn't. How many lives would have been saved if they'd never crossed paths?

It was 1976 when they first met, broke the ice, and began discussing their respective twisted fixations. By the time Lucas was arrested in Texas and Toole picked up for an arson in Florida, the arrests coming within months of each other in 1983, they were each prepared to talk. The police were soon able to link Toole to at least six murders, some carried out with the assistance of Lucas, some carried out on his own. The latter set of murders included a Florida man he had barricaded in his house and then burned alive after setting the place on fire, as well as—most infamously—the 1981 murder of Adam Walsh, kidnapped from a Sears store in Hollywood, Florida and later decapitated. The boy's murder turned Adam's father, John Walsh, into an unrivaled anticrime crusader, with the murder of his son leading him to spearhead the long-running *America's Most Wanted* series, followed by the recent *The Hunt*, which similarly uses reenactments to solicit tips on the whereabouts of wanted fugitives. Lucas's murderous exploits were, however, harder to pin down.

Claiming to be emissaries of a secret underground Satanic cult operating nationwide known as the "The Hand of Death," Lucas asserted that he and Toole had left a grisly trail of hundreds—possibly thousands—of victims, mostly hitchhikers, prostitutes, and truck-stop lot lizards all across the Lower 48. Lucas initially claimed to have killed twenty-eight people as part of his indoctrination into the cult, a number that quickly ballooned to over one hundred as soon as investigators from various states got a chance to sit down with him. Lucas reveled in the attention, and as dubious as some of his admissions were, he was hitting all of the hot buttons within the American psyche at the time: serial murder, interstate flight, and most importantly, Satanism. An unrepentant and malignant narcissist and attention seeker, Lucas was playing a nationwide consortium of cops eager to clear the books like a collection of Stradivarii—and it was working. By November '83, the Lucas Task Force was officially formed. He was set to be the most prolific serial killer in American history. He'd make sure of it, and the cops would do their best to help make it so.

In the end, Lucas was convicted of "only" eleven murders of the roughly *three thousand* to which he had confessed. Experts who've examined the cases in detail and are able to see the forest through the trees amid his many confessions, often later recanted, have sanded down his admitted number to roughly forty slayings where there appear to be actual linkages. For ten of these murders Lucas was sentenced to terms of life imprisonment. The sole murder to which Lucas conclusively could be linked and which sent him to death row was that of an unidentified Jane Doe found in a culvert off I-35 near Georgetown, Texas. Apparently thrown off the freeway overpass to the pavement below, the body had no identifying or distinguishing features other than two missing front teeth, a distinctive ring, and two matchbooks, including one from a dive motel in Henryetta, Oklahoma, some four hundred miles away. Discovered on the afternoon of Halloween '79, the victim was also wearing a fittingly themed set of orange stockings, the only clothing left on the body. The unidentified woman was soon assigned a new name. They called her Orange Socks.

Eventually sentenced to what the inmates call the "stainless steel ride"—death by lethal injection—at Huntsville for the sexual assault and murder of Orange Socks, Lucas would later have that sentence commuted because of concerns raised about his confession to the murder. These concerns centered on his penchant both for grandstanding and for recanting confessions. Moreover, lawmen bet on the fact that, in the Orange Socks case, carrying out an execution under these circumstances would not be judged favorably by history—even in Texas. It seems that many people, all the way up to then Governor George W. Bush signing off on the commutation, had their doubts about the confession and Lucas's actual involvement in the death of Orange Socks—today still an unidentified Jane Doe. Prior to receiving executive clemency in 1998, Lucas had spent the better part of fifteen years on death row. All the while, he was still ready and willing to talk to anyone who would listen.

In the meantime, cops in plain clothes with trunk loads of banker's boxes full of manila folders, each folder containing a cold-case murder book and an array of gruesome murder scene pix, were happy to make the drive to Texas to obtain Lucas's confession, clear the books, and be gone again. For many a weary and ethically pliable homicide cop, Lucas's compulsively blabbing about the Hand of Death, murderous road trips with Toole from coast to coast, and dabbling in Satanic ritual and torture seemed to loosely fit just about every MO of every unsolved case in America. Before long, word of Lucas's self-proclaimed exploits, his road trips through flyover states as a murderous drifter, and the likelihood of his having the highest body count of any serial killer in national history—maybe even toppling H. H. Holmes—had made its way to the Mad City. As 1983 drew to a close, fifteen years after the Rothschild murder, the first in the series of Madison's cold campus and area slayings, opportunity seemed to be knocking. The Wisconsin police would answer. Soon Lucas would be happy to oblige them.

Senior Year

As the Major Case Unit back in Madison dusted off old manila folders—more than a decade's worth of pain and torment relegated to the pages of handwritten reports, photostats, teletypes, and carbons—the Mad City and its beloved UW wondered if they might finally be out of the woods. Although the year 1983 had elsewhere brought about interesting times, in Madison, things seemed relatively sedate. Things still more or less seemed as they used to be or at least as people *thought* they used to be. Unfortunately, as 1984 came into focus, the UW campus, the common denominator in at least six sex murders dating back to the spring of '68, was about to pivot toward a new and unforeseen connection. Soon, those who didn't know or who'd forgotten that UW had other campuses outside the Mad City would find the fall of '84 to be a revelatory time. The events of that same autumn would also set in motion new theories—new spook stories and scattershot conspiracies—that in coming years would propel the entire UW campus system back into the national spotlight.

That same August of '84 would mark the start of the fourth and final fall term—the start of senior year—for twenty-year-old Janet Raasch. Like Donna Mraz before her, Janet was a business major; like Julie Ann Hall, she also worked in an administrative position on campus. The distinction in Janet's case was that she was based at UW's lesser-known campus at Stevens Point, a small city about a hundred miles north of the Mad City in Portage County and roughly the same distance due west of Green Bay. Despite the change of venue, by October of that year, the similarities to the other UW girls before her would soon reveal themselves.

In the fall of '84 UW's Stevens Point campus had been a university in the traditional sense for just a little over twenty years, having been founded originally as a "normal school" in 1894 by Portage County to train teachers. Unlike the Madison campus, UW's flagship venue, Stevens Point was and remains a comparatively rural area with its just over four hundred acres of rolling green campus lying between State Route 66 and I-39. With less than a quarter of the students hosted by the Mad City campus, it also remains a place—apart from the nature reserve and twenty-five-acre lake within the campus boundary—that typifies the state's scenic veneer. In addition, it's isolated enough that, once word got out, a number of NFL teams used the campus and surrounding areas as an off-season training ground, the so-called "Cheese League" to rival Major League Baseball's spring training "Grapefruit League" in Florida.

Simultaneously balancing her senior-year studies with her part-time job at the DeBot Center on campus—the principal dining and conference hall—Janet Raasch was, like so many of the victims before her, someone never afraid to burn the candle at both ends. A farm girl born and raised, young Janet wasn't afraid of hard work, or afraid of getting her hands dirty, or afraid of much of anything. She was also too young to remember, much less likely even know of, what happened to the girls back at or near UW–Madison—girls hitchhiking, walking, or simply going about their daily business when they were found by their killers. Then again, that was Madison, and Stevens Point was *not* the Mad City. The Capital City Killer stuck to the capital as his name implied, and those sorts of things simply didn't happen in agrarian Portage County. UW–Stevens Point, like UW–Madison, was a *decent* place—or so it was thought. The reality is that, in 1984 Middle America, nowhere was safe. It was an inconvenient truth few would admit.

On the afternoon of October 11, 1984—a Thursday in broad daylight—an acquaintance from campus dropped Janet off at a county road junction along State Trunk Highway 54, just outside the Stevens Point city limits. Janet told the man that she was going to head home for a few days, likely just for the weekend, back to her family's place in the town of Merrill about fifty miles north of the campus. Yet the driver, as he later reported, had picked her up hitchhiking while carrying a small satchel in Stevens Point and driven her beyond the city limits to the south, not the north. In fact, it was never clear—never reported by the media, never clarified by police—why exactly Janet was brought to that particular intersection to be dropped off. It was also never clear why, on a Thursday barely into her final fall term, she was already headed back home. Perhaps most curiously, no one ever explained—or bothered to ask—why she was dropped off roughly fifteen minutes away, near the town of Buena Vista, when she was actually headed in the opposite direction. Unlike Julie Speerschneider, the vanishing hitchhiker who disappeared into the night less than a block from her destination, the intended final stop defied the drop point. Unlike Speerschneider, Janet was also left at the roadside alone and nowhere near where she was headed—in fact, in the opposite direction entirely. Yet, precisely like Speerschneider, it was in the rearview mirror of a car speeding away that Janet was last seen alive.

Four days later, October 15, the manager at the DeBot Center made a call to Janet's room at Watson Hall on campus to ask her to come in for a shift, only to find she wasn't there. She *always* answered the phone during the week; she *never* missed the opportunity to work an extra shift. It was a simple but revelatory turn of events. One thing led to another—and to another—and before long, friends and coworkers started piecing together that Janet never made it to her family's home in Merrill. Her family had some concerns of their own and eventually called the university administration and staff at Watson Hall. In the first critical few hours, it seemed that her family had assumed she was back in Stevens Point, either working at the DeBot Center or out with friends and otherwise delayed in leaving. Her friends on campus and the staff at DeBot assumed at the same time that she had arrived safely back in Merrill. All the while, she was somewhere else entirely.

Before long, Stevens Point was Madison from fifteen years earlier, transplanted. Though the circumstances surrounding the disappearance of Janet Raasch were vaguely reminiscent of the Julie Speerschneider case, the vigorous leaflet campaign certainly had the makings of an encore of the community closing ranks in the aftermath of Julie's disappearance in March of '79. Posters bearing Janet's smiling visage—the quintessence of rural innocence—went up on the front doors of grocers, hardware stores, and greasy spoons across three counties. The media reported as best they could on the case but the timeline and even a theoretical itinerary was difficult if not impossible to nail down. Why did she choose to get dropped off in Buena Vista? Why was she going home to Merrill? Whom might she have been waiting for on Highway 54? An appeal for witnesses and fresh tips came up dry, other than a reported sighting in Marshfield, a town located about a forty-minute drive west of the campus. The cops chased it down and, like so many false sightings that waylay investigations, it was ruled out as bunk. As Janet's name and details were flagged as endangered missing on the National Crime Information Center and her face became a fixture on every lamppost, mailbox, and storefront across central Wisconsin, all anyone could do was wait. All the while, the man who'd dropped her off in the middle of nowhere—the last to see her alive—was sticking to his story.

Hunting Season

The morning of November 17, 1984, marked the start of a seasonably cold Saturday in Portage County, one week before the Thanksgiving weekend and within that narrow window when it was open season on the state's bird population before they flew south for the winter. With that, a small hunting party set out into the woods southwest of Highway 54 and County Road J near the village of Plover, dried autumn leaves rustling beneath their feet from the trees above, which had long since been rendered bare. The hunters were only a dozen paces or so into the bush when they happened upon a partially clothed and partially decomposed body lying on the forest floor. It was the remains of Janet Raasch, found a mere three turnoffs east down Highway 54 from where she had purportedly been dropped off near Old Amish Road.

The total distance from where she was last seen alive to where she was found dead was less than two miles. The total time elapsed between when she was last seen by her friend at the roadside to when she was found by the bird hunters was thirty-seven days. She had been dead since the day she was last seen, and, in the intervening weeks, the weather and local scavengers had made the identification process difficult. The missing-person poster circulated throughout the area and the local news reports, however, had specified the clothing she was last seen wearing, and in the early hours of the investigation, it allowed for a tentative identification. Janet's sister and father back in Merrill had just finished a day of hunting that same Saturday when they returned to the homestead and the phone rang. It was the dreaded call that changed everything and allowed the Raasch family to join the Rothschilds, the Bennetts, the Halls, the Speerschneiders, the LeMahieus, the Stewarts, and the Mrazes as the collateral damage of the Capital City Killer's mayhem. Only now, it was no longer the Capital City. The scourge knew no limits other than, as some speculated, restricting the hunt to on or near additional UW campuses.

A subsequent autopsy and cause of death determination was slow going. Two months after the body had been discovered, the crime lab in Madison still hadn't completed the full postmortem exam and report, nor conducted tox screens on the victim's blood and hair. In fact, it wasn't until the final days of January '85 that Portage County Coroner Scott Rifleman was prepared to confirm that Janet's death was a homicide at all. He speculated that the girl had been strangled to death, though the state of the body—as with so many of the others—made it impossible to say for certain. Investigators on the case who refused to be named conceded that "partially clothed" meant that Janet's pants had been removed, and that she had likely been "sexually molested," as they discreetly leaked to the press.

With that, Janet Raasch, missing person, became case number 84-I-1548—homicide. Over the years that file number would become engraved into the minds of countless investigators. Unlike the quagmire back in the Mad City, the case was a Portage County affair from start to finish. The Sheriff's Department maintained sole custody of the case and worked it as best they could given the investigative and technological limitations of the era, and for a small agency actually managed to punch above its weight and give the case a serious effort. But just like back in Madison, detectives came and went, banker's boxes piled up, tips were reviewed and vetted—all to no avail. No one would admit it, but by the close of 1985 the case was already cold.

Seventeen years later, in 2002, Janet's remains were, like Donna Mraz's body, exhumed as part of a desperate attempt to probe for new evidence—offender DNA in this case. They found none. Later, in July 2013, the *Stevens Point Journal* printed new information—once again leaked, but with the best intentions—that cops were working a new angle: that Janet was pregnant at the time of her murder. It might explain the sudden unscheduled and unannounced return home that autumn, the odd drop point—perhaps a meeting spot—and could certainly yield one or more people with a motive. The other possibility is that the removal of the clothing, the pregnancy, and the cops staying mum on the cause of death all converge. It could be that their refusing to cough up the precise cause of death, refusing to confirm or deny—or refuting altogether—the coroner's earlier proclamation that she was strangled, reflects the fact that the theory of a botched abortion matches injuries observed at the scene thirty years earlier. The theory might even explain why, over a month after she was discovered, a precise cause of death couldn't be determined for certain. It may, in fact, explain a lot. If the tip is indeed genuine, the suspect list should have been—and still should be—a short one. The driver who was the last to see her alive should also still be at the top of that list.

As unlikely as it seems, there are indeed tragic cases—many cases, in fact—where missing-person and murder investigations end up being revealed as accidental deaths. They often then end up as criminally negligent homicides rather than murders per se, but horrific losses of life no less, and typically at the hands of someone the victim trusted—or was simply duped into meeting before a procedure, such as a high-risk abortion, being forced upon them. In Janet's case, it might explain the drop point, with the story of going home for the weekend being subterfuge. It would certainly explain why the cause of death was never publicly revealed. Unlike the other Mad City victims, many of whom were found months or years later, a single month over the course of a cold Wisconsin autumn wouldn't be enough to render a cause of death determination impossible if carried out by a competent pathologist. The more likely scenario is instead that the cause of death is the most significant piece of holdback information the cops had at the time—and still have. It would mean that the cause of death was central to the motive and to the probable offender-victim relationship. Either way, the revelation of the new theory by the local press got someone talking—or more accurately, writing.

Within a few months of the hidden pregnancy theory, the Portage County Sheriff received an anonymous letter, and suddenly the plot thickened. Just shy of the mystery's thirty-year anniversary, it was 1984 all over again. Like the cause of death and condition of Janet's body, with this latest development the police followed the lead of their compeers in the Mad City's Major Case Unit and simply said nothing. All that was publicly stated by 2014 was that whoever wrote the letter should come forward—that cops were interested in talking to the author. No kidding. Whatever details were contained in the letter, it piqued investigators' interest; it somehow suggested knowledge of some, if not all, of the holdback information on the case.

But the problem with letters is that, hoaxes and sadistic quacks simply looking to sabotage cases aside, even well-intentioned letters can turn out to be red herrings when the police are desperate for morsels. It's happened before and will no doubt happen again. Cops get an unsigned letter, some investigators dismiss it outright, and others think they're sitting on a gold mine. Then, police brass kick it around for a few months and make a perfunctory plea for the author to offer himself or herself up. Later, a redacted version of the letter, or simply piecemeal excerpts, gets released to the media in a bid to solicit new tips or to simply ferret out the author through a system of dry snitching. Before long, the whole thing snowballs and becomes its own sideshow, with one red herring after another—anonymous letters inspiring more letters—and the cops chasing down bogus leads while the real truth drifts farther and farther away. The cases of Beverly Potts in Cleveland, the Grimes sisters in Chicago, Thomas Wales in Seattle, and Linda Shaw in Canada: these are but a few of the hundreds of murder investigations that, once cold, compel someone wracked by guilt to put pen to paper. Sometimes the information is sent straight to authorities, sometimes—like in the Potts disappearance in Cleveland—it's a dead letter drop, the incriminating note in that case left beneath the wall-to-wall carpet in a home for the future owners to discover decades later. Either way, anonymous letters usually hurt more than they help. Nevertheless, in Janet's case, it seems the local cops are still betting the farm on the cryptic note they received in 2013. Since then it's been radio silence. The Janet Raasch murder remains the only cold case in Portage County history.

Cooking the Books

The final days of Janet Raasch's life—in the offices of the DeBot Center, her suite at Watson Hall, and the classrooms of UW–Stevens Point—coincided with the final days of a remarkable shakedown in the state of Texas. It was a legendary roust courtesy of some Madison and area Major Case Unit cops looking to button up six nagging cold cases. A year earlier, Ranger Phil Ryan had busted Henry Lee Lucas and ran him in on a simple gun beef. Before long, the whole thing morphed into a veritable carnival of confessions—dubious admissions of Satanic ritual and interstate murder that brought cops from far and wide to go under the big top. Lucas was a strike-anywhere match who could be used to light up any dormant case, give it a named suspect, and allow the books to be cleared in record time. With the colossal tide of confessions already piling up and the certainty of guilty verdicts, a death sentence, and an expedited execution, there was no worry about ever having to pin the more questionable—if not logistically impossible—cases on Lucas heard before a court of law. There was not much point in even indicting him with the murders to which he confessed given the diminishing returns on prosecuting an already-condemned man. He was a dead man walking—or so they hoped.

The whole matter soon became a runaway train where Lucas proved himself to be perhaps the most compliant, pliable, and convincing of suspects ever interviewed, for weeks and months accommodating a never-ending receiving line of homicide detectives from across America. Lucas not only admitted to any and all unsolved murders that the cops laid out in front of him, but also to files they hadn't even brought with them. He was just vague enough on the locations, just close enough with respect to the MO, signature, and victim description, that his confessions couldn't be disproven. He even confessed to murders for which the bodies of the victims hadn't been found, in some sense future proofing investigations for years to come and allowing cops to clear murders to him perhaps even from beyond the grave. He provided general directions to where bodies were buried or dumped, or vague landmarks—tall trees, farmhouses, old wells—that could be found just about anywhere a body might turn up across the Lower 48. It was all a performance, but no one with the Lucas Task Force saw fit to stop him.

Most of his murder confessions required no coaxing—Lucas would just start talking and detectives would start writing. Many, like Orange Socks, were also Jane Doe cases, suspected prostitutes or young girls disowned from their families and hitchhiking aimlessly across America—perfect victims for someone like Lucas and his purported Hand of Death mandate. It all seemed to make good sense. Lucas and the police investigators who came to see him were good for each other.

Two of the victims Lucas confessed to killing, confessions that were taken at face value until only recently, included one Caledonia Jane Doe, found at the side of US Route 20 in New York in November of '79. The girl had been shot in the back of the head and had tan lines and pollen on her clothes that indicated she'd recently come from a sunny vacation spot. None of this matched with Lucas's MO or preferred victimology, but it was taken as fact for over thirty-five years. In 2015, Caledonia Jane Doe was identified as sixteen-year-old Tammy Alexander from Florida. Never reported missing by her family when she dropped off the radar in 1979, a high school friend unable to find her on social media in 2010 initiated her own freelance investigation and eventually pieced it all together with the help of modern-day police investigators. The ensuing timeline all but ruled out Lucas as possibly being the killer, notwithstanding the fact that Tammy was last seen with a clean-cut, bespectacled man driving a brown station wagon—details known in 1979 but later glossed over when Lucas confessed.

The other Jane Doe that was erroneously pinned on Lucas with his okay also wasn't positively identified until 2015. Known as the Bossier Doe for nearly thirty-five years, Carol Cole's body was found in Bossier Parish, Louisiana, in the winter of '81, stabbed to death and left in a stand of trees since likely the previous summer. Given how the details of the case failed to line up with earlier confessions by Lucas to other confirmed crimes committed in other states between 1980 and 1981, investigators knew that Lucas wasn't really in Louisiana—much less in San Antonio, Texas, where Cole had been reported missing in the summer of '80—and thus couldn't have been her killer. He confessed anyway, and the confession was recorded, at least for the short term, as credible. The murder was cleared to Lucas's name even though the cops knew it stunk. In the meantime, the real killers of these girls walked the streets and claimed who knows how many others. Lucas's methods and his ability to hold court while languishing in prison and have decorated cops hanging on his every word also proved contagious once the term "serial killer" took on a certain cachet value in coming years. Before long, Lucas would inspire a contagion of false confession to serial murder.

Embellished criminal exploits, spooky backstories about cults and conspiracies, and falsely confessing to the murders of innocents in a bid for tabloid fame became a cottage industry for the desperate and deranged the world over throughout the 1980s. Later, in the early 1990s, a Swedish man named Sture Bergwall, using the more media-friendly pseudonym Thomas Quick, was imprisoned for armed robbery and soon started confessing to various unsolved murders. In a country where one of the cold cases still on the books is the 1986 assassination of its own prime minister, Bergwall was a Scandinavian Henry Lee Lucas who investigators were more than happy to sit down with and let talk. By the time they were done, he had confessed to over thirty murders. The problem came when they went to verify his accounts. In addition to many of the confessions being immediately refutable, some of the people he confessed to killing were actually still alive and well. After more than a decade in a psychiatric facility, Bergwall, as of 2008, recanted all of his confessions, and the reality now appears to be that he never murdered anyone.

However, for many years, Bergwall's rants were taken at face value by giddy and opportunistic investigators for long enough that the real killers in those genuine unsolved cases to which Bergwall falsely confessed all walked free. Bergwall and the police alike unwittingly gave them the breathing room they needed to get away with their crimes, many of the files not only being "cleared" to Bergwall but also later expunged from police records altogether. Like wrongful convictions, few people consider the aftermath of false confessions for the victims, and how miscarriages of justice—whether in the courtroom or in the interview room of a jailhouse—once revealed for what they are, summarily turn falsely solved cases into instant cold cases with no prospect of closure.

But in 1984, when Lucas had confessed to being the killer of Caledonia Jane Doe and his admissions were becoming increasingly erratic, the Major Case Unit's interjurisdictional task force would be reactivated for the sole purpose of hitching its wagon to the Lucas Task Force before it was too late. Unlike some of the murders to which Lucas was now confessing—confessions that had even the most enthusiastically flexible of investigators scratching their heads and in an ethical conundrum—the Mad City murders all seemed to plausibly square with Lucas's MO. In fact, they seemed to be a better fit with Lucas in terms of the sexual sadism, organization, and transportation seen in each case than they were with either William Zamastil or shoplifter-turned-child killer Robert Lange, by then serving time for the Paula McCormick slaying in March of '82. It was out with the old and in with the new—Lucas could be the new poster boy for the Capital City Killer.

The victims in Lucas's admissions were also all young women, and there was a comparatively organized—psychopathic versus psychotic—element present in every slaying; the victims were transported over long distances before being dumped naked or almost naked in wooded areas off rural routes and county roads that Lucas had admitted he would frequent during the course of his murderous journeys. With that in mind, the cops figured the gory, fiery disposal of Debbie Bennett's remains could also arguably be chalked up to something pseudo-Satanic or ritualistic in keeping with Lucas's purported Hand of Death cult, and Madison's central location within the United States—a jump-off point to so many routes to the southern states preferred by Lucas—might be why he kept intermittently returning there. Maybe, they pondered, Madison's coed campus offered Lucas a steady supply of his preferred type of victim. The cops also knew that every Madison murder, other than perhaps Christine Rothschild, had relied on the use of a vehicle—an element central to Lucas's mobile offending.

The truth is that Christine Rothschild's murder never made the short list of cases to be artificially cleared to Lucas. The fact that in 1968 Lucas was serving time for beating his mother to death ruled him out for the Rothschild murder, but everything from 1976 onward—once he was sprung from prison on the attempted abduction charges—was fair game. But to bring the open/unsolved cases bookended by Bennett and Mraz to the oracle, a total of six stranger murders that aligned with Lucas's MO, a certain leap of faith first needed to be made. Someone had to officially acknowledge for the first time that all of these sex slayings in Madison were connected. Someone had to go on record to say that the Capital City Killer—a mythical local Ripper long since denied by authorities—was actually real. For Lucas to confess to the murders was to mean that one man was in fact responsible for all of them. For his confession to be taken as fact—even if it was little more than a spoon-fed lie—the murders would first need to be deemed connected in order for the ploy to work. As the books were set to be cooked and six murders "solved" with a single signature by Lucas, the local legend had to first and foremost be admitted as real. With his confessions, Lucas would become the Capital City Killer of past lore. It would amount to an official about-face that the police knew was guaranteed to have cascading legal, economic, and political ramifications for generations to come.

Time and Punishment

In the end, it simply wasn't meant to be. It was too rich for their blood. The suggested last-ditch effort to cobble six murders together and acquiesce to the local legend of the Madison serial killer was flawed from the get-go—too little too late. Four of the cases—the binary Julie Murders, as well as the LeMahieu and Stewart homicides—should have been linked from day one, but the attempt to have them baked in with the Bennett and Mraz killings was doomed to fail, even by Lucas Task Force standards. By the summer of '84, critics were already pulling on the barren threads of Lucas's so-called "confessions," and a new system of due diligence and fact-checking by the task force was in effect. The result was that his confessions were no longer being taken at face value, no longer could he be lobbed basic hints about open/unsolved murders and then led by the hand to fill in the blanks as detectives cued him on right and wrong answers. Cops in Madison and the surrounding area, including the four discrete agencies that comprised the Major Case Unit, and the even more flaccid Intra County Investigative Squad before it, had squandered years saving these cases for a rainy day. Ed Edwards had always been a long shot and a tough sell, but with Lucas, they figured their ship had come in. They guessed wrong; they had missed their window; they were back to square one—again.

The other problem was that, although tarring Lucas as the Capital City Killer might have played well back in Wisconsin had he actually first been nabbed in the Dairy State rather than Texas, there were simply too many eyes on the matter by that point. As a result of efforts by the FBI, the national press, and victim and prisoners' groups alike, Lucas's specific whereabouts over the years, both independently and in concert with Toole, had been largely confirmed by the time the Major Case Unit was thinking of going to the table. His confessions were becoming more and more suspect. Not only had the window closed on any opportunity the Major Case Unit might have had, by 1985 many of Lucas's self-proclaimed crimes were already back open as reactivated investigations, his list of three-thousand-plus killings now winnowed to about forty at most. There was simply no way in this climate of doubt that a few more murders were going to be credibly added to the tally. Mad City and Dane County authorities went back to the drawing board and the cases went back into the boxes—returned to languish in abeyance.

But in the years following the murder of Janet Raasch, a sense of eerie quiet was slowly restored to the UW campus system and the Mad City. By the late 1980s, people, as they so often do, seemed to have moved on beyond what had happened and a tenuous equilibrium had been restored. Janet would be the last of the victims fitting a certain serial pattern for many years, indeed for over a generation. As the tide washed over Dane County, Portage County, and the whole of Wisconsin, the vector of the Capital City Killer story began to change course. As the 1990s brought with it primitive, first-generation Internet iterations of chat rooms and message boards, soon topics and threads relating to all things crime and punishment—cold cases, missing persons, and serial killers—became dominant mainstays of fledgling Web 1.0. From there, true crime became the new long-form narrative of the late twentieth and early twenty-first century.

In time, as the story of the Mad City and UW murders made its way around the world, the tone actually became more rather than less moderate, a distinction that few unsolved crimes of the contemporary era can claim. In time, the Capital City Killer—singular proper noun—became more popularly known as the Capital City killings—pluralized common noun. In other words, an expanded dialogue and the revelation of the Lucas effect as the main determinant for the myth becoming reality led many to question the plausibility of a single offender being responsible for all of the murders—murders that began either with Christine Rothschild or Debbie Bennett. In time, the dialogue shifted from "Killer" to "killings," and new questions began to emerge. One of those questions was: If the murders weren't the work of a single offender, how could a total of up to seven different sexual murderers—each claiming one victim at random—be walking the streets of Madison and its picturesque UW campuses at roughly the same time? Or at least in immediate succession?

Worse yet, how could so many offenders be operating either concurrently or consecutively and *all* manage to elude capture? They were questions that deserved answers. They still do.

The semantics of what happened once upon a time in Madison also began to change as the 1980s became the 1990s, and Linda knew that she too was running out of time—that she was now, more than ever, on a clock. Jorgensen's put-upon mother and author of the now published *The Love Pirate*, Heidi, died the same month that Janet Raasch disappeared. Her scant obituary detailed an October 23, 1984, death from natural causes. Later, as his Sierra Singles consort Ezra Jameson peddled copies of Jorgensen's late mother's manuscript, which served as a carefully varnished recitation of some of the past, Jorgensen filled the void left by his mother's death by clearing out her room and putting it up for rent. As Linda waited for Jorgensen's next move via their proverbial long-distance chess match, she made one final road trip to LA to see what might become of the monster now that his mother—the penultimate of the surviving Jorgensen clan—was in the ground. Linda guessed it would be one of two extremes. One theory was that Jorgensen's manic behavior might stabilize as he tried to blend into upper-middle-class California society and present himself as a self-made man, using his inherited estate as a cover story for the material and professional success that he never had. She well knew that façades and taking credit for the successes and possessions of others was the raison d'être of the psychopath. Alternatively, she feared, much like the similarly twisted love-hate obsession Norman Bates had with his mother in the film *Psycho*, Jorgensen might completely unravel—that he might decompensate to the point where he'd need to kill again. It was, not surprisingly, the latter.

As Linda hit the road to California, she didn't know it, but the past, present, and future were all about to converge. The Age of Aquarius and the Information Age were on a collision course. The impact would be seismic. It would change everything. It would wake the dead.

Chapter 10

Scattered Ashes

The reward of a thing well done is having done it.

—Ralph Waldo Emerson, *The Conduct of Life*

Endgame

The 1990s were a blur. Arguably the nadir of twentieth-century Western civilization—the doldrums of artistic and intellectual advancement save the rise of the Internet—most of the decade was spent by Linda regrouping in what seemed like an endless state of in-between. By the summer of '94 she was well into emotional overdraft, her life consumed by press clippings and adversarial correspondences with police brass who couldn't be bothered, and by the preoccupation that she might be tasting defeat, having let Christine down after all. Back in 1968, few people understood the root of her obsession with seeing the case through, essentially mortgaging her own life for Christine—a girl she'd only known a few months. But by 1994, people understood it even less, and most were tired of hearing about it. Linda was herself tired of trying to explain it all—the fire in the belly that no one else seemed to have. Whether she'd known Christine only a few months—not quite a full UW school year—or for a lifetime was immaterial, she thought. Christine's case was a mantle that Linda picked up when no one else would. It was a calling few people ever have the guts or the moxie to answer; it was the reason the two of them met in the first place—it had to be. Or so Linda told herself, now over a quarter century later. Time had gotten away from her while riding slipstream in Jorgensen's dark wake for most of her adult life. When others gave up, she refused. Even she didn't know why. Or, by the summer of '94, perhaps she'd forgotten—she'd chosen to forget. It was now an end in itself. Jorgensen had to go down.

By August of that same summer, fifteen hundred miles west of Linda's home in Dallas-Fort Worth, it had also been ten years since Heidi Jorgensen had died. By then, her son—now nearly seventy—was an old man in body and even older in mind. Timeworn and turned out, Jorgensen could be found routinely wandering Marina del Rey in one of his now old, yellowed, and tattered white coats—like Dr. Corcoran's "hunting" outfit in *The Love Pirate* that had seen better days—as the cliché local eccentric. His daily routines consisted of hassling people on the boardwalk while trying to solicit donations for a phony foundation he'd set up for the brother he'd murdered, Linda believed, over four decades prior. Jorgensen was played out—or so it seemed.

Why he, apparently with the blessing of his mother years earlier, set up the Søren B. Jorgensen Foundation was nothing short of puzzling. As for the foundation's ostensible goals, no one seemed to ever know. What is clear is that by that summer of '94, for Jorgensen, money had already become tight as a drum. Yet, while he might have been a husk of a man and down to his final few dollars, Jorgensen's predatory instincts were still intact—razor sharp and laser focused. That same year, he had also made some interior adjustments to his mother's former one-bedroom place, moved out the Rickie and Lucy beds in their once-shared quarters, and started sleeping in the bedroom that had been previously used as a den—that housed the now hardcover edition of *The Love Pirate*. He then listed the bedroom as a rental accommodation for tourists or those in town on business—a want-ad hotel alternative twenty years before Airbnb. In due course he had a taker, an Argentinean immigrant—a Seventh-day

Adventist hailing from somewhere else in California who had come to Marina del Ray for some church business—who had been referred to him by Ezra Jameson. Sometime that summer the now nameless Argentinean arrived but the circumstances of any departure remain a mystery, with Jorgensen ignoring all questions about whatever became of him in later years. Whatever actually happened to the young Argentinean, Jorgensen had in the meantime managed to find God. Or, as he would later describe it, God had found *him*.

Newly obsessed with penance and forgiveness, Jorgensen came to embody what is known as religious mania—a curious condition that has accompanied the homicidal impulses of a number of infamous serial killers and necrophiles making up some of this era's most cruel and depraved murderers. Commonly seen during periods of compensation, the condition crosscuts both psychotic and psychopathic killers alike, from cannibal Albert Fish to Gary Ridgway and "BTK Strangler" Dennis Rader. The Babes of Inglewood murderer mentioned earlier, Albert Dyer, was a sadistic school crossing guard and opportunist who was hanged at San Quentin within a year of his arrest. Prior to his execution, however, he had also admitted to praying over the bodies of his victims after having posed them in a ravine while in a state of religious mania that accompanied his sexual arousal and sadistic bent. It was among the first of several key and largely consecutive cases in America and elsewhere to quantifiably suggest that while hyperreligiosity is not in itself necessarily linked to violence, the opposite might sometimes be true. Serial killers, it turns out, are often among the most God-fearing of people. They have good reason to be.

But unlike other sexual sadists and serial killers hiding behind a façade of religion, Jorgensen, it seems, came to genuinely believe. Like Dennis Rader, a deacon in his Kansas church admonishing members of his flock for their minor sins on one hand and a twisted sadist torturing and murdering entire families on the other, Jorgensen began using religion first as a crutch, then as a defense and, before long, realized it also made for a solid offense—an enabler. Almost two decades since his last maneuver against Linda on their proverbial chessboard, she would become the target of his first ecclesiastical assault. But not only was Linda ready for it, it was also just what she'd been waiting for.

Over twenty years earlier, Linda had sent her first cryptic Valentine card, providing not only her name—her *full* name—but also her address and telephone number, inviting, or more accurately daring Jorgensen to call. It soon became an annual tradition, each correspondence becoming increasingly pointed, ever more vexatious. She had crossed over the threshold and was now poking the bear—goading and provoking him with a thumb to the eye but also offering him a pool to reflect in, one that every malignant narcissist craves. Jorgensen, after two decades of stewing and historically accustomed to getting the drop on his victims, in 2006 finally had the fortitude to mail Linda a greeting of his own. Of all things to send as a rejoinder, it was the newly published pocketbook by Lee Strobel titled *The Case for Easter*—the follow-up to *The Case for Christ*. Linda first wondered if this was Jorgensen's attempt to get inside her head as she had his—a veiled reference to her time at St. Mary's Academy before leaving Milwaukee for UW where she later met Christine. She soon realized she was giving him too much credit. It turns out he was just losing it.

Linda dug into the book. Manically scribbled inside on nearly every page, the innards of what was for many years in the 1990s a supermarket checkout-line staple, were various screeds and streams of consciousness in Jorgensen's chicken scratch annotating the text of the otherwise pristine and thoughtful book. Some annotations in the margins seemed to, along several points of basic comparison, match to penmanship of the "St. Donna" Christmas card from December '70 that had been sent to the sister of the still-missing Donna Ann Lass. Other entries looked to be written by another person entirely, Jorgensen experimenting with both dominant and nondominant hands, masking his penmanship, maybe even adopting different personalities while writing and adjusting that writing accordingly. By then, anything was possible. And while most of these same rambling annotations related to the author Strobel's existing content, Jorgensen also cited verbatim passages from the New Testament, the general theme being that Linda's soul needed saving from a lake of fire.

Other entries were either illegible or inscrutable. Some of the inscriptions were also more specific, but esoteric:

> *To Linda: Do you really comprehend? Who pushed the button?*
> *The day of wrath, when the dead shall awaken. YES, very dead.*
> *The forgiveness of life everlasting OR death . . . and lies.*

It was a cryptogram, or so it seemed. Everything about it could lead to an answer at last—or it could all be nothing. When desperately looking for purpose in the words of the deranged, we so often want their madness to mean something. The Zodiac's ciphers sent to the press were similarly subterfuge—most were pure nonsense. The Zodiac, an avid reader—quoting Richard Connell's 1924 novel *The Most Dangerous Game* in one of his letters—may also very well have been an aficionado of Edgar Allan Poe's works. As best can be determined, this theory—the connection between Poe and the Zodiac's writing styles—has never been previously explored in detail; however, it's worth noting that Poe, in the December 1839 issue of *Alexander's Weekly Messenger*, challenged readers to write to the newspaper using a substitution cipher of their choice, a cipher that Poe vowed he could solve without a decoder ring. This mirrors what the Zodiac himself did, almost as if he were sending the communication to Poe via the San Francisco press over a century later. The problem is that the Zodiac's decoded letters were just ramblings. He was a pure amateur; he was certainly no Edgar Allan.

The same was the case for Eric Harris, the alpha male and malevolent psychopath of the pair of shooters behind the Columbine High School massacre in 1999—the progenitor to what later became a wave of school shootings that still haunt America. In the hours leading to the mass murder at the Colorado high school where he was soon set to graduate, Harris left an audio-recorded manifesto on a microcassette labeled "Nixon" for posthumous discovery after the rampage was over—to be found along with his deranged journals and video recordings after he and his accomplice Dylan Klebold committed suicide. Experts analyzed and were particularly confounded by the "Nixon" title of the cassette, for months searching for some meaning—a window into Harris's twisted mind that might disclose a motive, a trigger point, or an intended legacy. In the end, the label was determined to be meaningless and no more than further manipulation and game playing. It was purely random, the net sum of a pathologically disordered mind in its final hours on Earth. It also underscored the reality that the words of killers are so often either pure subterfuge or amount to an arcane worldview that only they and they alone will ever be able to comprehend.

Be that as it may, Linda would still try to make some sense of the book's annotations in this rather belated and bizarre move by Jorgensen. She cross-referenced the ramblings and ominous declarations and questions scribbled in *The Case for Easter* against *The Love Pirate* as a possible decoder ring. Before long, however, she was underwater and had lost her bearings—worse off than when she had started. For all she knew, that had been Jorgensen's intent all along—perhaps he knew full well she'd take the bait. But after having spent the 1990s boning up on the evolving MOs of serial killers, Linda by then also knew the missing Argentinean seemed to fit the methodology of what is now known as a "trapper" offender—an often aging killer who brings victims to familiar turf under false pretexts. It's a calculated deathtrap scenario where a weaker or more tentative killer can exploit home advantage.

In suburban Chicago during the 1970s, John Wayne Gacy had once lured young men to his home with job offers and other ruses before plying them with alcohol, having them volunteer for a "handcuff trick," and then raping and murdering them while immobilized. When he was finally busted in December '78, Illinois cops found twenty-nine bodies buried either in the crawl space or under the driveway of the modest house to where he'd lured the boys, many of them daily laborers at Gacy's construction company. After running out of room to accommodate further bodies, Gacy dumped his last four victims in the local river.

Fifteen years later, John Edward Robinson, widely cited as the Internet's first serial killer, trolled sex-fetish chat rooms on early versions of Web 1.0 social media in order to lure victims to his home for role-play and kinky bondage. Once victims were restrained, Robinson—by then in his fifties as had been Gacy—would murder his guests much like H. H.

Holmes did a century prior. Linda knew this same MO when she saw it. Jorgensen was trying to draw her in just as she had spent over a decade trying to draw him out into the light. She also knew that Jorgensen had resurfaced after all this time for some particular reason.

Although he might have begun his criminal career as a "hunter" (a killer who stalks outdoor areas familiar to him) or even a "poacher" (a killer who uses the pretext of legitimate travel to slip in and out of cities and murder anonymously), Jorgensen, like others before him, had transitioned, it appeared, to become a textbook trapper. Linda knew that Jorgensen's manic writings, as cryptic as they appeared, were also warnings. Maybe he knew that Linda of all people was the only one left who might stop him. He was right. But if the Wisconsin police wouldn't follow her lead and follow Jorgensen to make him pay for the past, she could at least stop him from what he might do next. If she couldn't bring him to justice, she would bring justice to him—one way or another. It was then that Linda made a new friend while briefly back in California—the LAPD. In the meantime, what she didn't know about Jorgensen was that *The Case for Easter* wasn't a book he chose at random. It seemed that he might be starting a new tradition of his own.

Remnant

Back in Madison, the Capital City Killer began as an urban legend to try to make sense of the senseless. It became a legend that was later buoyed, like the Ripper myth before it, with "can neither confirm nor deny" public reticence that only fanned the flames of paranoia and intrigue at once. Once the Lucas Task Force hit the ground running and no state seemed to be out of bounds with respect to Lucas's binge confessions of serial murder and Satanism, delegates from the Major Case Unit now handling most of the Madison and UW murders were forced to consider consolidating their open/unsolved cases. Consolidation meant connection—connection meant a common offender.

It began with a slow trickle when the simultaneous brutality of the Rothschild and Bennett murders seemed to connect the campus area as an unlikely hunting ground. By the mid-1980s, the dam had burst and both Dane County and the entire state of Wisconsin were subsumed in talk of a serial killer. In time, with clear outliers like Donna Mraz and certainly Janet Raasch, talk of two more killers—operating either discretely or as a murderous dyad—came to dominate a new narrative. As "Killer" became "Killers," and then simply "killings" with a lowercase "k," theories became more and more erratic. The Internet didn't exactly help.

As unsolved crime forums and similar threads and chat rooms came to dominate the web from its outset, the story of the Madison campus killings transmuted into something that should never have been—what should not be today. Like the Ripper legend, the facts of the cases—the faces and names of the eight young girls whose lives were snuffed out and subjected to horrific atrocities—have become the inconvenient backgrounds to all sorts of off-the-wall theories proffered by all forms of wannabe detectives and general troublemakers. In time, people stopped caring about what really happened and preferred the version that would transform the cases into a ghoulish Madison spook story. As legendary film director John Ford said about how he made films depicting the heroes and villains of the old west: "When it's a choice between writing the history and writing the myth, write the *myth*."

The problem is that myths, legends, and criminal supposition, once alchemized into "real" history, can have additional unforeseen consequences. In Madison, on the UW campus, and throughout the entire state of Wisconsin, this is exactly what happened. By the mid-2000s, cresting at the same time that Linda was receiving her threatening cryptogram from Jorgensen as part of their slow, ongoing chess game, a new UW myth was taking hold: the Smiley Face Killer.

As a byproduct of the same local predisposition to legend that spawned the Capital City Killer before it, the Smiley Face Killer was yet another theory borne out of conjecture. It was one also sourced in numerous deaths associated with UW but, unlike the Madison slayings, deaths less clear in their origin. In fact, for many years, none of these deaths had been reported, much less investigated, as murders at all. The legend of the Smiley Face Killer came about insidiously following a series of bizarre and tragic drownings that some conspiracy theorists decided were more than coincidence. There was even some patently ludicrous suggestion that the Smiley Face Murderer and the Capital City Killer, one and the same, had used the Raasch murder near the Stevens Point campus to transition. That the murder marked a turning point from UW–Madison to UW–La Crosse—another state campus located about two hours northwest situated on the Mississippi—where the killer supposedly resumed his murders with a new MO and signature. The idea that the two sets of deaths were linked was nothing short of preposterous, as was the idea that the La Crosse campus deaths to follow were murders at all. It didn't, however, stop the legend from becoming fact in the minds of many. But contrary to the Ripper and Capital City Killer myths, proponents of this legend, unfortunately, included those who should have known better. Those whose jobs it was to know better.

The UW–La Crosse campus, like the Stevens Point campus, had been founded as a normal school and operated as such until 1927 when it was opened up to offer other baccalaureate degrees. Today, with just over 10,000 students and as one of the most populous of the eleven smaller "comprehensive" campuses within the UW system, it has produced a number of notable alumni, mostly with respect to pro sports. The town of La Crosse itself, with just over 50,000 people—a total of 150,000 residents in the metro area—also boasts its own notable distinction: more bars per capita than anywhere in America for a metro area of its size. Not surprisingly, the combination of an unprecedented supply of watering holes, a college campus, and city streets that in many cases slope toward one of the most majestic and unforgiving rivers in the continental United States has often proven to be a deadly confluence of circumstances. Enter the legend of the Smiley Face Killer.

Beginning in 1997 through to the most recent case in 2014, at least nine UW–La Crosse undergraduate students—all male—have drowned in the Mississippi River, all tragic cases that the diligent La Crosse PD rightfully ruled as being accidental. In nearly every case, the men, last seen at or near bars close to the waterfront, were found to have blood alcohol concentrations of two to three times the legal limit for driving following postmortem toxicology tests. While the bereaved families of these same young men were incredulous that the victims, many of whom were varsity athletes and accomplished swimmers, could drown, many were also neophyte drinkers or previous abstainers seemingly unprepared for the effects of alcohol after what may have been an evening of predictable college bingeing.

The path of least resistance for many inebriated and confused students would have been a downward trajectory toward the river with the risk of accidentally tumbling in. Add in drunken horseplay and showing off, and a deadly combination ensues. Water temperature at nearly any point in the school year combined with the effects of alcohol would lead to near-instant immobility leaving even the most seasoned swimmer quickly at risk under such circumstances. With drowning as the second leading cause of accidental death in America (after traffic accidents and ahead of firearms) for males within the same age range as these students—at the rate of about ten a day according to the Centers for Disease Control—and with alcohol consumption a leading contributor in these drownings, the La Crosse water deaths reflect a constellation of circumstances that, while horrible and no doubt preventable, actually mirror larger trends in the data nationwide with respect to lives lost to the water. The cases should have been open-and-shut with a discourse geared toward waterfront safeguards and the perils of immoderate alcohol consumption by college students. Instead, by 2008 that common sense narrative veered in another direction—toward the florid and the implausible. Toward that of a serial killer.

Perhaps it was the ever-looming public myth of the Capital City Killer and the mysterious spate of UW-related murders within recent memory that fueled such talk. Perhaps it was something else entirely. Either way, talk of men being murdered—lured to the water's edge, held underwater, thrown in the water, killed elsewhere and dumped in the river, you name it—began to gain unlikely but predictable momentum. Soon people started looking for a broader pattern, an MO and signature that could be belatedly or retroactively used to suit the theory—that might lend credence to the latest UW legend and justify the latest bandwagon conjecture.

Two unlikely people aboard this same bandwagon—and unfortunately later driving it—included retired NYPD detectives named Kevin Gannon and Anthony Duarte. While selectively collating data from across the US, the retired cops apparently found a total of at least forty young men with similar demographic backgrounds—mostly white, mostly college students, mostly jock types—whose drowned corpses had turned up in bodies of water across a total of eleven states. While La Crosse and its campus students led the pack in terms of an overrepresentation of victims, the erstwhile detectives went public with what they thought was the signature of the killer or killers—spray-paint graffiti. Not just any graffiti, in fact, but rather graffiti images, or "tags," depicting smiley faces. And so, with a flick of the switch and just like the Capital City Killer before it, the Smiley Face Killer was born. With that, a new era of speculation and storytelling began.

The two retirees, having persuaded many of the dead teens' parents to believe this, later went on to reference an undetermined number of cases where at least one smiley face graffito had been found at or "near"—in the most liberal sense of the word—where a body had been recovered. Some bodies turned up on shore with a smiley face tag anywhere from feet to miles from that location. In other cases, the tag was in the general vicinity of where it was believed the men had fallen into the water. Either way, the deaths, like all drowning deaths in fluid and moving bodies of water, made it difficult if not impossible to determine the precise point of entry and point of drowning. Also, because graffiti turned up at various locations adjacent to the river or in the surrounding urban area—in some cases, either miles upstream or downstream and blocks inland from the waterfront—this coincidence was summarily considered "proof" of the common signature. It was said to be the Smiley Face Killer's calling card.

But the truth is, just as drowning is the most common cause of accidental death among young men of this age group, so too are smiley faces the most common non-gang-affiliated graffiti image according to the FBI's database, notwithstanding the fact that no two of the smiley faces appearing "near" the drowning sites are remotely similar in style, size, paint color, or drip pattern—the graffiti vandal's, or "artist's," equivalent of a fingerprint. Some have tried to account for the latter detail, the overwhelming discrepancies between the tags, by actually suggesting that the

Smiley Face Killer is actually a composite offender, a larger underground movement shoehorned into a single public persona. That it amounts to some kind of murderous syndicate or occult group targeting collegiate jocks and their lookalikes across America.

Some murder-enthusiast and armchair-detective hobbyists have even theorized that the different murderers in different cities are all connected by a common goal and ideology with the "Smiley Face" members themselves—much like the shadowy hacktivist group Anonymous—being intentionally unaware of the real identities of their collaborators spread across America. The difference in this case of course is that, instead of launching distributed denial of service (DDoS) attacks against news corporation websites and exposing child predators like Anonymous does, the Smiley Face syndicate is stalking and luring students to the water and then drowning them. Especially, it seems, UW students. Especially, for whatever reason, Midwestern jocks. At some point, someone—either the killer or an accomplice—then spray paints a smiley face on an exposed surface somewhere in the surrounding vicinity to taunt authorities and leave the group's calling card. The pattern continues from there, from city to city, campus to campus.

The theory was and remains pure fiction. It's also a combination of sheer opportunism and exploitation at its worst. Greater emotional toll is exacted upon families already devastated by the drowning death of a loved one by being told that death was at the hands of a murderer, possibly a serial killer or member of some occult group targeting young men. The Smiley Face Killer theory has been disproven wholesale by a number of expert bodies, most notably the Homicide Research Center located across the river from La Crosse in nearby Minneapolis, as well as countless independent subject matter experts. Referring to the "Midwest river deaths," the FBI, in a 2008 press release, also described the Smiley Face hypothesis regarding the drownings as having no "evidence to substantiate the theory" that the deaths were anything more than alcohol-related drownings. Famed criminal profiler Pat Brown, in her own interview about the theory back in 2009, was less measured in her choice of words, calling it "ludicrous." Yet, despite these same findings and an endless list of irrefutable rebuttals to the theory, for some, this modern-day reincarnation of the Ripper myth—one that has once again been transplanted to Wisconsin—lives on.

Night Class

On the morning of May 26, 2008, Linda hosted a fortieth anniversary memorial she had organized to commemorate Christine's life—and death—at the Bell Carillon Tower at UW. Although the turnout four decades later was predictably scant, some UW PD and Madison cops—both old and new—showed up as a sign of support and respect. After Christine's one-time philosophy professor offered a few solemn words, former UWPD Chief Ralph Hanson—now looking like Father Time in a pair of balmorals—stepped to the podium. He spoke honestly and reverentially. He said he'd wished he'd run the race that was the Rothschild murder as a younger man. What the current complement of officers on the force never told him is that Linda had already run it. She'd had tabs on Jorgensen the whole time, the department's official all-points want long since evaporated.

As the ceremony closed and the bourdon bell in the campus belfry rang eighteen times—one toll for each year of Christine's brief life—Linda scanned the small crowd and saw that none of Christine's surviving family had made it out, save her sister Arlene. Christine's mother, Patria, was by 1968 long since dead. Now, forty years after what should have been Christine's original vigil had been denied, an aging Arlene approached and spoke to Linda. She described how the murder, the third child of the family being taken—stolen—too young, was the veritable end of her parents. She told Linda how, after that day, Christine's name was seldom if ever mentioned again in the home; how everyone on Kenmore Street died with Christine that day.

While Linda was never contacted by any of the Rothschilds between 1969 and 2008, the promise she kept was not to them but to Christine—a commitment made to Christine and only Christine. Her sister, Arlene, understood it all where others didn't. She knew Linda had done—and was still doing—what the rest of the family simply couldn't. They were simply all too broken. True to form, Arlene confirmed that Christine's parents both died largely as strangers in the same house from different causes in later years. The attending pathologists offered some medical mumbo jumbo with respect to the specific reasons for organ failure but in layman's terms it was a set of broken hearts that claimed them both. They both checked out early.

After Arlene quietly stepped out of the room, some cops in addition to former Chief Hanson stepped forward as the rest of the modest crowd dispersed. But, unlike Hanson, they weren't there to pay their respects, at least not as much as they were to keep tabs on Linda—to eavesdrop on the types of conversations she'd just had with Christine's sister. To find out how she might upstage them, embarrass them. One detective with the campus PD in particular took Linda aside, ending the emotive occasion on a crassly sour note with a dire warning: that her "meddling" might just very well compromise their "very active" investigation on which they were working "very hard." He warned her flat-out that she "outta" back off, mind her own business, and stop monkeying with their case—that she was flying too close to the sun.

That's all he could tell her; or, more accurately, all he *would* tell her. The latest generation of UW cops, it seemed, wasn't interested in the most recent and actionable information on Jorgensen, including his current address, his unsettling correspondence, the missing Argentinean, or any of it. Ironically—or not—within a couple of years, that same detective purportedly working so "very hard" on the Rothschild case was revealed to be himself a high-risk paraphiliac and exemplary campus creep drawn to UW for all the wrong reasons. He was soon tossed from the department and criminally charged, as his career ended in disgrace, his so-called "very active" investigations had, as confirmed by 2010 and likely earlier, come to include the use of hidden up-skirt cameras while interviewing female victims in his office. Victims who, like Christine Rothschild, had approached the UWPD for help about stalkers and other issues that plagued just about every college campus, no matter how neatly preened. Like Jorgensen, whose updated details the same cop had refused to hear, he had been drawn to the Mad City under the pretense of public service—a position of trust and authority—for reasons we may never know. He's since slipped off the map. Whatever was left of the Jorgensen case seems to have gone with him.

Two months after the fortieth anniversary memorial organized by Linda, as the conspiratorial rhetoric surrounding the Smiley Face Killer, as the millennial version of the Capital City Killer, was gaining momentum, Linda decided to pen another note—not to Jorgensen but to William J. Bratton, chief of the LAPD. As a walk-in, she'd spoken to a desk officer at the closest station to Jorgensen's condo, the Pacific Precinct on Culver Drive, when she was last there in the summer of '94 to conduct one final stakeout. It's where and when she first learned of the MIA Argentinean. With Jorgensen now living adjacent to Chief Bratton's expansive jurisdiction—though officially LA Sheriff's Department territory—and apparently gearing up, once again, for something sinister, Linda e-mailed Bratton a synopsis about the monster hiding in plain sight next door to his department. Linda, leapfrogging over the LA Sheriff's Department with official jurisdiction in Marina del Rey, knew that the LAPD's resources and street savvy would be needed to contain Jorgensen, even as an old man. Although he had thus far outwitted or otherwise eluded every police force in every city he had ever lived in or passed through, including the venerable NYPD, Linda hoped that the tenacious pedigree of LA chiefs might help to advance her cause.

In LA and beyond, the names of the city's previous police chiefs were synonymous with the annals of American crime fighting and winning the new west. One was William H. Parker, a native of the gunslinger capital, Deadwood, South Dakota, who moved to America's "white spot" and joined the force in '27. Wounded at D-day in '44, he had become chief in August of '50.

Parker, unfortunately known for his racism and hard drinking, is also known for his zealous efforts to combat crime and to modernize the department, the creation of the department's Gangster Squad to crush West Coast mobsters being one example. No doubt unknown to him at the time, Parker also had a stable of future talent under him. Day drunk 24/7 by the time he got his brass buttons, Parker was also smart enough to know he had no business trying to drive or write his own speeches. Those were the first two tasks that would require full-time assistants once he made chief. The first spot filled was his speechwriter: a young public-information officer named Gene Roddenberry. Later, his chauffeur would be a rookie cop named Daryl Gates. Roddenberry quit the force in '56 to develop, among other projects, the original *Star Trek*—Mr. Spock is reportedly modeled on Parker's cerebral but no-nonsense disposition. Gates later went on to become chief himself, first cocreating the original SWAT team in America and then later retiring to design first-person shooter video games after watching LA burn on his watch in the riots of '92.

By October of '02 Bratton was sworn in, and by '07, he was the first chief to receive a second term in over two decades. Linda, sensing that he'd want to know about Jorgensen, was confident that Bratton and his force were *not* the Major Case Unit of a generation past. Police work had grown up—at least a little—with serial killers, psychopaths, and criminal paraphilias now all part of the law enforcement nomenclature. She knew what buzzwords would get his attention. In an e-mail dated July 6, 2008, Linda laid out a brass-tacks summary of the last four decades, the names of witnesses, a timeline of events, and Jorgensen's current lair. She laid out what had been done by Jorgensen, what was likely done, and what would no doubt be done again if left unchecked. It wasn't a presumptive, sanctimonious missive. Linda's lifetime of communiqués to the UWPD and other stakeholder law enforcement agencies never were. Rather, the letter was a concise and effective appeal to logic. She hit "send" and transmitted it to a general handle for the department's senior brass and then waited. In two days, she had received a reply from a Captain Jackson on behalf of Chief Bratton. They were interested.

They were also circumspect. The reply disclosed that there were, predictably perhaps, a slew of cold-case hospital-related murders, most in the city proper—LAPD jurisdiction—that seemed to square with the time Jorgensen had returned to the area. Although the department would look into a possible connection, she was told, it would take time. After waiting forty years, another few years, Linda thought, wouldn't matter. At least now someone was paying attention. But it wasn't just the LAPD.

In the fall of '08, two months after the LAPD got back to Linda, a class convened in a lecture hall over a thousand miles away in Canada on the grounds of Western University, one of the nation's so-called "Old Four" colleges and distinguished institutions of higher learning. It was the first cohort of a new criminology-meets-communication class designed and taught by this author for senior undergraduate students. In lieu of a conventional term paper, students, after analyzing a series of five cold cases from across the United States, were to provide a report with a hypothesis on the solvability of the case today by the use of contemporary methods and technologies to reignite the case and—if possible—to create a suspect profile in the process. Although the students, other than what had been taught in the course, had no training in criminal investigative analysis, forensics, the tabling of preparatory and attack paraphilias, or criminal signature reading, that was exactly the point.

It was to be a fresh look at the cases through the eyes of civilians exploiting the resources of modern technology—a think tank unconstrained by the forces of bureaucracy or the egos of blow-dried politicos. The class, mostly Dean's honors students with advanced technological skills, hadn't even been alive when the assigned cases had occurred. They consequently held no existing opinions or suppositions, none of the biases or inflated notions of expertise. Such biases or notions, often cited as a recipe for investigative "tunnel vision," tend to occur when cops think they already know the ending. They can also occur when new attempts to investigate cold cases within the same department lead to what's known as an institutional memory—the same missteps being repeated when new cops on the case still follow the same flawed playbook. Inspired in part by groups such as the Vidocq Society—a Philadelphia-based unsolved crimes club made up of subject matter experts—the class was an experiment as much as it was a credit course.

Since the course was headed by me while still a cop at the time, and also moonlighting as a professor while completing a doctorate, it commingled law enforcement and academia so that students were effectively part of civilian reactivated homicide investigations. Offered as a night class—a pragmatic decision to accommodate personal scheduling—it quickly filled to capacity. In a regal, old lecture hall, perhaps reminiscent of ones at UW that Linda and Christine attended, students soon found themselves poring over files and workshopping murders that time had forgotten. Vetting and compiling suitable cases for the students had taken some serious legwork, and the goal was to select those cases that seemed to offer either one of two outcomes. Either the cases conveyed some semblance of solvability through the benefit of new technologies, or they were cases, woefully investigated the first time around, that might benefit from a fresh set of eyes and renewed enthusiasm without the type of intra-agency factionalism often bogging them down—in part why those same investigations seemed to have fizzled out and failed in the first place. Why they were to some extent doomed from the outset as products of a flawed system.

Some of the cases assigned for the class were obscure and others were better known, but all were serial cases—either known or suspected. The objective behind the serial classification was to teach students distinctions to be made between an MO and a signature, and the way to vet the accuracy of purported linkages based on the context, vintage, and quality of the criminal investigative analysis at the time the murders occurred. Because of the evolving body of knowledge some decades later, the training amounted to more than anyone in the Major Case Unit or any of the departments surrounding Madison ever would have received or had at their disposal. The same would hold true for most police forces across America investigating cases where bodies fitting Jorgensen's MO might have turned up over the previous forty years. The cases analyzed included grisly whodunits such as the Alphabet Murders, a series of child slayings in 1970s Rochester, New York, where victims were apparently selected because their first and last names began with the same consonant. As a case badly bungled from the outset, the investigation was now in deep freeze with families of victims still waiting for answers. Other older cases included the crimes of the so-called "Mad Butcher" of Kingsbury Run, otherwise known as the Cleveland Torso Murderer, who dismembered at least twelve and as many as twenty or more victims between 1935 and 1938 in the so-called Sleepy City. It had been a foundational case in geographic profiling and what's known as criminal propinquity—the spatial affiliation of crime scenes, victims, and evidence recovery locations. The class delved into some of the quack theories as to the killer's identity while at the same time winnowing canonical victims from probable copycat victims. There was one case, however, that really stumped students, a case they had never heard of prior to that same autumn—the Capital City Killer.

The first time the course was offered, the students didn't fare so well. Cases that should have been linked were not and other cases that shouldn't have been linked were wrongly connected. It was, in fact, symptomatic of the same predictable linkage blindness that has felled many an official police task force, including the one formed back in the Mad City in the wake of the

Bennett murder and burn job. Over the next two years, as word of the course spread and it filled up more and more quickly, students came more and more prepared—and from more varied backgrounds and disciplines. Although cold cases earmarked for class analysis were rotated in and out, the eight Madison murders beginning with Christine Rothschild endured as a constant that nagged at me and everyone who ever tackled them. Just as it seemed that each new cohort managed to get a bit closer when an old reporter or retired cop could be coaxed to talk to them as part of their research, any hope for leads would later dry up, people would die off, and e-mail and forwarding addresses would no longer be available. All the while, the LAPD was, if taken at its word, still looking into an entirely separate set of nurse and nursing student murders in LA County, which had seemed to spike with Jorgensen's return to the area. At the same time, Linda, waiting for a report on any progress, fully hoped that this time the cops were doing their job and might even put Jorgensen under surveillance. With the advent of DNA evidence, she even imagined the possibility of DNA in a previous case being eventually matched with a Jorgensen public discard and then surreptitiously seized by police. Maybe it would all soon be wrapped up once and for all, or so she still hoped. By January of 2011, when the Western course began its third full-time offering, I had no idea who Linda was. The identity of Jorgensen and his past misdeeds, both known and suspected, were equally unknown. I knew nothing about *The Love Pirate* or the Sierra Singles, Valentine Sally, Donna Ann Lass, or Māori justice. Then, only a month in, a switch was thrown.

Cold Call

It was February 2011 when the past caught up to the present in double time. It was then that a course student, twenty-one-year-old Jillian Clair, met Linda on social media. Although a previous cohort in the class had managed to unearth Linda's name from a microfiche cache of Associated Press and *State Journal* articles referencing Christine's thwarted memorial service back in '68, an Internet search at that time was a dead end. By that winter, however, Linda had decided to create a Facebook profile and she was located. It was good timing, maybe beginner's luck for young Jillian. Either way, it was pay dirt.

After e-mail exchanges were volleyed back and forth without my knowledge, a plan was subsequently devised. From toiling in the art room of the *Sentinel* after hours to the lonely road treks in the early days to the now instant access offered by the Internet, Linda saw a yawning chasm in time and space closing and an opportunity—maybe the final one to ever avail itself—to perhaps at last change the sluggish course of events with the help of Jillian and her group. With the end of the term drawing near, there was little time left to act. Linda, however, didn't need any convincing. After giving Linda the brief backstory of what the class was doing and why, Jillian and her crew were armed with the same information that every police department in Madison and area had been provided over a decade prior concerning Jorgensen's precise whereabouts and activities—what he had done and what he might still be capable of doing. It was the same information the LAPD had also been given and, by that time, had been noodling for a little over two years. A road trip was out of the question—and too dangerous—not to mention that if I knew about it, I would by policy have to put the kibosh on any direct contact. Among the students a consensus was reached to go dark—to go rogue.

The next best thing to actually going to see Jorgensen would be to call him. Better yet, Jillian and the students knew that because they were *not* the police, certain rules of engagement didn't apply to them. Namely, they could covertly record the conversation without notifying Jorgensen, what's known as a one-party consent recording, which is a recording that, when obtained in secret by a civilian, is not only legal but also very much admissible in court. Reporters do it all the time, that's why when speaking with the press, it's actually best to assume one is always being recorded and that there is often no such thing as off the record, unless the reporter agrees. Some reporters will extend the courtesy of asking if they can record but what they're really doing is *telling* you they are—providing advanced warning. In Jorgensen's case, no such warning was needed.

The reason for the call would be made clear to Jorgensen—Jillian would be doing the talking and using a pseudonym for her own protection, on Linda's advice. There was no need to disguise the reason or nature of the call, the students had received a crash course in Jorgensen's malignant narcissism and psychopathy from Linda in the early days of exchanging Facebook messages, and later more detailed e-mails and phone calls of their own. If Jillian could get Jorgensen talking, she was told, conflicting and coded versions of events would soon follow, and he would, in a fashion, inculpate himself. It would be the polygraph interview of forty-three years earlier that never happened. The difference was that reliance was no longer to be placed on a lie detector, an inadmissible and gimmicky prop easily defeated by psychopaths who generally lack deception stress responses. This time it would be the disembodied voice of a coed who would bring Jorgensen back almost forty-three years to a murder in the spring of '68 at UW—the ghost of Christine Rothschild.

On the afternoon of March 15, 2011—a Tuesday—the cold call was placed to the number for the landline at Jorgensen's Marina del Rey condo. It was the same number listed for the dubious Søren B. Jorgensen Foundation. A male voice answered on the third ring. While Jillian was clearly startled and perhaps even a bit rattled, she kept it together and played it cool. It's not every day that an undergrad ends up in direct conversation with a serial killer in a skip tracer role—the unofficial representative of nearly half a dozen police departments. The call lasted a total of fifty-four minutes. It was the first time since 1968 that anyone had asked Jorgensen about what happened the day of Christine's murder. What follows are some of the more noteworthy exchanges:

> JC: I am doing a project on the Capital City Murders and I was wondering if you wouldn't mind answering a couple questions for me, to help me with my project?
>
> NJ: Capital—Capital City Murders? Is this someone shooting students from a tower, or something, or what? *(laughs)*
>
> JC: Umm . . . well, the Capital City Murders were a series of deaths which occurred at the University of Wisconsin at Madison between, I think it was like, 1965 to like, 1987?

Something like that? *(feigning ignorance)*

NJ: I was there briefly to get a chance to be chief survey resident but I left because the politics at that school were so rotten that I left and got my chief residency somewhere else.

JC: Oh, okay I completely underst—*(interrupted)*

NJ: I didn't get to socialize much. I was very busy and I had some really, really big personal problems among the big professors . . . well, I'm not sure. I really didn't get to know the students. The people I got to know were graduate students and that's about it.

JC: Uhh . . . well, Mr. Jorgenson, I understand that at one point you were suspect in one of these mur—*(interrupted)*

NJ: That's because of a jealous . . . well not jealous, I'll say invective surgery chief who I exposed to be negligent in his duties. I had a patient which I was watching with the chief surgery—chest surgery chiefs—and I called him to let him know that the patient's pressure—blood pressure was dropping and his systolic pressure was falling below numerically that's the pulse rate. It's the Oxford rule of shock, ma'am, I was an intern at Children's Hospital in New Orleans. I notified this guy and he was miffed that I bothered him at a party.

JC: Oh my!

NJ: And I embarrassed that son of a bitch—smart aleck—and he took [it] upon himself, who didn't know anything about student affairs, even less than I, and dropped my name as a suspect. And that was just particularly vindictive as I exposed him as an arrogant son of a bitch who—I exposed him for what he was where as I did my duty and informed him.

JC: How come you've never cleared your name then?

NJ: I didn't have to clear my name! I did have an FBI clearance because I have certain connections when I was sergeant major of Air Force headquarters.

JC: Right.

NJ: That's how I cleared my name because I was actually with a couple of students—student nurses who came over to see me and took me back to their abode. So, this is a matter that I embarrassed the idiots of the socialist and the socialist mind on campus who seemed to think that Christians, Christian missionaries, were like Elmer Gantry: hypocrites. Whereas the hypocrites are the socialist student bodies which have taken over some of our best colleges in the country. Harvard, Yale, UCLA, and Stanford and Berkeley.

JC: Were you familiar with Christine Rothschild at all? Did you have any relationship with her?

NJ: I never met her; I might have seen her; she might have made a spectacle of herself at the restaurant across the street from the university—we heard about her. I didn't even know her name until some years later. One of my track associates introduced me to his cousin, Amelia, in San Fernando who was nineteen years of age. I was only fifteen, shot up tall for a fifteen-year-old—she was such a wonderful girl that a lot of the girls who wanted to date me too. I said "I'm sorry I've got somebody else." So I never even dated any high school girls because I found older women, and I found them much more valuable. They were *(laughs)* so the thought that I would even date these teenagers—which I've never done—that's ridiculous. They would bore the hell outta me.

MS: Okay.

NJ: And—MRCS, military royal college surgeons I had an associate in Zululand, Dr. Anthony Barker, really a wonderful man and I was going to come back to the mission field in Africa but I got distracted by the mission field in the ghetto in Brooklyn. I didn't even know who this Christine Rothschild was, but I did know some of the Rothschild family in Berkeley in the University of California. We used to go flying with Bertram Rothschild of the Rothschild family branched in South Africa, in fact his father had proceeded the stock exchange in Johannesburg.

JC: I see, and—*(interrupted)*

NJ: And when I was in Africa, I was with him. I was a guest at his home in Pretoria. I don't know if they knew the branches of the family, if this was even the same family if this, what do you call her? Christine Rothschild?

JC: That's right.

NJ: They talk about several victims but I only heard about this one person who was a similar name to the, my friend from Berkeley, the *real* Rothschild family.

JC: Now, Christine Rothschild was stabbed fourteen times. Do you have any idea what would compel a person to stab a person fourteen times?

NJ: Well maybe she refused some boy or something and he took it out on her. Sounds like that's an act of rage. You would really have had to have some personal relations to make one or two stabs but fourteen! That's an act of rage, wouldn't you say? *(laughs)*

JC: I—*(interrupted)*

NJ: You don't have to have a PhD in psychology to figure that one.

JC: She also had her gloves shoved down her throat.

NJ: Her what?

JC: Her gloves shoved down her throat. I was wondering if you had any opinions about that.

NJ: Her gloves!?

JC: That's right.

NJ: Hand gloves?

JC: Yes.

NJ: That's bizarre. What is that supposed to mean, that she talks too much or tells people the wrong thing or exposed him? You could run wild with your imagination on that one. That's pretty wild. *(laughs)*

JC: Okay, so do you believe these Capital City Murders were connected?

NJ: I don't know this local stuff. I had no interest in Wisconsin. I was just interested in getting my chief surgery residency, and I got overwhelmed by the local hassles there, and I left.

JC: Okay . . .

NJ: And good riddance! All your . . . backbiting little hassles going on and your incompetent handling of a serial killer and God knows what else. You should have taken some officer from New Orleans or New York or San Francisco or something where they handle real crime instead of this whatever you call it police in Madison trying to handle it.

JC: Okay. Well, I really appreciate your time today and I have one last question for you—did you murder Christine Rothschild?

NJ: I never even knew her. I have no reason to kill her or any other teenager. I had no interest. One good thrust would do the job if you had the knowledge of anatomy to do it anyways, you know? It doesn't take that much knowledge. Any good swordsman knows where to find a place.

JC: She was stabbed with a medical tool and that just makes me curious if maybe you have some suspicions as to who it might have been?

NJ: Medical tool? You mean like a Humvee knife or something?

JC: Like a scalpel.

NJ: An amputation knife? . . . my own attitude was to try and avoid using an amputation knife. This I learned from being stabbed during combat during the European, central European campaign. Battle of the Bulge, you know they call it.

JC: Anyways, I—*(interrupted)*

NJ: They can't quite solve it, she may have contributed to . . . the failure to solve it. The justice on the case of this sixteen-year-old or whatever girl who was probably a pretty bright girl. But, she may have crossed somebody in the wrong way. And these things happen. *(laughs)*

JC: Alright then. Well, have a great afternoon. And thank you again for your time.

NJ: Alright.

The recorded call is as revelatory as it is chilling. As research into the intricacies of the psychopathic mind tells us, it is a *continuance commitment* to a certain contrived narrative—and web of lies—even well into old age. Firstly, Jorgensen provides a hypothetical motive for Christine's murder in spite of his insistence that he never met her. He later revises this when he confirms that he did in fact know *of* her, and that she had made a spectacle of herself (an oddly specific visual term for a Peeping Tom and somnophiliac) at a nearby restaurant. This confirms, as Christine had dreaded and shared with Linda—and the UW police—that she was being stalked in her daily routine, the "restaurant" in this case undoubtedly being Rennebohm's where she was a regular. Jorgensen, offering an oddly specific explanation for the symbolism of the gloves being inserted in her throat, also suggests that he knew that Christine had mentioned his name to others as her stalker. Secondly, aside from sticking to his absurd and disproven backstory of having been a sergeant at the Battle of the Bulge, he seems to genuinely believe it was Sandy Mackman who alerted authorities that Jorgensen might well be a suspect in Christine's murder. While incorrect, the assumption seems to have been logically drawn from Jorgensen's recollection of a confrontation in which Mackman was embarrassed, by inference, the gun-pointing incident when Jorgensen's behavior unraveled in the aftermath of the murder. He also retreads the importance of his missionary work in Africa, referencing South Africa in particular and links to the Rothschild name most notably in both Berkeley and Africa, two locations where he admitted or is otherwise suspected of killing before. This is a not-uncommon psychological process in which offenders, particularly serial offenders, may transpose and commingle dates, faces, names, and places not as a matter of confusion but as part of a preferred internal narrative. These, however, aren't the most telling take-away points of the interview.

When confronted head-on with the question of whether he murdered Christine Rothschild, Jorgensen offers what is known in investigative interviewing and investigative psychology as a *weak* denial. Rather than actually denying it, he instead rationalizes why he would have no interest or need to have killed her. It's as if he were perhaps being asked to respond to something as bland as a survey question, not a question about whether he had murdered and mutilated someone he had already arguably admitted to noticing and remembering over forty years later. Also telling is his reference to Christine as part of a group consisting of "any other teenager," a rationalization and preemptive denial process also common to compulsive liars. The telephone interview Jillian and her classmates conducted, while not a smoking gun, was certainly enough to warrant the formal police interview that never happened. Killers have certainly been named as prime suspects and even arrested in cold cases based on less. In addition to providing more information about his knowledge of and possible motive for Christine's murder, the Berkeley reference, although perhaps coincidental and clearly inconclusive as to any confirmed linkage to the Williamson murder, is nonetheless curious. The interview had elicited more information than anyone other than Linda had amassed—not to mention from a suspect whose whereabouts were known the entire time. Maybe that's why he did what came next.

On Good Friday, 2011, five years almost to the day after he'd mailed Linda a marked-up copy of *The Case for Easter* and a little over a month after he received the cold call from Jillian Clair, Jorgensen finally and belatedly took Linda up on the offer to chat about the old days at UW. It was the offer she'd made in writing when she mailed the first of twenty-five consecutive Valentine cards to him beginning a quarter-century earlier. No one knows what finally prompted him—what the timing of it all meant. Maybe it was the earlier call from Jillian and the vaguely exculpatory statements he'd made once caught off guard, statements he might have made that would have been useful four decades earlier had anyone bothered to officially follow up. Either way, he chose over the Easter weekend, perhaps as a corollary to his previous ramblings inscribed in *The Case for Easter* or maybe at random. Either the way, the call was a brief one.

Linda picked up the landline in the living room on the second ring that day. It was a little past 3:00 p.m. CT when she answered with the same customary "Hello?" she always did, doing so on the same landline she'd had for almost thirty years. But this time was different. On the other end was only breathing, at first. It was the same sound—the same ominous inhales and exhales—that Christine had listened to when the calls first started in room 119 of Ann Emery Hall back in April of '68. It was the sleepwatcher *modus operandi* all over again. Linda sat and listened—patiently. She didn't resort to a second and more panicked "*hello?*" She did nothing but waited—waited him out. Somehow she knew; she wasn't sure how, but she knew it was *him*. And he knew that she knew. Decades upon decades on, the jig, it seemed, was finally up. Then, after close to a minute, a rickety, weathered voice came on the line to break the standoff of silence. "The Rothschild girl," the voice said—the same depersonalizing epithet used in his call with Jillian Clair. "No one was smart enough to check the autoclaves. That day, no one looked at the autoclaves. Tell Josephson, tell him he wasn't smart enough." *Click*—dead air. End call. Endgame.

To this day, there is no way of verifying it was Jorgensen for certain who called Linda's house in Texas that Good Friday. The references to the "Rothschild girl" and Detective Josephson by name—pairings going back to the original investigation of 1968 that few living people then or now would know of—and the unusual syntax corresponding to the call with Jillian just a month earlier is, however, glaring to say the least. Linda also used a directory callback feature with Ma Bell to confirm that—immediately after the hang-up—the call in question came from a landline in Marina del Rey, one that matched the listed address for the Jorgensen foundation

Linda never called the number back. The utterance in itself was enough. An autoclave, she already knew from her interviews of hospital staff back in the fall of '68 and onward while getting acquainted with surgical jargon, was a pressure chamber used to sterilize medical equipment—like scalpels, like the "medical utensil" once described as the murder weapon in Christine's case. She knew that those same autoclaves were plentiful in both the surgery suites and nearby research labs at the same campus hospital where Christine was pronounced dead. The same hospital where Jorgensen worked and was seen proclaiming it was, after all, a nice day for a murder. She knew that autoclaves blasted bloodied surgical tools with saturated steam somewhere in the neighborhood of 250 degrees F for upward of fifteen minutes per cleaning cycle. It was more than enough time and heat to render those same implements safe for reuse in other surgeries. It was also more than enough time and heat—and interference—to make those same tools once co-opted as murder weapons essentially useless as evidence, both then and now. But especially then.

That's how he did it, how he got away with it. Linda marveled at the evil genius of it: he hid in plain sight, he hid among the frenetic cops failing to see the forest through the trees, he carried the murder weapon to where death was pronounced and then returned it to its point of origin in pristine condition. It was a sterilized needle in a haystack, one he could never be connected to, even if it was ever found. She had been right all along about one thing in particular; it was one that Jorgensen himself confirmed verbatim—*no one looked*.

The interview with Jorgensen, its transcript and a full report on the case—in fact, *all* of the Madison cases—was sent to the UWPD by Jillian and her classmates in the summer of '11. At last, it seemed, the case had been brought in from the cold. The interview had raised red flags that at least warranted the formality of a police interview—or more. The report and accompanying recording's receipt was acknowledged with thanks and that was that, and there the case sat, again. As that package made its way from the Toronto area to Madison, another envelope made its way from Dallas to Marina del Rey. It was the 26th and final Valentine's Day card Linda would send—one that referenced the call Jorgensen had finally made to her. By all estimates, it too—like the report to UWPD—went unread.

By February 16, 2013, it was officially over. That same day Jorgensen dropped dead. With a coroner's certificate that listed cardiac failure as the official cause of death, the precise circumstances of his demise were destined to remain shrouded in mystery. With the help of Metro Cremation Service, Jorgensen kowtowed to his Scandinavian heritage and did the Viking thing—a funeral pyre lit on the quick. He was cremated almost immediately, his ashes scattered over the Pacific Ocean outside LA. All arrangements, likely previously discussed, were handled by Ezra Jameson of the Sierra Singles who had brought him the Argentinean and peddled the small run of copies of *The Love Pirate* for him. Ezra, his only loyal friend—Quong Sha in the flesh—reportedly later cleaned out the condo and very shortly after sold it. There would be no DNA to recover and nothing left to follow up on should a match ever be attempted. Jorgensen would leave this world without a trace. An obituary replete with lies—some of the same ones told upon his '68 arrival in the Mad City plus some new ones, including that he was still a practicing physician and was divorced—would be the final and inaccurate reminder of the wound that Jorgensen's existence left on the world. Or so, at least for a while, it seemed.

Cardsharps

It was 2013 before I actually met Linda for the first time. In the aftermath of Jorgensen's death and receipt from Linda of his trumped-up obit, I found myself conflicted about the way it all ended. Linda was less ambivalent, saying such things as "and so the monster is dead" and "we stopped him." *We* stopped him. She remains convinced that the cold-call interview was something of a Trojan horse that had foiled whatever it was Jorgensen was planning in the final year or two of his life. What caught him off guard as a random, though apparently innocuous, cold call no doubt became something that tormented him in later months, she believed, once it dawned on him that now, at long last, others knew—others were watching him. He would be aware that for the first time ever, there was an expanded audience, people monitoring his actions, who knew him for what he was. Linda's chess game, as the two of them grew older and wearier, had transcended the virtual board that had become the distance between LA and Dallas. Linda, by enlisting the willing assistance of others—much as Jorgensen had conscripted Ezra to do his bidding—had changed the rules of the game.

After Jillian's recorded telephone call, Linda and Jorgensen never had any further contact before his death. Whether the call fundamentally altered the course of events and did in fact interrupt whatever it was Jorgensen may have planned as his curtain call will never be known. Whether or not it had a bearing on his wish to be cremated out of fear that a possible exhumation of Christine Rothschild and other potential victims—the possible discovery of the bodies of Donna Ann Lass or the unnamed Argentinean—might yield new biological evidence will also never be known. But it prevails as being very curious.

The LAPD in retrospect probably found no real reason to approach Jorgensen and may have simply been placating Linda in their e-mail exchanges. Despite the red flags his telephone ramblings raised and their having the transcript, the UWPD never followed up on the information of the March 2011 interview with a more formal one. They never followed up on the confirmed whereabouts of Jorgensen who, for over four decades, purportedly had a locate flag on him as a person of interest, which a UW cop had once stressed police were working "very hard" to find—working very hard to close the case. The cold-case civilian activism of Jillian Clair and her peers at the university, exploiting modern technological resources, was possible in large part because of the digital age in which we live. As a well-intentioned and useful effort to assist the police in a long-stalled investigation, no one was attempting to usurp the police function. All results were promptly turned over to them for follow-up on a suspect they claimed to be looking for in anything but a real-time investigation. Whether this is a harbinger for a new cultural phenomenon remains to be seen.

Innovative approaches and a fresh set of eyes, civilian or not, could well benefit other dormant investigations, including both unsolved murders and cases of known or suspected wrongful conviction. The latter always ensures the former since every founded wrongful conviction inevitably creates a new cold case. It's the backstory to infamous American cases like those of Kirk Bloodsworth, the first American on death row spared in the nick of time after he was exonerated by DNA after serving eight years for a murder he didn't commit, and, of course, the West Memphis Three—the eponymous trio of teens who served eighteen years for a triple murder they never committed in their home state of Arkansas. In addition to the injustice of innocent people being incarcerated for years or even executed, the real killer still roams free, able to kill again, and families of victims lose any sense of closure they once may have had.

By the time the procedural errors in such cases are revealed—and begrudgingly admitted by authorities—many of the original files and exhibits are purged, the derailed investigation too far gone to start over. The truth is that criminal investigation and public oversight and accountability are today light-years ahead of the circumstances found in the Mad City and its college campus beginning back in the spring of '68. With that, police are able, when willing, to exercise a variety of new "stimulation" strategies to inspire public interest, renew a call for tips and other information, or to sweat the suspect by putting the case back in the public eye. In the 2000s, a changing of the guard in Madison led to a wholesale eradication of dead wood, from the basic incompetents to the criminal voyeurs who had been tasked with these investigations and, at last, there now seem to be some innovative new attempts to get right with the city's dark past.

One initiative, believed to have been the first of what later became a series of similar campaigns across America, is premised on the idea that criminals, serial murderers included, either can't or won't keep their mouths shut. It's also rooted in an understanding that the notion of honor among thieves—much less sexual murderers—is an entirely mistaken concept. Police informers for instance, arguably the lifeblood of criminal intelligence gathering and particularly in the areas of organized crime, fugitive recovery, and drug offenses, will often dime out their own mothers, brothers, and even their children in exchange for the few hundred dollars paid by a police handler. A further reality is that being a jailhouse snitch in high-profile cases is often a rewarding vocation for inmates looking to plea-bargain their charges. The cold-case playing card deck was a rather inspired idea that seeks to leverage these realities.

With Julie Speerschneider as the three of diamonds and Donna Mraz as the two of clubs, the hunt for the Mad City Killer or killers of old lives on through an innovative new cold-case program, now widely adopted across the United States, that integrates the faces and names of murder victims on playing cards distributed to penitentiary inmates.

With a deck of cards being one of the few legal mainstays of state and federal prison populations, someone somewhere—the confirmed first use is unclear and unclaimed—realized that the best method of cultivating intelligence on cold cases among existing offender populations was to put the facts of the case into the hands of other thieves, rapists, and killers—literally. Although themed decks of cards bearing all variety of images are nothing new, using prisons to circulate decks of cards featuring the faces, names, and details surrounding the deaths once attributed to the Capital City Killer was nothing if not innovative. It was rooted in the hope that inmates, when looking at the cards they're dealt, will have their memory jogged by one or more of the details mentioned on the cards. Criminals, now a captive audience to the facts of these cases, might see an opportunity, it was hoped, to come forward with information of use to stalled investigations. Whether playing solitaire in solitary confinement or three-card draw in the prison yard, every card displays the face of a life extinguished too soon. An abridged version of the story that goes with it, complete with dates, is also provided.

Since card decks generally detail cold cases by state and are distributed within that same state, inmates in Wisconsin today may very well find themselves dealt a hand containing one or more cards bearing the face and name of a victim whose killer they know either on the outside or with whom they may be doing time—a killer with whom they may even be playing cards. Although in some cases the victim's name might not ring a bell, the details and dates could, especially if the prisoner recognizes the general timeline as one corresponding with a crime an acquaintance or even a cellmate has previously bragged about getting away with. It's a remarkably creative guerilla tactic that creates an underground economy of cold cases within the correctional system and which, strangely enough, unites citizens on the outside and crooks on the inside toward a common goal of cold-case closure—of resolution, of absolution.

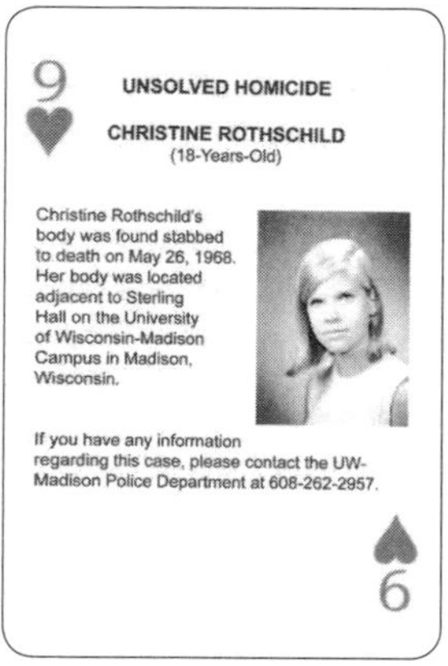

The same set of Wisconsin cold-case playing cards distributed across the Midwest features Christine Rothschild as the nine of hearts—the oldest cold case of the fifty-two card set. It remains unclear how suits and ranks were assigned to cases and victims, and whether it is a reflection of either investigative vintage or priority of the cases. In truth, the assignments appear to be, like much of what happened in these investigations proper, entirely random.

Linda has a set of the cards she managed to obtain from the Madison PD some years back. Christine is the nine of hearts. Today her face turns up in pairs, flushes, and four-of-a-kind hands in places like Fox Lake, Black River, and Kettle Moraine—all of the thirty-plus adult prisons and correctional institutions scattered across Wisconsin. When an inmate ends up with that card in his hand today, he's unlikely to know—like most others—that Christine's case, while officially still unsolved, is nonetheless considered resolved by many. Those people include Linda and me. The other seven slayings once attributed whether in whole or in part to the Capital City Killer remain, however, both unsolved and entirely unresolved. They are cases, answers still outstanding, for which closure is needed. There's little question that the Julie Murders are connected to the near-analogous slayings of LeMahieu and Stewart. That killer, unless dead, is no doubt still out there—whether in Dane County or elsewhere—roaming free. Because there will have been other victims in other cities either before or after the set in Madison, it can only be hoped that he's been caught and incarcerated elsewhere for at least one of these crimes—somewhere where his crimes were taken seriously. It can only be hoped that he is perhaps looking into the eyes of one or more of his victims, their images emblazoned on the same playing cards he is using within the Dairy State penitentiary system or elsewhere in America. The other Madison murders—Bennett, Mraz, and Raasch—are also still solvable but for some reason languish as cold cases. Then again, much of what happened in the Mad City over that seldom talked about and willfully forgotten quarter-century period never ceases to surprise me or anyone else who learns of it.

It has been in part the purpose of this book to set the historical record straight about what happened once upon a time in the Mad City—to clear the air and offer a valediction to a period many would prefer to forget on one hand and open up a renewed discourse on the other. There is no shortage of theories about how or why this all happened in an unlikely place like Madison in the first place, and why it kept on happening—and why it still does today. The cold-case playing cards have some new editions in recent years, the names of young UW coeds like Kelly Nolan and Brittany Zimmerman whose deaths, in spite of modern technologies, investigative methodologies, and improved police recruiting and training efforts, remain as cold and confounding as the spate of murders that began with Christine Rothschild on that drizzly Sunday morning in May of '68. Those detectives working those cases today, the families still waiting for answers who, like the Rothschilds, sent their daughters to UW because it was a safe school, should know about what came before. And what no doubt will come again.

Epilogue

Saboteur

> And now I may dismiss my heroine to the sleepless couch, which is the true heroine's portion—to a pillow strewed with thorns and wet with tears.
>
> —Jane Austen, *Northanger Abbey*

While Niels Jorgensen was a consummate psychopath who spent much of his life knitting together lies about his various exploits, and even tried to take credit for being a Purple Heart recipient and vet of the Battle of the Bulge, there is a lesser-known story of real heroism from the final days of the Second World War that in many respects squares with the equally lesser-known story of Linda's forty-year campaign. It was called Operation Gunnerside, or the Norwegian heavy water sabotage.

Norway's first hydroelectric plant in the small town of Rjukan had the capability to produce heavy water, soon to be determined as a key component in the creation of nuclear weapons. After the Nazis conquered Norway in 1940, Hitler began mobilizing troops and equipment toward the region with the intent of shipping heavy water to Germany to beat the Americans to the punch in the construction of an atomic bomb. Gunnerside was officially a British military campaign intended to sabotage such a shipment. A previous Allied attempt to infiltrate the plant had, however, failed miserably. It took the efforts of six novice Norwegian saboteurs, the true heroes of the day, for the heavy water sabotage mission to finally succeed. The six of them, all civilians with no official military or special ops training, relied on a certain brand of intuition, cunning, and patience not taught in any field manual, and pulled it off by detonating charges they had attached to massive heavy water drums awaiting shipment to Germany. That shipment would have provided more than enough heavy water for Nazi scientists to develop an atomic bomb and ensure global supremacy for Germany. It remains difficult to assess just how many lives they saved, but they no doubt prevented an atomic invasion of Britain and America and a much different future for the world. Yet no one has ever heard of them or their mission.

Although military historians consider it one of the most successful acts of Allied sabotage of the Second World War, the story is virtually unknown outside of Scandinavia. Equally, Linda's story and her forty-year dogged pursuit of Jorgensen—in fact, the larger story of Jorgensen as a serial killer no one else ever bothered to notice—has until now never been properly documented. As with the Rjukan saboteurs, a debt is owed to Linda. She was a woman on a quest imbued with a passionate urgency to track Jorgensen, to have him brought to account for Christine's death, the murder for which he was undoubtedly responsible. Linda, beyond trying to do right by her friend, at the same time knew that psychopathic murderers, once started, seldom if ever stop. She left no stone unturned as she searched for possible linkages to Jorgensen in other cases. These included Jorgensen's brother Søren, Donna Ann Lass, the Jane Doe known as Valentine Sally, Judith Williamson, and the disappearance of the mysterious Argentinean. Jorgensen's bottom of the ninth decision to opt for cremation ensured that DNA evidence, if existing or later found, would never be matched. Just as it is unlikely that any conclusive connection will or can ever be made in these cases, so too will it never be known if Jorgensen, looking over his shoulder in later years, reined himself in on account of someone else watching. It is all bound to forever remain a matter of conjecture.

Not unlike the heavy water saboteurs, Linda started out unskilled, untrained, and in way over her head—barely nineteen and traumatized to the hilt. Embarking unknowingly on an over-four-decade campaign for justice, it ended up being a matter of learning on the fly and playing it by ear, a perilous maze of twists and turns that she taught herself to navigate and negotiate. In so doing, she willingly forfeited much of her own life in the process, out of loyalty and as part of a debt she owed—a vow she had made—to her best friend Christine in death. It was, just as how the saboteurs had seen their mission, simply something of necessity that had to be done, a risky task with no material reward—one that few would ever know about.

There would be no blue ribbons, no television deals, none of the electroplated plaques like the cops who ignored her efforts and ensuing tips were accustomed to getting. The mission came with no glory either sought or received. Linda never expected it to be otherwise. With this book, however, it is hoped that, through the lens of the past, we can start to look toward the future. With that in mind, once you're done with this book, consider recommending or passing it on and spreading the word about those Madison cases still waiting to be solved, cases that it seems will otherwise remain condemned to the obscure footnotes in American history. Perhaps it will increase the odds that someone will step up to the plate with his or her knowledge about killers who have, until now, escaped justice. Perhaps something in these pages will jog something useful in someone's memory. So many years on, this is the best we can hope for. Somebody always knows *something*.

Today, Linda—the unsung saboteur of the countless other crimes likely to have been committed by Jorgensen—lives an overdue quiet life in suburban Fort Worth. Now well into her sixties, she is, at the moment, learning Japanese, following several years of part-time teaching English as a second language. With Jorgensen's death, she now finds that she has more available time to devote to other projects that, being Linda, she will inevitably see through to fruition. Even today, Linda herself can't explain what drove her—what the prime mover was, if any—that propelled her on her quixotic and, as some have said, foolhardy, thankless, and often dangerous journey pursuing a serial killer across Middle America and back again. The point is that she can't explain it and that's why it matters. More importantly, she doesn't need to explain it.

As Linda once told me, that moment in the dean's office in the autumn of '67, when she and Christine first met by chance, they were like surrogate sisters, perhaps even *real* sisters reunited. There is no single thing that can ever explain it. She saw Christine's soul and who she really was, spot-on and no strings or prior assumptions attached. Neither of them, having lived amid rehearsed etiquette and false niceties, had ever met a real friend of their choosing before that day. It was, perhaps, their first autonomous act as adults. Most people can imagine this type of epiphany moment as a young adult away from home for the first time; most can remember in Technicolor the nostalgic and emotional resonance of happenstance friendships and adventurously liberating experiences first undertaken while in college. Yet, few if any can understand experiencing that, and then having it so summarily and mercilessly taken away—having it end in murder. And not just any murder. A murder like the one that punctuated Christine Rothschild's brief, bright, and gentle life. Add to that a murder that went officially unsolved—not to mention trampled upon time and again. That's why there will be people who understand why Linda did what she did—those who get it—and inevitably also those who don't. Like so many of the tragicomic detectives—at least one a peeper himself—who bungled the case from day one, there are those who quite simply will *never* get it.

Jillian Clair, on the other hand, following completion of the course during which she interviewed Jorgensen, has gone on to graduate school, and works as a music and talk show producer at an independent radio station. As the families of the other Mad City and UW victims wait for answers, many of the others mentioned in this book have died. Ezra Jameson, for legal reasons, is a pseudonym. As he was Jorgensen's veritable bosom buddy, we can only hope that someone, like Linda, is keeping a watch on him for the rest of us.

AUTHOR'S NOTE ON NAMES

Some of the key or otherwise recurring secondary sources are listed in the selected bibliography at the end of this book; however, the multitude of newspaper accounts of events in Madison and elsewhere, obtained almost exclusively through records held by the Milwaukee *Journal Sentinel*, the *Wisconsin State Journal*, the Madison *Capital Times*, and the *Stevens Point Journal*, are not each individually indexed. Most of these sources are cited directly within the narrative. When inline references are not given for an account of a crime, in most cases it means that the details have been obtained from primary sources both named and unnamed. Whether I named a primary source depended on a number of factors. Most primary sources expressly asked not to be named. Even if a person did not ask for anonymity, there may have been other factors that caused me to omit or change the source's name. In fact, the need to strike a delicate balance between accuracy and the expectation of privacy that some of the historical bit players in this story still seek, whether rightly or wrongly, has strongly influenced how I crafted this narrative.

When a living person did not grant consent, or could not be located to provide his or her blessing about being included in this story, I have provided anonymity, not because of any legal obligation, but because it was simply the ethical thing to do—another departure from a great deal of true crime. I also preserved the anonymity of a number of people I would describe as bit players—they had not previously spoken on the record and their names had not been recorded in any secondary source The exception is Ezra Jameson, as mentioned, whose name I altered for legal and investigative reasons—and who quite frankly doesn't deserve his name in print. University and police officials, as well as those persons publicly associated with specific places and events discussed in this book are, however, named in every case, unless it was found to add nothing to the real objective of this book. For instance, the disgraced UWPD detective who was found to be surreptitiously recording students and victims of crimes for a sexual purpose and was sent packing doesn't deserve to eclipse the other more honorable members of the department, and his name has thus been omitted. Readers who want to identify him can search for his name based on the information in this book, and it's certainly a matter of public record. Once again, however, simply because I can provide names doesn't mean I felt compelled to, in every case.

ACKNOWLEDGMENTS

In learning of this book and its revelatory content, some people have expressed surprise that the story contained herein has never been properly told before now. There are actually a few reasons for that. Some of those reasons are underscored in the pages of the story that I've just told; namely, that until my students found Linda, the story's real-life heroine back in 2011, no one had bothered to ask—much less care. Until now, keyboard cowboys on various online unsolved threads—which in many cases actually do boast some logical and earnest contributors—have hijacked the dialogue about what happened in Madison, Wisconsin, between 1968 and roughly 1998. They have indulged in some revisionist history that for years would obfuscate any chance of the actual story seeing the light of day. This was of course made possible in large part by what remains the most puzzling set of police investigations and associated media-relations policies I've ever seen with respect to unsolved homicides anywhere in North America, at least after 1900.

Between indifference, recklessness, and a tragic interplay of incompetence and malevolence on behalf of everyone from elected officials to armchair detectives, getting to the bottom of what the hell happened in Madison and on and around its flagship college campus has not been easy. It's been a five-year undertaking that never could have gotten off the ground if, in addition to Linda, I had not been the beneficiary of the support, source material, research assistance, guidance, and insight of a great number of remarkable people, most of whom I consider contributors to this book and its mission to set the history straight. Ideally, it's a story that, now finally told as it happened, will begin a new dialogue on criminals and their victims, campus safety, investigative accountability, and the use of subject matter experts in stalled, inactive, or unsolved homicides that demand impartial analysis by those who know what they're doing—and are prepared to do what's necessary to begin thawing out cold cases.

The first up for thanks are the fellow scholars and advocates currently working with me at the forefront of innovation, professional and technical collaboration, and data accuracy with respect to historical homicides, as well as advocacy on behalf of victims and their families—people all too often forgotten about and even revictimized by the various institutions within the criminal justice system. These colleagues also in many cases provided peer review of this manuscript ahead of publication, as they did with my earlier book *Murder City*. The peer review is of course commonplace in the case of scholarly and scientific texts, but is a rarity for true-crime books—titles that in many cases tend to unfortunately focus less on the expert analysis of crimes and proper sourcing, with the view to help solve murders, as much as they focus on indulging in the lurid recitation of gory details and a certain infantile and downmarket giddiness. These peers of mine meriting thanks include, in no particular order, Enzo Yaksic and James Fox, directors of the Northeastern University Research Group for Atypical Homicide in Boston, for which I'm honored to be an invited member; as well as members Dr. Eric Hickey of Walden University and professor emeritus at CSU Fresno; Dr. Joan Swart at the Eisner Institute in Encino; Dallas Drake of the US Center for Homicide Research in Minneapolis; and lastly, Detective Helena Pereira of the Hamilton Police (Canada) along with Detective Steve Daniels of the Wisconsin Homicide Investigators Association and Detective David Bongiovani, formerly of the Dane County Sherriff's Office. I'd also like to thank Tom Hargrove, a fearless investigative journalist-turned-criminologist who founded and remains the head of the Murder Accountability Project (murderdata.org), as well as Detective Ken Mains, who founded and heads the American Investigative Society of Cold Cases, another two organizations with which I'm proud to have long-standing affiliations. In terms of my own unsolved crimes think tank, the Western University Cold Case Society, I acknowledge and thank Sharon Field-Brennan, as well as case managers Katherine (Kay) Reif, Professor Neisha Cushing, and Brikena Qamili. Particular thanks also to investigative members Jessica Karjanmaa, Cassandra Laperriere, Curtis Fisher, Ricky McDougall, and Ashurina Odicho. Their research and fact-checking with respect to many of the cases discussed in this book proved to be above reproach, and I wish them every success in their future endeavors after graduation, many of them moving on as practitioners in a criminal justice system that desperately needs men and women of vision and ingenuity like them. Special thanks also to Dr. Robert Barsky, Dr. Vickie Woolsley, and Dr. Martin Rapisadra at Vanderbilt University; Dr. Marcel Danesi and Dr. Paul Salvatori of the Victoria College Center for Research in Forensic Semiotics at the University of Toronto; Lisa Marine at the Wisconsin Historical Society; and Liz Mantz and her colleagues at the Western University archives collection.

Turning to the crime reporters and media stakeholders of the world, special thanks to Ashley Matthews, formerly of the NBC affiliate in Madison, as well as Elisa Fieldstadt of NBC Universal in New York, Michelle McQuigge of the Canadian Press, Dwight Drummond and Nazim Baksh of the CBC in Toronto, and freelance stringer Jared Linzod—also a former cold-case student—all of whom not only assisted in one form or another with this book, but who have also demonstrated remarkable integrity and an admirable commitment to furthering public interest in unsolved crimes and assisting victims of crime. I'd like to thank Ms. Matthews in particular for brokering my introduction to Mickey Mraz, brother of Madison murder victim Donna Mraz, and express my heartfelt gratitude to Mickey for trusting me with his family's story and providing the backstory to Donna's brief life that touched many.

I'd also like to thank my New York literary agent Grace Freedson, as well as Kevin Sullivan and Catherine Carnovale of Sullivan Entertainment in Toronto, two media aficionados swimming upstream in a world of socialized television, who seem determined to ensure—seemingly against all odds—that the cream can and will still rise. A special word also for my father, David G. Arntfield, Q.C., a retired prosecutor and tireless advocate for the law, who simultaneously instilled reverence for the power of language and the will to act where others will not.

Lastly, I'd like to thank Vivian Lee and the entire editorial team at Little A Books for their collective vision for my work and for recognizing the timely importance of this book—for enabling me to tell this story.

With gratitude,
Michael Arntfield, PhD

SELECTED BIBLIOGRAPHY

Adams, M. (2003). Cold Case Squad: Partnering with Volunteers to Solve Old Homicide Cases (July 2002). In *Subject to Debate* (pp. 1, 7). Washington, DC: Police Executive Research Forum.

Aggrawal, A. (2009). *Forensic and Medico-Legal Aspects of Sexual Crimes and Unusual Sexual Practices*. Boca Raton, FL: CRC Press.

______________. (2010). *Necrophilia: Forensic and Medico-Legal Aspects*. Boca Raton, FL: CRC Press.

Agnew, R. (2011). Crime and Time: The Temporal Patterning of Causal Variables. *Theoretical Criminology*, 15(2), 115–140.

American Psychiatric Association. (1968). *The Diagnostic and Statistical Manual of Mental Disorders, 2nd Edition*. Arlington, VA: American Psychiatric Publishing.

______________. (2013). *The Diagnostic and Statistical Manual of Mental Disorders, 5th Edition*. Arlington, VA: American Psychiatric Publishing.

Arntfield, M. (2014). Cybercrime and Cyberdeviance. In R. Linden (Ed.), *Criminology: A Canadian Perspective, 8th Edition* (pp. 500–516). Toronto: Nelson Education.

______________. (2015). The Monster of Seymour Avenue: Internet Crime News and Gothic Reportage in the Case of Ariel Castro. *Semiotica*, 207(1), 201–216.

______________. (2016). *Gothic Forensics: Criminal Investigative Procedure in Victorian Horror and Mystery*. New York: Palgrave-Macmillan.

______________. (2017). Necrophilia in Literature, Poetry, and Narrative Prose. In A. Aggrawal, E. W. Hikey, & L. Mellor (Eds.), *Understanding Necrophilia: A Global Multidisciplinary Approach*. San Diego: Cognella Academic Publishing.

Arntfield, M., & Danesi, M. (2017). *Murder in Plain English: From Manifestos to Memes, Looking at Murder Through the Words of Killers*. Amherst, NY: Prometheus.

Arntfield, M., & Danesi, M. (Eds.). (2016). *The Criminal Humanities: An Introduction*. New York: Peter Lang Academic Publishing.

Arntfield, M., & Gorman, K. A. (2014). *Introduction to Forensic Writing*. Toronto: Carswell.

Arntfield, M., & Mains, K. (2016). Cold Case Investigations: Challenges and Opportunities. In L. Mellor & J. Swart (Eds.), *Homicide: A Forensic Psychology Casebook*. Boca Raton, FL: CRC Press.

Ashilman, D. L. (1987). *A Guide to Folktales in the English Language: Based on the Aarne-Thompson Classification System*. Westport, CT: Greenwood.

Balousek, M. (2000). *101 Wisconsin Unsolved Mysteries*. Madison, WI: Badger Books.

Bates, T. (1992). *Rads: The 1970 Bombing of the Army Math Research Center at the University of Wisconsin and Its Aftermath*. New York: Harper Collins.

Becker, H. S. (1963). *Outsiders: Studies in the Sociology of Deviance*. New York: The Free Press.

Berlinksi, C. (2009). The Dark Figure of British Crime. *City Journal*. Retrieved from www.city-journal.org/2009/19_2_british-crime.html.

Bernick, M. S. (1982). On Crime and Conscience: Reasons for Confession Remain a Mystery. *American Bar Association Journal*, 68(3), 306–309.

Bohm, R. M., & Vogel, B. L. (2011). *A Primer on Crime and Delinquency Theory, 3rd Edition*. Belmont, CA: Wadsworth.

Brunvand, J. (2003). *The Vanishing Hitchhiker: American Urban Legends and Their Meanings, Revised Edition*. New York: W. W. Norton & Co.

Brussel, J. A. (1968). *Casebook of a Crime Psychiatrist*. New York: Bernard Geis Associates.

Bugliosi, V. (1974). *Helter Skelter: The True Story of the Manson Murders*. New York: W. W. Norton & Co.

Burgess, A. W., Regehr, C., & Roberts, A. (2012). *Victimology: Theories and Applications*. Burlington, MA: Jones & Bartlett.

Bursik, R. J. (1988). Social Disorganization and Theories of Crime and Delinquency: Problems and Prospects. *Criminology*, 26(4), 519–552.

Canter, D., & Gregory, A. (1994). Identifying the Residential Location of Serial Rapists. *Journal of the Forensic Science Society*, 34, 169–175.

Canter, D., & Youngs, D. (2009). *Investigative Psychology: Offender Profiling and the Analysis of Criminal Action*. Hoboken, NJ: Wiley.

Chan, H. C., & Heide, K. M. (2009). Sexual Homicide: A Synthesis of the Literature. *Trauma, Violence, and Abuse*, 10, 31–54.

Chan, A. C. Y., Beh, P. S. L., & Broadhurst, R. G. (2010). To Flee or Not: Postkilling Responses Among Intimate Partner Homicide Offenders in Hong Kong. *Homicide Studies*, 14(4), 400–418.

Cleckley, H. (1941). *The Mask of Sanity: An Attempt to Clarify Some Issues About the So-Called Psychopathic Personality*. Maryland Heights, MO: Mosby. 5th Edition Facsimile Reprinted in 1988 by Emily Cleckley.

Cohen, L. E., & Felson, M. (1979). Social Change and Crime Rate Trends: A Routine Activity Approach. *American Sociological Review*, 44, 588–608.

Coleman, J. S. (1988). Social Capital in the Creation of Human Capital. *The American Journal of Sociology*, 94—Supplement, 95–120.

Coleman, L. (2004). *The Copycat Effect: How the Media and Popular Culture Trigger Mayhem in Tomorrow's Headlines*. New York: Simon & Schuster.

Collins, P. (1964). *Dickens and Crime*. London: Macmillan.

Copes, H. (1999). Routine Activities and Motor Vehicle Theft: A Crime Specific Approach. *Journal of Crime and Justice*, 22(2), 125–146.

Cullen, D. (2010). *Columbine*. New York: Twelve Books.

Cullen, F. T., & Agnew, R. (Eds.). (2011). *Criminological Theory: Past to Present, 4th Edition*. New York: Oxford University Press.

DeLisi, M., & Conis, P. J. (Eds.). (2012). *Violent Offenders: Theory, Research and Practice, 2nd Edition*. Burlington, MA: Jones & Bartlett.

DiBiase, T. A. (2014). *No Body Homicide Cases: A Practical Guide to Investigating, Prosecuting, and Winning Cases When the Victim Is Missing*. Boca Raton, FL: CRC Press.

Doerner, W. G., & Lab, S. P. (2012). *Victimology, 6th Edition*. Burlington, MA: Anderson Publishing.

Douglas, J. E., Burgess, A. W., Burgess, A. G., & Kessler, R. K. (1992). *Crime Classification Manual: A Standard System for Investigating and Classifying Violent Crime*. New York: Lexington Books.

D'Ovidio, R., & Doyle, J. E. (2003). A Study on Cyberstalking: Understanding Investigative Hurdles. *FBI Law Enforcement Bulletin*, 73, 10–17.

Duncanson, J., & Pron, N. (April 2, 1992). Elusive Killers Leave Cold Trail for Police. *Toronto Star*, part 4 of 5 in series.

Eck, J. E., Clarke R. V. (2003). Classifying Common Police Problems: A Routine Activity Approach. *Crime Prevention Studies*, 16, 17–39.

Eck, J. E., & Weisburd, D. (1995). *Crime and Place*. Monsey, NJ: Criminal Justice Press.

Emsley, C., & Shpayer-Makov, H. (Eds.). (2006). *Police Detectives in History, 1750–1950*. Burlington, VT: Ashgate.

Farrell, H. M. (2011). Dissociative Identity Disorder: Medicolegal Challenges. *The Journal of the American Academy of Psychiatry and Law*, 39(3), 402–406.

Farrington, D. P. (2005). The Integrated Cognitive Antisocial Potential (ICAP) Theory. In: D. P. Farrington (Ed.), *Integrated Developmental and Life Course Theories of Offending: Advances in Criminological Theory, Volume 14*. New Brunswick, NJ: Transaction. 73–92.

Finn, J. (2004). A Survey of Online Harassment at University Campuses. *Journal of Interpersonal Violence*, 19, 468–493.

Fox, J. A., & Levin, J. (2014) *Extreme Killing: Understanding Serial and Mass Murder*. Thousand Oaks, CA: Sage.

Gatowski, S. I., Dobbin, S. A., Richardson, J. T., Ginsburg, G. P., Merlino, M. L., & Dahir, V. (2001). Asking the Gatekeepers: A National Survey of Judges on Judging Expert Evidence in a Post-Daubert World. *Law and Human Behavior*, 25(5), 433–458.

Gerbeth, V. J. (1996). *Practical Homicide Investigation, 3rd Edition*. Boca Raton, FL: CRC Press.

Girard, R. (1979). *Violence and the Sacred*. Baltimore: Hopkins Press.

Gunn, L., & Caissie, L. T. (2006). Serial Murder as an Act of Deviant Leisure. *Leisure*, 30(1), 27–53.

Hare, R. (1970). *Psychopathy: Theory and Research*. New York: Wiley.

______________. (1991). *The Hare Psychopathy Checklist—Revised*. Toronto: Multi-Health Systems.

______________. (1998). *Without Conscience: The Disturbing World of Psychopaths Among Us*. New York: Guilford Press.

______________. (2003). *The Hare Psychopathy Checklist—Revised, 2nd Edition*. Toronto: Multi-Health Systems.

Hayward, K. (2012). Pantomime Justice: A Cultural Criminological Analysis of Life Stage Devolution. *Crime, Media, Culture*, 8(2), 213–229.

Henn, F. A., Herjanic, M., & Vanderpearl, R. H. (1976). Forensic Psychiatry: Diagnosis of Criminal Responsibility. *Journal of Nervous and Mental Disease*, 162(6), 423–429.

Hickey, E. W. (2015). *Serial Murderers and Their Victims, 7th Edition.* Boston: Cengage.

Holmes, R. M., & Holmes, S. T. (2009). *Profiling Violent Crimes: An Investigative Tool, 4th Edition.* Thousand Oaks, CA: Sage.

Hughes, T., & Magers, M. (2007). The Perceived Impact of Crime Scene Investigation Shows on the Administration of Justice. *Journal of Criminal Justice and Popular Culture*, 14(3), 259–276.

Jackson, C. A. (2012). *The Tell-Tale Art: Poe in Modern Popular Culture.* Jefferson, NC: McFarland.

Jenkins, P. (1988). Myth and Murder: The Serial Killer Panic of 1983-85. *Criminal Justice Research*, 3(11), 1–7.

Kaplan, S., & Garrick, B. J. (1981). On the Quantitative Definition of Risk. *Risk Analysis*, 1(1), 11–27.

Karmen, A. (2007). *Crime Victims: An Introduction to Victimology, 6th Ed.* Belmont, CA: Thomson-Wadsworth.

Keppel, R. (2010). *Riverman: Ted Bundy and I Hunt for the Green River Killer.* New York: Pocket Books.

Keppel, R., & Walter, R. (1999). Profiling Killers: A Revised Classification Model for Understanding Sexual Murder. *International Journal of Offender Therapy and Comparative Criminology*, 43, 417–437.

King, R. N., & Koehler, D. J. (2000). Illusory Correlations in Graphological Inference. *Journal of Experimental Psychology: Applied*, 6(4), 336–348.

Kopley, R. (2008). *Edgar Allan Poe and the Dupin Mysteries.* New York: Palgrave Macmillan.

Krafft-Ebing, R. von. (1892). *Psychopathis Sexualis*. Philadelphia and London: F.A. Davis Publishing.

Kurland, M. (2009). *Irrefutable Evidence: Adventures in the History of Forensic Science*. Lanham, MD: Ivan R. Dee (Rowman & Littlefield).

Lamberg, L. (2002). Stalking Disrupts Lives, Leaves Emotional Scars. *Journal of the American Medical Association*, 286(5), 519–522.

Langley, T. (2012). *Batman and Psychology: A Dark and Stormy Knight*. Hoboken, NJ: Wiley.

Larson, E. (2003). *The Devil in the White City: Murder, Magic, and Madness at the Fair That Changed America*. New York: Vintage.

Laub, J. H., & Sampson, R. J. (2003). *Shared Beginnings, Divergent Lives: Delinquent Boys to Age 70*. Cambridge, MA: Harvard University Press.

Leyton, E. (2005). *Hunting Humans: The Rise of the Modern Multiple Murderer*. Toronto: McLeland & Stewart.

Livingston, J. (2004). Murder in the Juárez: Gender, Sexual Violence, and the Global Assembly Line. *Frontiers: A Journal of Women Studies*, 25 (1), 59–76.

Marriott, T. (2007). *Jack the Ripper: The 21st-Century Investigation*. London: John Blake Publishing.

McHoskey, J. (1995). Narcissism and Machiavellianism. *Psychological Reports*, 77(3), 755–759.

McHoskey, J., Worzel W., & Szyarto, C. (1998). Machiavellianism and Psychopathy. *Journal of Social Psychology*, 74(1), 192–210.

McNally, R. J. (2005). *Remembering Trauma*. Cambridge, MA: Belknap Press.

Meithe, T. D., & Meier, R. F. (1994). *Crime and Its Social Context: Toward an Integrated Theory of Offenders, Victims, and Situations*. Albany: State University of New York Press.

Mellor, L. (2012). *Cold North Killers: Canadian Serial Murder*. Toronto: Dundurn.

Money, J. (1986). *Lovemaps*. New York: Irvington Publishers.

______________. (1989). *Lovemaps: Clinical Concepts of Sexual/Erotic Health and Pathology*. New York: Prometheus Books.

Moore, A. B., Clark, B. A., & Kane, M. J. (2008). Who Shalt Not Kill? Individual Differences in Working Memory Capacity, Executive Control, and Moral Judgment. *Psychological Science*, 19(6), 549–557.

Moran, R. (1981). *Knowing Right from Wrong: The Insanity Defense of Daniel McNaughton*. New York: The Free Press.

Murder Accountability Project. (2015). *Tracking America's Unsolved Homicides*. Retrieved from http://murderdata.blogspot.ca/p/blog-page.html.

Mustaine, E. E., & Tewksbury, R. (1998). A Routine Activity Analysis Using Refined Lifestyle Measures. *Criminology*, 36, 829–857.

______________. (1999). A Routine Activity Theory for Women's Stalking Victimization. *Violence Against Women*, 5(1), 43–62.

______________. (2002). Sexual Assault of College Women: A Feminist Interpretation of a Routine Activities Analysis. *Criminal Justice Review*, 27, 89–123.

Pantaleo, K. (2010). Gendered Violence: An Analysis of the Maquiladora Murders. *International Criminal Justice Review*, 20(4), 349–365.

Paulhus, D. L., & Williams, K. M. (2002). The Dark Triad of Personality: Narcissism, Machiavellianism and Psychopathy. *Journal of Research in Personality*, 36, 556–563.

Perlmutter, D. (2000), *Policing the Media: Street Cops and Public Perceptions of Law Enforcement*. Thousand Oaks, CA: Sage.

Petherick, W. (2009). *Serial Crime: Theoretical and Practical Issues in Behavioral Profiling, 2nd Edition*. Burlington, MA: Elsevier.

Pettem, S. (2012). *Cold Case Resources for Unidentified, Missing, and Cold Homicide Cases*. Boca Raton, FL: CRC Press.

Phillips, P. D. (1980). Characteristics and Typology of the Journey to Crime. In D. E. Georges-Abeyie & K. D. Harries (Eds.), *Crime: A Spatial Perspective* (pp. 167–180). New York: Columbia University Press.

Pickering, M., & Keightley, E. (2006). The Modalities of Nostalgia. *Current Sociology*, 54(6), 919–941.

Pickersgill, M. (2010). From Psyche to Soma? Changing Accounts of Antisocial Personality Disorders in the American Journal of Psychiatry. *History of Psychiatry*, 21(3), 294–311.

Pintar, J., & Lynn, S. J. (2008). *Hypnosis: A Brief History*. Malden, MA: Wiley–Blackwell.

Porter, S., & Wrightsman, L. W. (2014). *Forensic Psychology, 2nd Canadian Edition*. Toronto: Nelson Education.

Rafter, N. (2006). *Shots in the Mirror: Crime Films and Society*. New York: Oxford University Press.

Ramsland, K. (2006). John George Haigh: A Malingerer's Legacy. *The Forensic Examiner*, 15(4). Electronic document.

Ressler, R. K., Burgess, A. W., & Douglas, J. E. (1988). *Sexual Homicide*. Lexington, MA: Lexington Books.

Ressler, R. K., & Schachtman, T. (1993). *Whoever Fights Monsters: My Twenty Years Tracking Serial Killers for the FBI*. New York: St. Martin Press.

Richardson, M. (2005). *On the Beat: 150 Years of Policing in London Ontario*. London: Aylmer Express Ltd.

Rosman, J. P., & Resnick, P. J. (1989). Sexual Attraction to Corpses: A Psychiatric Review of Necrophilia. *Bulletin of the American Academy of Psychiatry and the Law*, 17(2), 153–163.

Rossmo, D. K. (2000). *Geographic Profiling*. Boca Raton, FL: CRC Press.

Schmid, D. (2005). *Natural Born Celebrities: Serial Killers in American Culture*. Chicago: University of Chicago Press.

Seltzer, M. (2007). *True Crime: Observations on Violence and Modernity*. New York: Routledge.

Sewell, J. (2009). *The Shape of the Suburbs: Understanding Toronto's Sprawl*. Toronto: University of Toronto Press.

Sledzik, P. S., & Micozzi, M. S. (1997). Autopsy, Embalmed and Preserved Human Remains: Distinguishing Features in Forensic and Historic Contexts. In W. D. Haglund & M. H. Sorg (Eds.), *Forensic Taphonomy: The Postmortem Fate of Human Remains* (pp. 483–496). Boca Raton, FL: CRC Press.

Strand, G. (2012). *Killer on the Road: Violence and the American Interstate*. Austin: University of Texas Press.

Turvey, B. (2013). *Forensic Victimology: Examining Violent Crime Victims in Investigative and Legal Contexts*. Waltham, MA: Academic Press.

US Department of Justice. (2014). Federal Bureau of Investigation, Behavioral Analysis Unit. *Serial Murder: Pathways for Investigation*: A Report from the National Center for the Analysis of Violent Crime. Quantico, VA.

Vieraitis, L. M., Kovandzic, T. V., & Britto, S. (2008). Women's Status and Risk of Homicide Victimization. *Homicide Studies*, 12(2), 163–176.

Voss, N. (2011). *Mysterious Madison: Unsolved Crimes, Strange Creatures and Bizarre Happenstance*. Charleston, NC: History Press.

Walton, R. H. (2014). *Practical Cold Case Homicide Investigations Procedural Manual*. Boca Raton, FL: CRC Press.

Watt, M. C. (2012). *Explorations in Forensic Psychology: Cases in Criminal and Abnormal Behaviour*. Toronto: Nelson Education.

Woliver, L. R. (1993). *From Outrage to Action: The Politics of Grassroots Dissent*. Chicago: University of Illinois Press.

Wood, J., & Aldridge, M. (1999). *Interviewing Children: A Guide for Child Care and Forensic Practitioners*. Hoboken, NJ: Wiley.

Wortley, R., & Mazerolle, L. (Eds.). (2008). *Environmental Criminology and Crime Analysis*. Cullompton, UK: Willan.

Wright, A. M., & Holliday, R. (2005). Police Officers' Perceptions of Older Eyewitnesses. *Legal & Criminal Psychology*, 10(2). 211–223.

Wright, A. M., & Holliday, R. (2003). Interviewing Elderly Witnesses and Victims. *Forensic Update*, 73, 20–25.

INDEX

E

F

G

H

K

L

M

N

U

V

Y

Z

ABOUT THE AUTHOR

Photo © 2017 Richard Bain

Bestselling author Michael Arntfield is a veteran police officer, professor, and television host. Known by his students as "Profficer," an endearing blend of his academic and law enforcement professions, he teaches criminology at Western University and is a previous visiting Fulbright Chair at Vanderbilt University. With fifteen years of experience as a police officer, Arntfield offers a unique perspective into unsolved murder cases that combines suspenseful storytelling, academic knowledge, and investigative technology. He is the lead investigator on the true-crime series *To Catch a Killer* on the Oprah Winfrey Network in Canada and is the author of *Murder City: The Untold Story of Canada's Serial Killer Capital*. He is also director of the Murder Accountability Project in the United States and both the founder and director of the Western University Cold Case Society in Canada.

When he isn't teaching, investigating cold cases, or writing about them, he is researching long-term crime trends and developing new television projects. His latest research is on cyberbullying, social media, and psychopathy.